Rebuilding Story Worlds

Critical Graphics

Series Editor: Frederick Luis Aldama, Arts and Humanities Distinguished Professor, The Ohio State University

Volumes in the Critical Graphics series bring scholarly insight to single authors and their creator-owned graphic fiction and nonfiction works. Books in the series provide context and critical insight into a given creator's work, with an especial interest in social and political issues. Each book is organized as a series of reader-friendly scholarly chapters that precede the reprinting of short graphic fiction or nonfictional works—or excerpts of longer works. The critical insight and commentary alongside the creative works provide a gateway for lay-readers, students, and specialists to understand a given creator's work and life within larger social and political contexts as well as within comics history. Authors of these books situate the work of their subject within the creator's larger body of work and within the history of comics; and bring an engaged perspective to their analysis, drawing on a variety of disciplines, including medical humanities, environmental studies, disability studies, critical race studies, and women's, gender, and sexuality studies.

Rebuilding Story Worlds

The Obscure Cities by Schuiten and Peeters

JAN BAETENS

Rutgers University Press

New Brunswick, Camden, and Newark, New Jersey, and London

Library of Congress Cataloging-in-Publication Data

Names: Baetens, Jan, author.
Title: Rebuilding story worlds : the Obscure Cities by Schuiten and Peeters / Jan Baetens.
Description: New Brunswick : Rutgers University Press, [2020] | Series: Critical graphics | Includes bibliographical references and index.
Identifiers: LCCN 2019037920 | ISBN 9781978808478 (paperback) | ISBN 9781978808485 (hardback) | ISBN 9781978808492 (epub) | ISBN 9781978808508 (mobi) | ISBN 9781978808515 (pdf)
Subjects: LCSH: Schuiten, François. Cités obscures | Schuiten, François—Criticism and interpretation. | Peeters, Benoît, 1956– —Criticism and interpretation. | Graphic novels—Belgium—History and criticism. | Comic books, strips, etc.—Belgium—History and criticism.
Classification: LCC PN6790.B43 S393 2020 | DDC 741.5/9493—dc23
LC record available at https://lccn.loc.gov/2019037920

A British Cataloging-in-Publication record for this book is available from the British Library.

www.rutgersuniversitypress.org

Manufactured in the United States of America

To my friends of *Les Impressions Nouvelles*

Contents

Rebuilding Story Worlds

1

A New Series, a New Type of Author

First known by American readers under the unfortunate title of *The Cities of the Fantastic*,[1] *The Obscure Cities* (French: *Les Cités obscures*) by artist François Schuiten and writer Benoît Peeters is a long-running Franco-Belgian *bande dessinée* or comics series set on a Counter-Earth, a world that is similar to yet also different from the world we know. The official website of the work, Altaplana, states: "In this fictional world, humans live in independent city-states, each of which has developed a distinct civilization, each characterized by a distinctive architectural style. The word Obscure is somewhat misleading for English-speaking readers. In America, we tend to think of the word to mean 'little known' or 'odd.' The French use the word for multiple meanings, including 'mysterious,' 'hidden,' or even 'secluded.' ALL of these adjectives could apply to the world imagined in the minds of Benoît Peeters and François Schuiten" (Altaplana, n.p.).[2]

This statement on the home page of Altaplana already hints at some of the major features of the work of Schuiten and Peeters: the strange and the uncanny, the relationship between reality and fiction, the importance of spatial and urban settings, and the very singularity of a project that seems to be as much interested in world making as in storytelling come immediately to the fore, and most elements of this rough general presentation will be read in detail in the various chapters of this book.

The Obscure Cities is a series that is both very coherent and homogeneous thanks to the unity of its fictional world, progressively disclosed throughout each new volume, yet very complex and decentered due to the fact that each new volume introduces new characters, topics, story lines, and social and political issues. In that sense, the series functions as a laboratory to experiment with the often conflicting relationships between human characters and their environments—physical, cultural, social, and material, but also political in the many senses of the word. As Catherine Labio energetically puts it: "One of the most important series of the late twentieth century, *Les Cités obscures* has played a key role in the revitalization of *bande dessinée* that began in the 1980s. It has also found a worldwide audience. Since the publication of *Les Murailles de Samaris* in 1982, the series has grown in rhizomatic fashion into a multivolume universe" (2015, 318–319).

The originality and unique position of the series depend not only on style and content. This originality, which this book will also frame in historical and political terms, is strongly related to the way in which Schuiten and Peeters profoundly redefine the usual comics publishing policy as well as the relationships between comics and other media. As pointed out by the leading French historian and theoretician of comics studies, Thierry Groensteen:

> *The Obscure Cities* . . . The volumes that have been gathered until today under this generic term can immediately be distinguished in many ways from the cycles and book series with which the comics world is so familiar. Here, the proliferation of titles has not been programmed in advance. The first volume of the series, *The Great Walls of Samaris*, was not meant as the pilot of a series to be developed in case of success. The coherence of the whole enterprise does not depend on the presence of a recurring character or a group of characters, not even by the repetition of certain material aspects of the volumes (size, book design). (Groensteen 1994, n.p.; my translation)

Launched with the publication of *Samaris* in 1983 (first U.S. translation in 1987), after a run in the monthly *(À Suivre)* from June to September 1982, the chronicles of *The Obscure Cities* constitute a landmark series in European and world comics. The revised and final version of the various works in four "integral" albums released (in French) between 2017 and 2019 presents us with a timely opportunity for a first critical overview of the series as a whole, including many of the "peripheries" that were not realized in the host medium of comics (illustrated books, anthologies, catalogues, collector's items, lectures, posters, performances, and so on). We may begin this endeavor by considering what makes the series such a stunning achievement in modern comics and more generally in modern literature and culture. Much more than other works or series, *The Obscure Cities* has indeed a powerful literary dimension, which immediately makes it a good candidate in bridging the gap between two worlds, that of comics and that of writing.[3] As we will see later, the generic and media hybridization of *The Obscure Cities* goes, however, far beyond the sole fields of comics and literature.

Deeply rooted in Belgian and European comics culture, but with more than an eye wide open to global tendencies, *The Obscure Cities* has emerged at a watershed moment in modern comics culture and in modern or postmodern culture in general. This introductory chapter will give a historical presentation of the work and its context in order to build the necessary framework to better understand and critically examine not only the form and content, but also the real stakes of Schuiten and Peeters's contribution to the ninth art.

A brief practical note before getting started: Readers less familiar with the plot of the various volumes will be happy to discover that comprehensive plot summaries are available at the highly user-friendly and perfectly up-to-date portal site Altaplana,[4] where one will also find clear and circumstantial information on characters, places, events, and general chronology of the series.

In global comics history, 1983 may not be as pivotal a year as, for instance, 1978, the year that witnessed the launch of Will Eisner's *A Contract with God* and the first issue of the journal *RAW*, a publication strongly influenced by European comics avant-garde and rapidly influential in France as well as the UK, or 1986, which saw the simultaneous publication of *Watchmen*, *Batman: The Dark Knight Returns*, and of course the first volume of *Maus*—all books that strongly impacted the European comics market, introducing a conceptual tension between "comics" and "graphic novels" that was practically unknown before, when all European comics, whatever their style or content, were seen as part of the same medium. It is nevertheless a year that is at the center of a crucial period where the great structural changes in European comics culture during the 1950s and 1960s, both in content and in institutional terms, resulted in a new Golden Age of adult storytelling.

After World War II, European comics witnessed two fundamental and strongly linked transformations: one in its publication formats, another in its commercial and industrial infrastructure. First of all, the classic publication venues—comics pages or sections in daily newspapers, weeklies, and monthly magazines—were challenged by a new format, that of the specialized

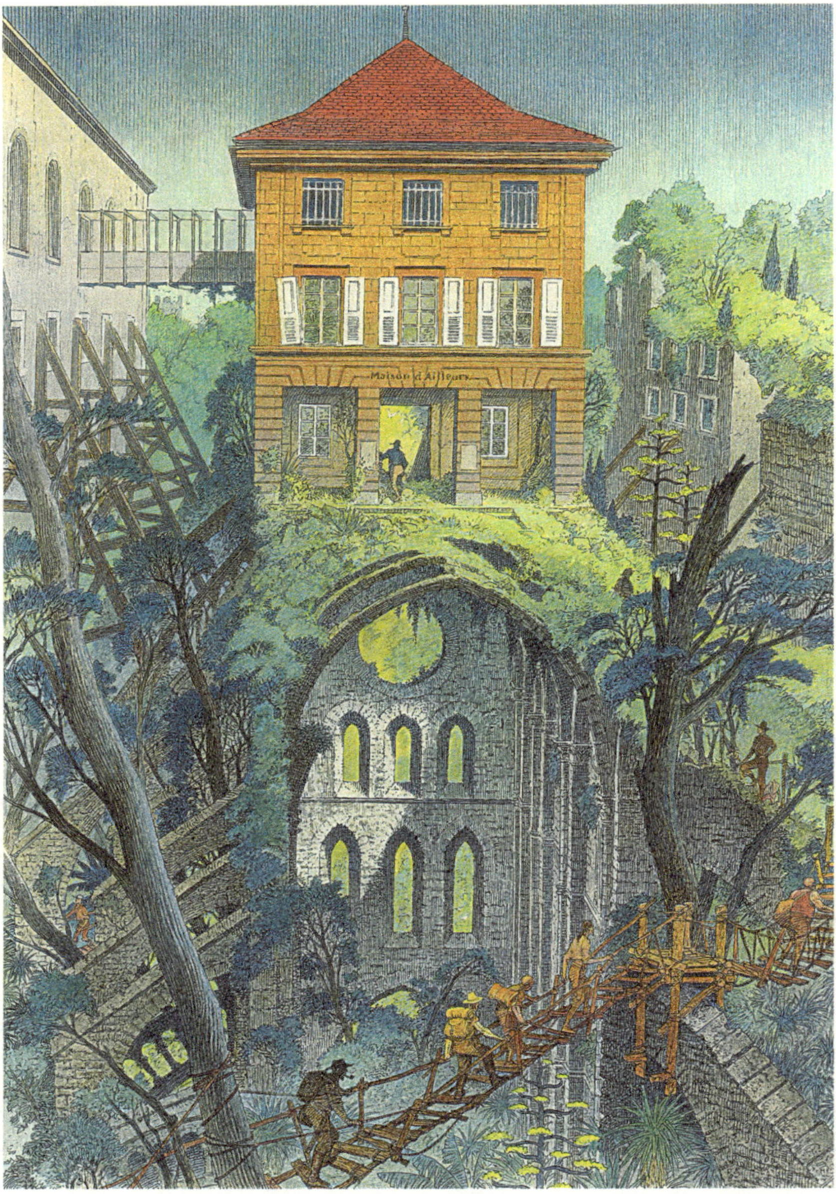

FIG. 1.1 Illustration for the exhibit *Im-possible Worlds* at the science fiction museum La Maison d'ailleurs (November 2019–October 2020) in Yverdon-les-Bain, Switzerland (© François Schuiten)

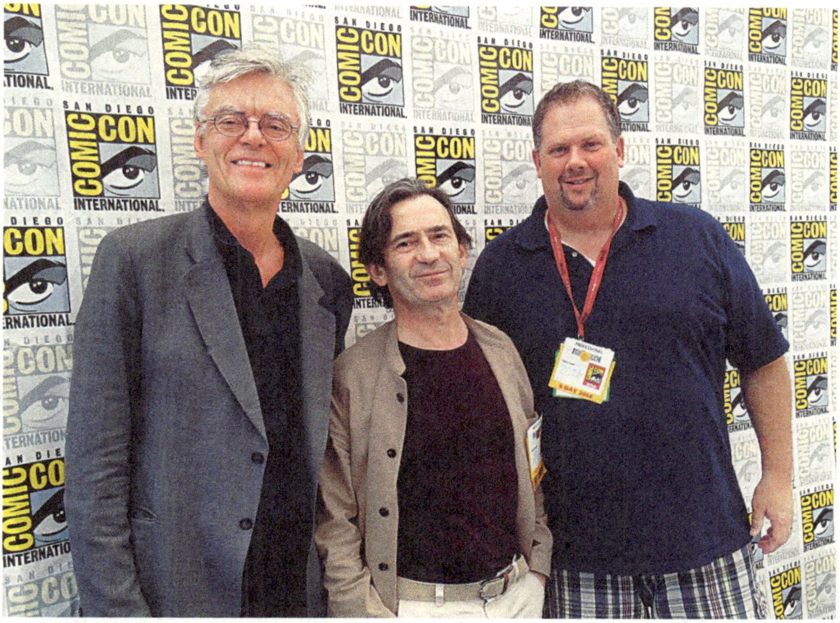

FIG. 1.2 François Schuiten, Benoît Peeters, and their U.S. publisher, Steve Smith, at Comic-Con 2014 (© Benoît Peeters)

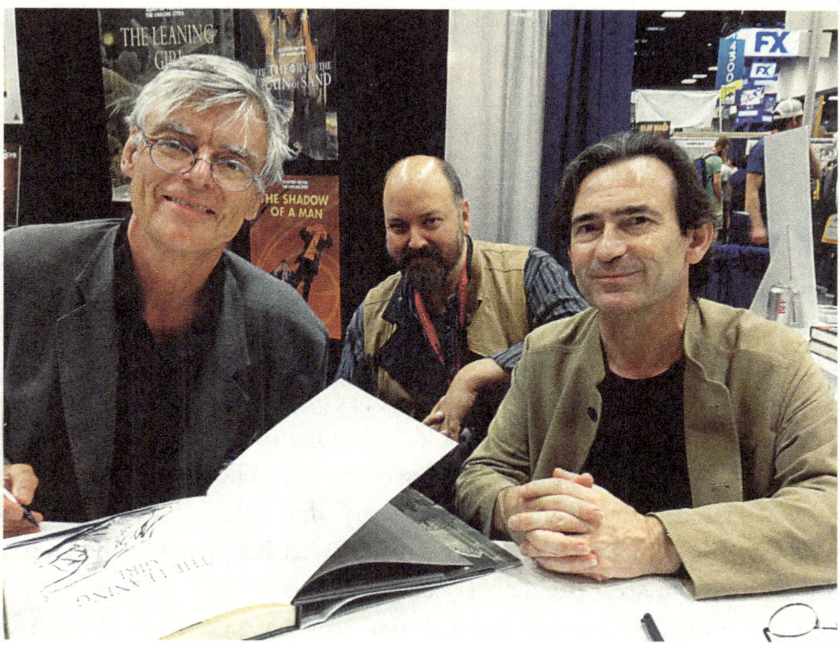

FIG. 1.3 François Schuiten and Benoît Peeters (background: Dave McKean) signing *The Leaning Girl* at Comic-Con 2014 (© Benoît Peeters)

comics magazine, that is, a weekly publication of sixteen to twenty-four pages offering a combination of gag strips and serialized adventure strips, generally complemented with smaller editorial contributions. Granted, comics magazines already existed before the war, but their number and importance strongly increased after the mid-forties and fifties, with *Tintin* (the journal) as the flagship publication in the field. Each of these magazines had its own look and feel, tone, and ideology, but this internal streamlining did not prevent artists from adding a personal touch. Magazine editors tried to seduce their readers with maximal diversity and thus a mix of genres as well as visual and narratives styles. This variety was a must in the competition between the countless journals on newsstands; the number of subscribers being generally very low, accounting for between 5 and 10 percent of the copies sold (Michallat 2018), necessitated an industry aversion to routine. This openness to individual creation within the comics cultural industry encouraged artists to create and develop their own characters and story worlds, which were normally not continued or rebooted when the series was abandoned (for a counterexample, see Baetens and Frey 2018). Obviously, this creative freedom proved an essential feature in the emergence of the adult comics of the sixties, when authors—more attuned to catering to juvenile audiences—obtained greater freedom to move to other types of content and storytelling.

Subsequently, the dominant publication format ceased to be the periodical publication, be it in general publication formats or in specialized magazines (GREBD 2013). During the 1950s the hegemonic model for the album format, the so-called 48cc format ("48 pages, cartonné, couleur" [48 pages, hardback, full color]). For many years, the reissue of a serialized comic in album format had been rather exceptional—here as well the most famous example was *The Adventures of Tintin*, almost immediately released in book form. Things changed, however, during the fifties, so that by 1960, serialization had actually become a form of prepublication of a subsequent album. Economically speaking, such a system proved attractive for authors, who thus received double pay: first, a fixed amount per page in the daily or the magazine; second, a percentage per copy sold. This system offered many new opportunities for starting authors, producing thus a large pool of creators capable of answering demands from new, specifically adult but not necessarily countercultural audiences of the sixties. Unlike what happened in the United States, with the great divide between superhero comic books and underground comix, the European *bande dessinée* production not only allowed for more internal diversity; it also prepared the birth of adult or serious comics in an almost organic way, most journals and authors trying to progressively express less stereotypical forms of storytelling and responding to a clear social demand for more mature material. The new comics that emerged in the 1960s were not only the result of a reaction against the limitations of the industry but came about as the result of the industry's effort to meet the new demands of both the authors and the public.

The widespread acceptance of comics in Europe, where the industry did not specialize in the horror genres that had exposed U.S. comic books to wide social and political repression, as well as the dynamic distribution policy of magazines and publishers in Belgium and France—the core countries of the European production in that period—contributed to an enlargement of the field from general and juvenile publications to adult publications. The range and scope of these new comics were extremely diverse. Some were traditional comics that progressively targeted a more mature audience (the works published in a magazine such as *Pilote*, founded in 1959, are a good example of the rise and fall of the attempts to convert a youth journal in something else [Michallat 2018]); others were from the very start oriented toward a political agenda.[5] Yet none of the works—some of them masterpieces, such as Moebius's *The Airtight Garage* (1976–1979)—were labeled "graphic novels," mainly due to the presence of a wide range of styles and genres and thus the absence of a clear-cut opposition between mainstream and nonmainstream publications. The general awareness of the appearance of new forms of comics did not materialize in a need for a new label.

(À Suivre) (1978–1997), the monthly magazine that prepublished *The Obscure Cities*, is often seen as the epitome of the new comics that had flourished in 1960s and 1970s. At the same time, *(À Suivre)* also established a new format. On the level of the publication format, it initiated the notion of the chapter: contrary to previous forms of serialization, which delivered the story in daily strips or weekly single or double pages, the magazine introduced the "literary" unit of ten- to twenty-page segments, at the perhaps inevitable cost of loss of color, a major break with the full-color policy of other magazines. The literary influence is, however, not limited to purely formal aspects of segment or chapter length: "As Mougin [the magazine's editor] daringly asserted in the preface of the first issue, which also served as a manifesto for the magazine's artistic ambitions, '*(À Suivre)* will be the bold entrance of comics into literature.' This programmatic pronouncement contained a double aspiration: it implied not only a desire to accentuate the literary dimension of comics, but also, and as a consequence, to leave the devalued domain of youth and popular culture in order to integrate the more legitimized sphere of literature" (Leroy 2018, 252).

The often very lengthy "novels" in *(À Suivre)* were always purely fictional stories, more specifically adventure novels. One of their great classic models was Robert Louis Stevenson, clearly present in Pratt's *Corto Maltese* series. In that sense, these "novels"—the specific label appeared on the cover of the reissues in album format—were quite different from the focus on autobiography or semiautobiography propagated by the yet-to-come "graphic novel." *(À Suivre)* had a decisive influence nevertheless on the institutional characterization of comics as a form of writing, that is, as a new form of literature, and *not* as caricature or fine art. On the one hand, *bande dessinée*'s emphasis on (long) storytelling and fiction set it apart from the various traditions of cartoon press drawings, satirical visual journalism, or agitprop illustration, as made, for instance, in the context of Situationism before and after May 1968 (Chollet 2000). On the other hand, *(À Suivre)* also opposed attempts to legitimize comics by linking them with the world of painting and fine arts, an idea first triggered by the exchanges between comics and pop art, which eventually, but not always successfully, were reinforced by repeated initiatives to bring comics into the museum or the art gallery (Beaty 2012).

As already stated, the art of Schuiten and Peeters is at the same time classic (and even to a large extent already canonical) and groundbreaking (and in some regards definitely anti-mainstream). Illustrative of this position is that *The Obscure Cities* will almost immediately obtain the "best album prize" of the Angoulême International Comics Festival, always on the lookout for new yet undisruptive authors. The award given to the second volume of the series, *The Fever in Urbicand*, can therefore by seen as the symbolic inscription of the work by Schuiten and Peeters at the crossroads of tradition and innovation.

Although always very clever and sophisticated, the page layout of *The Obscure Cities* is for instance clearly nonrevolutionary. Any reader would spontaneously recognize it as classic *bande dessinée*. In a similar vein, reading for the plot will never be a disappointing enterprise. At the same time, the series is also cutting-edge, and much of the effort of this book will go toward unpacking the work's novelties. The basic stance of the authors is nevertheless not radical. Their position is somewhere in between the two extremes of the traditional and the avant-garde. In literary terms—and the literary dimension of their work makes this a natural reference—one could say that *The Obscure Cities* is an example of a flank guard,[6] similar perhaps to the "rearguard of the avant-garde" position cherished by Roland Barthes, the major spokesman for French modernism of the 1960s and 1970s, who played a crucial role in the intellectual formation of Benoît Peeters as the supervisor of his MA thesis, which applied the reading method of the famous book *S/Z* (Barthes 1974) to the world of Hergé (Peeters 2015).

Avant-garde, rear guard, flank guard: these terms may seem abstract or abstruse, but in the context of 1983, they can be positioned within a heated debate on the "end of modernity" in France, and although the Brussels-based Schuiten and Peeters are much indebted to the specifically Belgian branch of Franco-Belgian comics, one should not forget that *(À Suivre)*, in spite of being published by a Belgian company (Casterman),[7] had its headquarters in Paris and contributed in more than one way to the cultural life of, and social debates happening in, France. The year 1983 is often seen in France as an ideological turning point, not between modernity and postmodernity (the latter term was not yet widely used in these years, and much of what the French called "modernity" would be seen in Anglophone contexts as typically postmodern), but between two decades of exceptional social and cultural innovation—if not revolution—and a sudden return to more traditional forms of writing and thinking. The most explicit illustration of this return was to be seen in the literary field, with the radical move by Philippe Sollers, the editor in chief of *Tel Quel*, the journal that had epitomized all things new and revolutionary since the early sixties. Autobiography and "celeb culture" suddenly replaced antihumanist poststructuralism and the belief in the death of the author and of the subject (Sollers 1990 [1983]).

The case of Sollers is exceptional for the extreme violence of his move, which his enemies interpreted as a shameless betrayal due to political opportunism and marketing reasons, but his novel *Women* is clearly a sign of the times. The typically New Novel credo exemplarily theorized by Alain Robbe-Grillet in his *For a New Novel* (Robbe-Grillet 1992 [1963]), with its blatant rejection of the worn-out categories of character, plot, psychology, causality, or spatiotemporal coherence, has run out of steam by this point and is being replaced by more traditional forms of storytelling.

Although straightforwardly narrational at first sight, *The Obscure Cities* occupies a much more subtle and rewarding position, upon which writer Benoît Peeters has clearly elaborated in several critical interventions, among which can be counted the afterword to his second novel, *La Bibliothèque de Villers* (Peeters 2012a [1980]), and a much-quoted lecture at the first international conference on the work by Georges Perec (Peeters 1985). A great fan of the New Novel, as shown by essential criticism on Robbe-Grillet (Peeters 2001b) and a delectable pastiche of Claude Simon in his first novel, *Omnibus* (Peeters 2001a)—in which he imagines Simon's Nobel Prize some ten years before the actual award—Benoît Peeters is also a great defender of the pleasures of classic storytelling and strongly plot-based literature. A book must be readable and exciting at plot level, while also being written in such a way that the reader can progressively discover new aspects and levels so that she can truly become the coauthor of the work. Peeters quotes Nabokov as one of his models, but also Agatha Christie, Edgar Allan Poe, Hergé, and Alfred Hitchcock, the master of suspense whom he also presents as the master of creative reading or viewing. As the detailed analyses within this book will show, this is exactly the reading attitude that *The Obscure Cities* aims to produce. The historical position of the series is therefore that of the flank guard, saving many achievements of avant-garde writing while also demonstrating the necessary merits as well as pleasures of classic storytelling. In 1983, Schuiten and Peeters start a collaboration that tactically and practically opts for a reconciliation between the old and the new.

Yet plot and story are not the only dimensions of *The Obscure Cities* that display a creative tension between past and present. Visually speaking as well, there is a refined merger of styles and techniques borrowed from the drawing and comics tradition and the ambition to appropriate them in new, challenging ways, as a springboard rather than as a straitjacket or an asphyxiating cultural superego. Regardless of the props and settings of the story, a topic that will be addressed in the next chapter, the drawing style of *The Obscure Cities* clearly shows the threats and opportunities Franco-Belgian comics artists are facing in 1983, the year Hergé died and the *bande dessinée* world stood still.

In the Franco-Belgian context, the Clear Line technique and its aesthetics of stylization and legibility had achieved a solid hegemony since the postwar period, either in the Hergé/Tintin version of it or that of the competing Spirou group, the former being considered a slightly more academic form of Clear Line drawing, the latter often seen as a more spontaneous and humoristic type, more open to personal variations and tempted by individual brio and exuberance (the so-called atom style). Most attempts to supersede Hergé and his Clear Line aesthetics are not as revolutionary as one might expect—a phenomenon that perhaps repeats the not-so-conflictual relationships between old and new comics in the previous generations. Many young artists, eager to liberate themselves from the stylistic constraints of the Clear Line, did not do so by a radical overthrow of this aesthetic, but by a kind of ironic mimicry or overplay, a characteristically postmodern reuse and pastiche thoroughly documented by Bruno Lecigne in an influential monograph, *Les Héritiers d'Hergé* (Hergé's heirs; Lecigne, 1983), a study that relied on Jean Baudrillard's "simulacrum" as its theoretical backbone, while using the creative work of artists such as Yves Chaland or Jean-Claude Floc'h and François Rivière.

Here as well, Schuiten and Peeters adopt an interesting intermediary position, quite distinct from the explosion of Clear Line parodies, often hyper–Clear Line exaggerations, in the post–Clear Line era. While respecting a whole set of Clear Line constraints, such as, for instance, the use of contour lines and the practice of monochromatic color zones inside these lines, François Schuiten's artwork introduces two changes: first, a much more realistic drawing style, which breaks away from the sometimes caricatured stylization inherent to most Clear Line types; second, the systematic and highly integrated use of hatching lines, which abandons the general Clear Line resistance to shadowing and crisscrossing. Furthermore, *The Obscure Cities* mixes color and black and white, sometimes even within single volumes. Technically speaking, one also notices a rapid abandonment of coloring devices: in *Samaris*, Schuiten still uses the Hergéan technique of "blue print coloring," that is, of adding colors to separate prints deprived of any black line to which the black contour lines were added afterward. In later works, he will use the direct color technique as well as utilize a different kind of black, a color no longer limited to contour lines but which evokes more ancient engraving techniques.

The blurring of boundaries between stylistic features and media will prove fundamental in the series, within the books themselves but also in the many expansions and continuations of the series outside the printed volumes. The absence of color in certain books and drawings immediately foregrounds the other model that is competing here with Hergé's Clear Line: the nineteenth-century engravings by Gustave Doré and others. Less frequently mentioned in the histories of comics, yet no less important a forerunner of twentieth-century comics than, for instance, Rodolphe Töpffer or Wilhelm Busch, Doré is constantly in the background of Schuiten's drawings, as clearly shown by a comparison with Doré's famous illustrations of world literature: the Bible, Cervantes's *Don Quixote*, or Dante's *Divina Commedia*.

Next to other references such as the tradition of architecture drawings—an aspect that will be discussed in more detail below and in the next chapter—or the illustrative style of *fin de siècle* art nouveau and Jugendstil, still very present in Brussels's architecture today, the mix of Clear Line elements on the one hand and references to *engraving* techniques on the other hand engenders a new way of superseding Hergé while staying within the canonical forms of drawing and illustrations as well as the conventional format of narrative comics. In other words, *The Obscure Cities* is not a work that yields to the purely aestheticizing and nonnarrative tendencies that

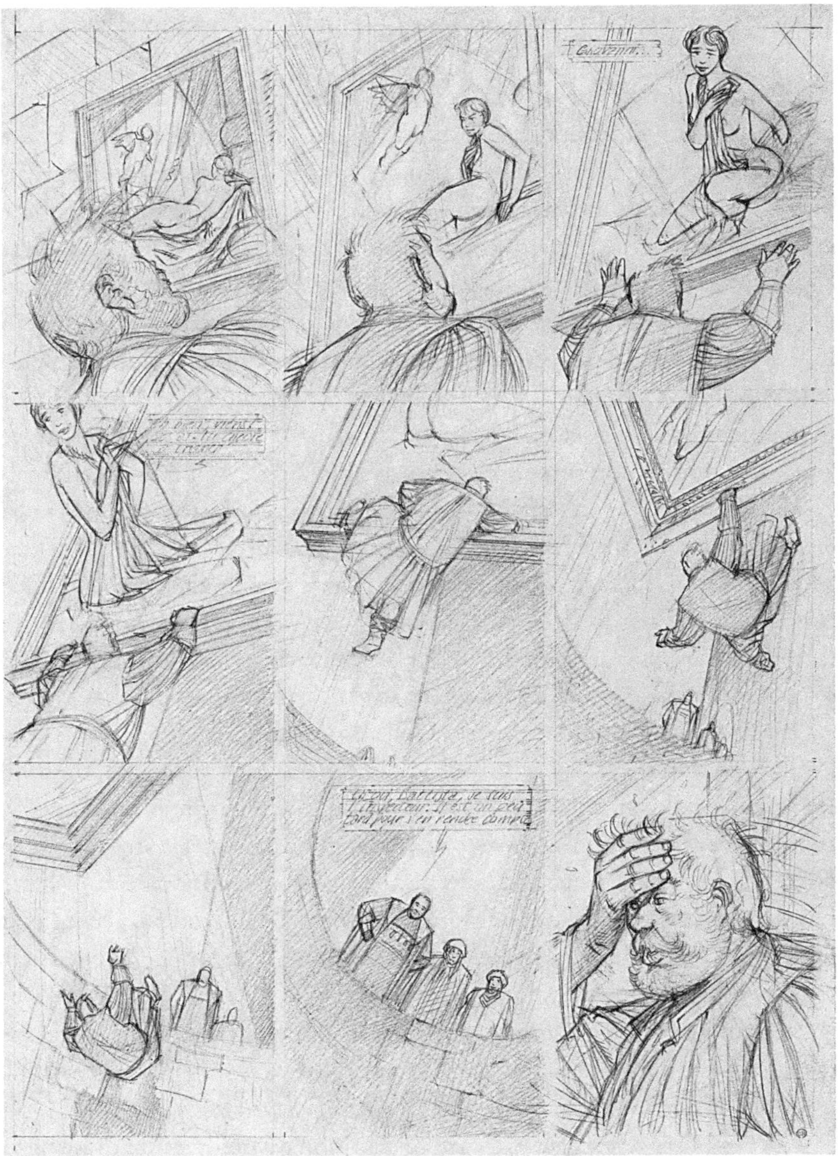

FIG. 1.4 Penciling of page 41 of *The Tower* (© François Schuiten)

grow in importance during the 1980s; that is, the period that sees the emergence of "direct color," a way of drawing that allows for the direct integration of color on the page, unlike the old-fashioned ways of comics drawings characterized by the radical split between drawing and colorizing, the latter often done by underpaid female workers (Groensteen 1993). In spite of the

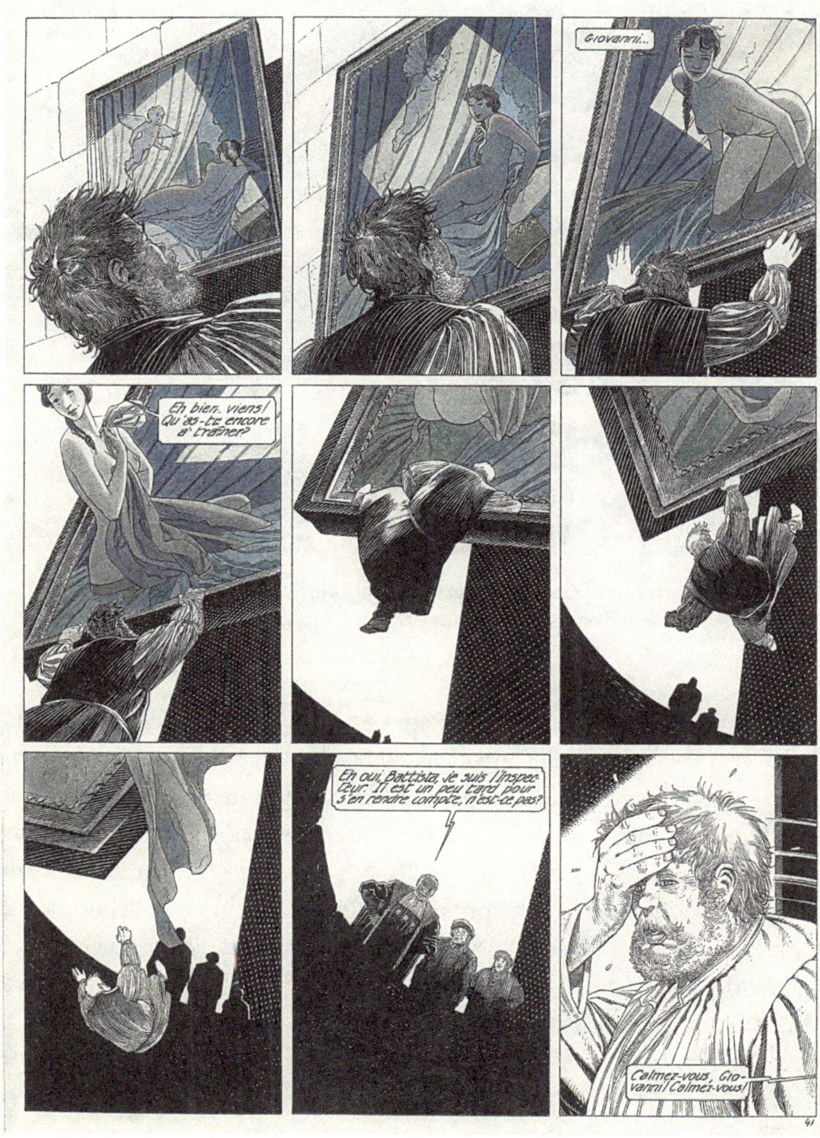

FIG. 1.5 Final version of page 41 of *The Tower* (© Casterman, with kind permission of the authors and Editions Casterman)

strong presence of panoramic views and large panels, often covering a full page, *The Obscure Cities* is anything but a sequence of poster art images. It takes storytelling very seriously, although the stories told introduce totally new ways of focusing on story worlds and, in so doing, address the relationship between character and story world.

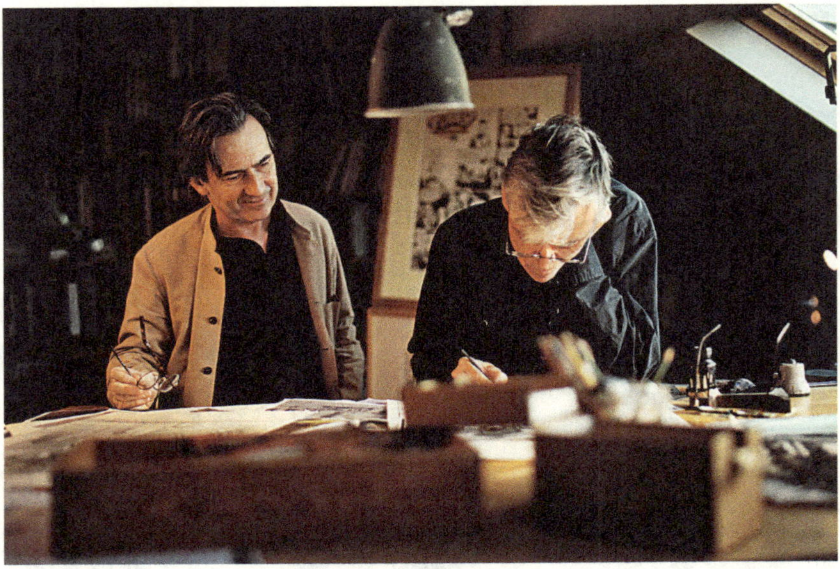

FIG. 1.6 Benoît Peeters and François Schuiten "co-working" at *The Obscure Cities*, photograph by Vladimir Peeters (© Vladimir Peeters)

One of the most salient characteristics of *The Obscure Cities* is the special collaboration between its authors. The hyphen between the names of the two authors, who sign their work with the pen name Schuiten-Peeters, is indeed more than a typographical whim. It symbolizes instead the hybridization of the functions of writing and drawing. *The Obscure Cities* is the result of a duo that is at the same time highly specialized, since both François Schuiten and Benoît Peeters have their own very successful careers as multimedia visual artist and writer and filmmaker, respectively.

Besides being a scriptwriter for various comics, photo novels, and cinema artists, Peeters is also a highly acclaimed biographer (2011, 2012b),[8] fiction writer, and essayist[9]—not to mention his strong commitment to a wide range of cultural policies and cultural management duties and functions, as well as teaching assignments.[10]

Born and raised in a family of artists and architects (Marion 2009), François Schuiten has almost instantaneously developed multiple career paths. Besides his work on *The Obscure Cities* and as an illustrator and drawing artist, he has been in charge of the visual design and scenography for countless events, public spaces, cultural venues, and premises all over the world: for example, metro stations in Brussels and Paris, murals in various cities,

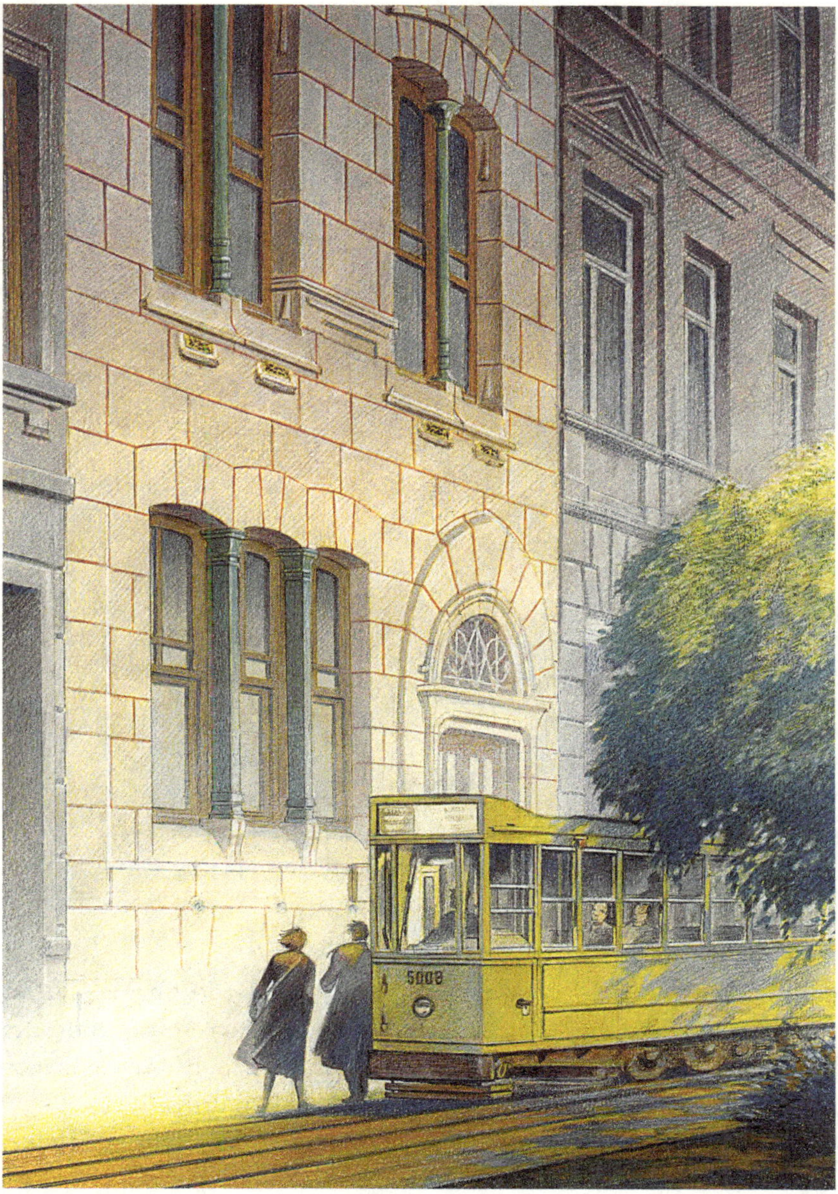

FIG. 1.7 The Autrique House in Brussels, serigraphy by François Schuiten (© François Schuiten)

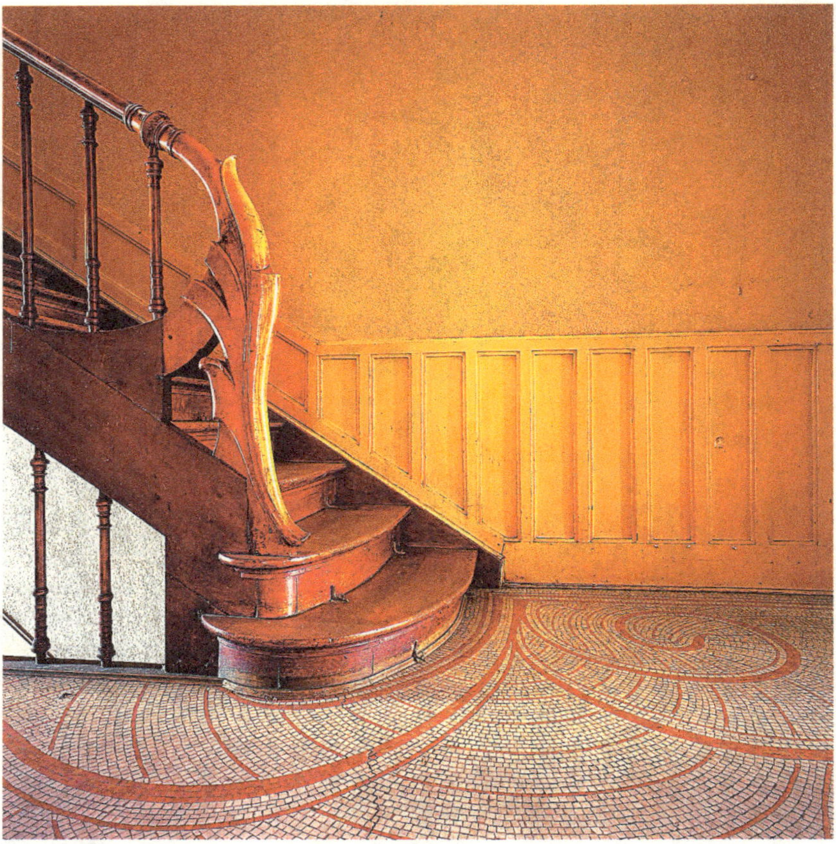

FIG. 1.8 The Autrique House, photography by Marie-Françoise Plissart (© Marie-Françoise Plissart)

pavilions at the Hannover World's Fair and at Expo 2005 in Aichi, Japan, and the restoration, with Benoît Peeters, of the Maison Autrique, the first house designed by art nouveau architect Victor Horta in Brussels, and more recently the new train museum, Train World,[11] also in Brussels.

In order to fully grasp the singularity of the collaboration between Schuiten and Peeters, it does not suffice to insist on their multiple and systematic exchanges during the elaboration of *The Obscure Cities*. As a writer, Peeters constantly advances proposals for the visual look and feel of the story world, the drawing style, and the page layout of the series, whereas Schuiten no less frequently makes suggestions at the level of plot, characters, and fictional universe. No less important is the fact that the authorial "posture" of Schuiten-Peeters is at the same time an illustration as well as a critique of auteur theory, currently still one of the strongest underlying ideological models of the shift

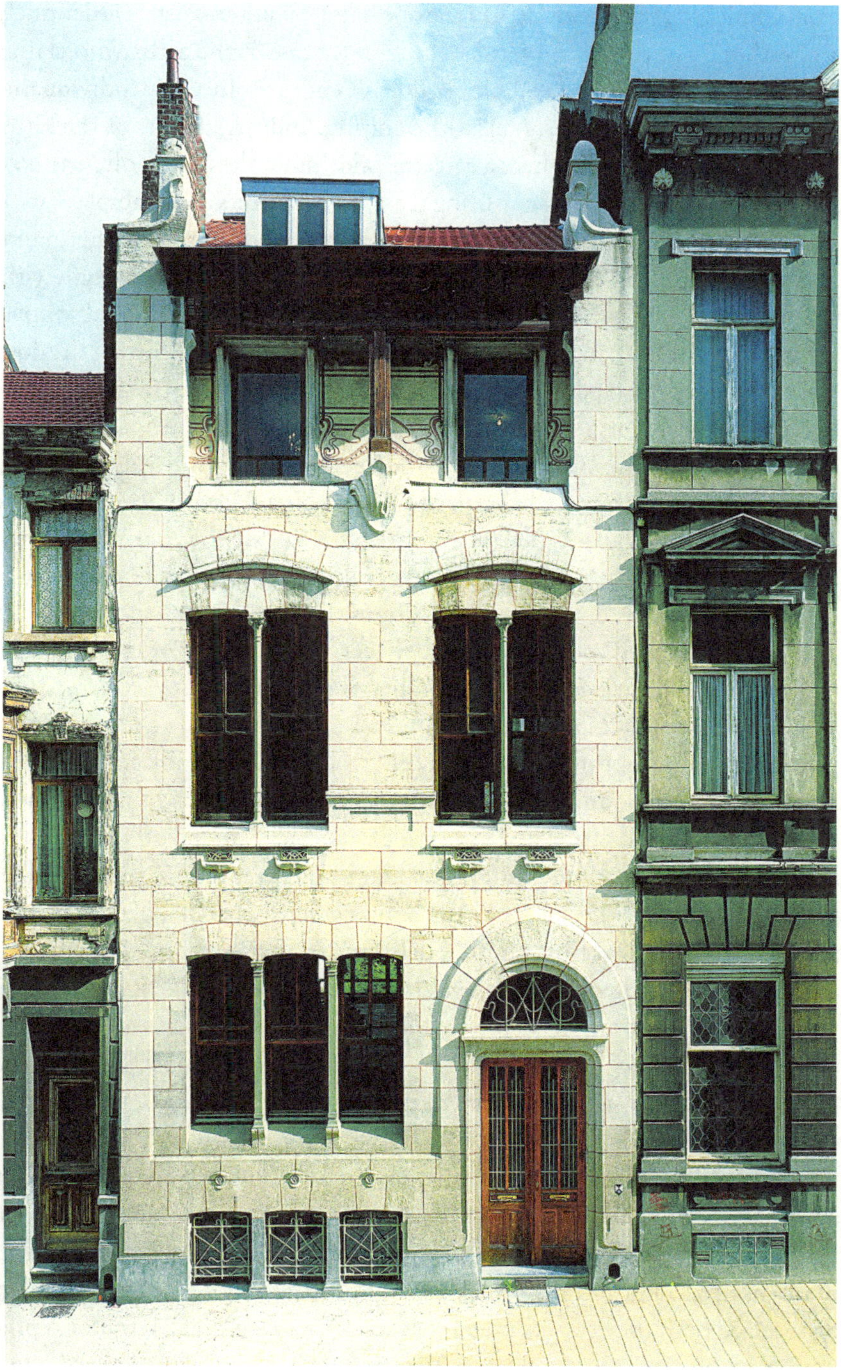

FIG. 1.9 The Autrique House, photography by Marie-Françoise Plissart (© Marie-Françoise Plissart)

from comics to graphic novels. On the one hand, Schuiten-Peeters is definitely an "author"—in the strong sense of auteur, that is, of the artist who claims to supervise and control a complex collective endeavor in a very individualistic sense—since both artists reject the cultural-industrial logic of the series as developed by a studio where a certain "pilot" is endlessly and often almost anonymously continued by a shifting team of freelancers and employees with no real participation in decisions regarding the work. On the other hand, Schuiten-Peeters is an author duo truly different in conception. To begin with, the duo does not present itself as a "complete author," as the new graphic novel aesthetics would like to have it; that is, the single author combining the double competences or expertise of drawing and storytelling, the two major functions of comics storytelling that the traditional studio always tended to carefully distinguish. Both Schuiten and Peeters in their individual projects and Schuiten-Peeters, as the hybridized author of *The Obscure Cities*, prove very critical of all generic boundaries and the high-low divide that has not disappeared with the shift from comics to graphic novel. From the very start of their personal as well as their joint careers, François Schuiten and Benoît Peeters have crossed the boundaries between high and low, text and image, the stability of print and the ephemerality of performance. *The Obscure Cities* is also a series that is resolutely transgenre. It is a mosaic or patchwork of genres, all strongly profiled and competing for the reader's attention: science fiction, encyclopedic and archival writing, pseudo-documentary, radio drama, travelogue, political satire, and psychological drama, among others. It is also a series that is increasingly transmedial, not in the sense initially coined by Henry Jenkins—as the "process where integral elements of a fiction get dispersed systematically across multiple delivery channels for the purpose of creating a unified and coordinated entertainment experience" (Jenkins 2007, n.p.)—but as the result of successive incursions in unceasingly new forms of world making beyond print, both online and offline. Finally, *The Obscure Cities* is also a series that continues to explore in novel and radical ways audience participation, for instance by challenging the institutional gaps among original work, authorized fan fiction, and rogue—that is, appropriationist, activist, noncanonical, often politically radical—expansions (De Kosnik 2016).

To summarize: *The Obscure Cities* is a series that appeared after a period of intense and radical transformations of European comics culture and that epitomized both the literary and modern classic take on serious comics as promoted by the magazine *(À Suivre)*. The great novelty of the series resides not only in the exploration of aspects rarely addressed in the European tradition, such as the tension between story (plot, action) and story world, but also in the subtle hybridization of many conventional dichotomies, such as high versus low or one-shot versus serial publication. These characteristics are reflected in the special collaboration of its two authors, who have managed to deepen their personal careers while also producing a form of narrative agency that blurs the boundaries between the verbal and the visual.

2

A World of Its Own

The Obscure Cities is not born out of a mere idea—a plot, a concept, a character, a universe, a storytelling technique. Nor was the series triggered by an image or a set of images, fixed or moving. In spite of the ubiquitous intertextual references to all kinds of visual models and examples or the immediately recognizable touch and feel of the work, the starting point of *The Obscure Cities* was an actual experience, that of a very special place, the monumental, even pharaonic Brussels Law Courts building, the chief work of the architect Joseph Poelaert (1817–1879), which continues to dominate the city even today (in comparison, the Royal Palace, well known to the readers of Tintin's *King Ottokar's Scepter*, is nothing but an operetta construction). As revealed by Benoît Peeters in the introductory page to the Integral Edition, the origins of the series can be situated in 1979, when the two friends, Schuiten and Peeters, visited the Poelaert building. Yet this visit was more than an example of mere chance or preparatory research; it was from the very beginning an actual experience of the *Obscure Cities* world, the Law Courts building being one of the hidden contact zones between Earth and Counter-Earth: "On a rainy November day of 1979, we have opened a tiny door in the unlikely labyrinth of the Brussels Law Courts building. It was by this chance event that we discovered the world of the Obscure Cities. We have longtime traveled from Xhystos to Urbicand and from Pâhry to Blossfeldstadt. How could we ever have imagined the places these explorations would bring us to and the encounters they would allow us to make?" (vol. 1, p. 5).

Thus everything started with the visit to this neoclassicist but highly eclectic building with its more than 1,000 rooms and countless number of windows, corridors, and stairways. Whatever the singular status of Peeters's opening statement, in which he describes the *Obscure Cities* world not as the author of a work of fiction but as an actual visitor and witness of Counter-Earth,[1] it would be difficult to find a more fitting example of what Russian formalist Mikhail Bakhtin (1981) understood by the notion of chronotope or "time-space," referring to the fact that different literary genres operate with different configurations of time and space, each genre presenting a specific combination of setting and plot lines and thus obtaining its particular narrative character (the classic example of the gothic store, where ghost stories and caves or crypts are two sides of the same medal). The Poelaert building not only triggers a narrative—after all, any picture can tell a story—or a whole range of narratives; it is itself a structure that produces an overlap of space and time while being also the product of such an overlap itself; since it is not possible to see it, one can only wander through it—and immediately become lost—both by the monumental character of the construction and by the labyrinthine nature of its structure. In a chronotope it is impossible to tell the story from the place and vice versa. In this case, the visit to the Brussels Law Courts building put the whole work in motion, and *The Obscure Cities* can be read as the personal and fictionalized transposition of a day at the mesmerizing and bewildering palace (in French, the Law Court is known as the *palais de justice* or Palace of Justice). It is the visit to the building, not the image of the building, that sets the creative work in motion. The trigger of the work is the actual embodied experience of the Law Courts, not the all-too-familiar outside view of the monument that still dominates the Brussels skyline and that all city dwellers know, but not always in their flesh and bones (for one does not visit a court of law as a tourist attraction, and the reputation of the building, the construction of which involved the destruction of an entire low-income area, remains highly ambivalent).[2]

This Ur-moment of the series, perhaps reimagined after the event in order to rationalize the shock of the moment, is a real knot of meanings and experiences. The Poelaert building proves to be much more than just a spectacular edifice; it immediately foreshadows some of the major characteristics of Schuiten and Peeters's work. However, the real stakes of the Law Courts chronotope may not all be present or readable from the first episode: *The Obscure Cities* is, oxymoronically, a permanent work in progress—in the same vein as the unfinished and perpetually renovated Poelaert building—and several aspects and significations of the place can only be discovered in a very slow

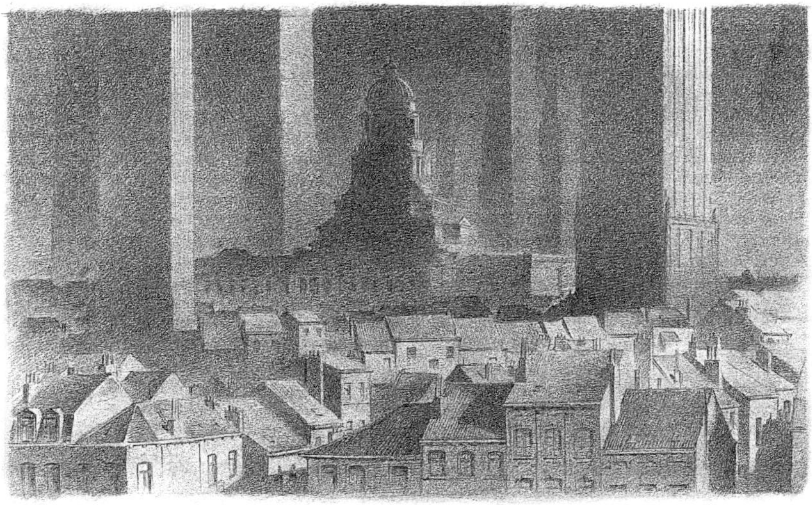

FIG. 2.1 The Brussels Law Courts House, by François Schuiten (© François Schuiten)

and progressive way, almost by trial and error. What is clear from the very start, however, is the awareness of the architectural theme in *The Obscure Cities*. When the first volume of the series was published, the promotion of the book—highly anticipated after a successful first run in *(À Suivre)*—emphasized its unique selling proposal: *Samaris* was the first comic whose main character was not a human or animal character but . . . architecture. Not in the sense of an anthropomorphic or humanized setting or indeed a prop that achieves human agency—think of the famous July 26, 1908, episode of *Little Nemo in Slumberland*, where the little boy's bed comes alive and strolls through the city, stretching its "legs" over the skyscrapers as in a kind of panoramic steeplechase, or of the more recent examples of manga where buildings morph into robots—but in the less superficial sense of places, spaces, buildings, and settings where, animated or motionless, the architectural element is the fundamental driver of the action. In *The Obscure Cities*, the plot and more generally the whole structure of the work depend on the relationship between setting and action. More technically speaking, the series explores the hybridization of the two forms of diegesis that narratologists often distinguish (Genette 1983): diegesis in the broad sense as the action as plotted by a narrator (diegesis is then opposed to mimesis, supposedly direct and unplotted) and diegesis in the narrow sense of the word as the spatiotemporal setting in which the action takes place (here, in this narrow sense, action is excluded from the definition of diegesis). The very use of the notion of chronotope already hints at the blurring of boundaries between the action in the foreground and the setting in the background, but it is no exaggeration to say that the factor that actually dominates is the background—of which architecture is of course a vital aspect.

In the new *bande dessinée* world, this interest in architecture is anything but a surprise. In 1985, in between the first run of *Fever in Urbicand*, the second volume of *The Obscure Cities*, and its eventual publication in album format, the Angoulême Comics Center organized a reference exhibit on architecture and comics, whose catalogue appeared as a special issue of *(À Suivre)*.[3] *The Obscure Cities* occupied a prominent place in the exhibit, which at the same time was used as a marketing tool for the new album, which would receive an important award at the subsequent Angoulême festival. As all these publications and activities show, the link between comics and architecture has been always been very strong. For a better understanding of their relationship, it is, however, necessary not to reduce it to a kind of one-way traffic leading from architecture to comics but to go beyond the mere study of the presence of architectural themes and motifs in comics. Granted, this presence is important and long-standing, but it does not suffice to disclose what is really at stake in the encounter between buildings and drawings.

Let us first examine the question from the point of view of comics. The fundamental question in this regard is well raised by Catherine Labio, who makes a sharp distinction between the thematic, historical, and sociological approaches of architectural elements in comics and the analysis of the nonrepresentational architectural features of page and book. The former concerns the study of architecture "in comics," the latter has to do with the architecture "of comics," and the author argues that "there is an architectural unconscious of the comics page, an extradiegetic mirroring of domestic architecture that gives the page its basic structure and accounts in significant measure for the readability, emotional power, and popularity of the genre" (2015, 317). This strong theoretical hypothesis is then developed along two lines of research. The first one is static: the classic layout configurations of a comics page are similar to "the basic shapes and façade structures of residential buildings in their places of origin" (317). The second one is dynamic and compares the reading of a comic to the walk through a building: "The beholder has no choice but to begin by taking in the entire composition of the page, no matter how fleetingly. From that point on, if she decides to read the comic, she is automatically involved in a perpetual zooming in and out of the various frames that make up the page and shifts continuously between her role as spectator/viewer and her role as reader, an experience that makes reading a comic more like entering a building than reading a novel" (326).

In a second step, this innovative approach can be completed with the point of view of the architect. Modern architects turn more and more to comics, not only as a sales or marketing tool, but also as a medium that proves capable of doing what other types of visualization, theoretically more "serious," more prestigious, and more technical, often fail to do. In her remarkable study *Bricks and Balloons*, Mélanie van der Hoorn (2012) has brought together an amazing corpus of comics representations of architectural ideas and realizations as commissioned by architects, among which are some by the more famous ones, such as those by Jean Nouvel. In the lavishly illustrated overview she presents of these exchanges between bricks and balloons, two elements come strongly to the fore, which largely overlap, but from another perspective, with the claims made by Catherine Labio.

On the one hand, van der Hoorn convincingly demonstrates that there is a necessary analogy between the two art forms, which are both based on the practice of drawing. A building, before it becomes a tridimensional construction, has to exist as a drawing, and we know that in certain cases the architect considers her or his job "done" once the drawing is finished (perhaps not unlike Hitchcock, who liked to boast that the real work was done once the storyboard was finished, the actual shooting being nothing more than a boring duty having nothing to do with the real creativity of the director). Yet van der Hoorn's examples clearly establish that the relationship between architectural drawing and comics drawing is not necessarily that of master and slave: comics can achieve a dynamic form of drawing that the static, single-image, monoperspectival architectural drawings can only dream of. In addition, comics also propose drawings that are a critique of architecture, that is, of certain forms of architecture—for instance by showing the gap between the theoretical perfection of the design and the practical problems it may induce. Conversely, the drawings can also have a rhetorical power that no technical description can equal, certainly if they combine words and images, as demonstrated in the following anecdote by François Schuiten, himself a scion of an architectural family:

> As a small boy, Schuiten sometimes accompanied his father on a visit to a client. "The client would pour some whisky, drank one himself, and then my father began to draw the house and—very smart—he introduced the dressing table of the lady of the house, the favorite chair of the man of the house, the dog, and drew it all probably four times as large as it would ever turn out to be.

> Then he sprayed fixative over the pastels, pulled out a *passe-partout*, framed the drawing and set it over the dresser of the lady. 'So,' he would say, 'just think it over.' Sometime later the phone would ring: 'Yes Mr Schuiten, we agree to your proposals.' What did that mean? He drew their dreams, he opened a window on what could be their future." (Marion 2009, 13)

On the other hand, van der Hoorn also suggests that comics are an appropriate medium when it comes down to revealing the interaction between mankind and building, as well as in establishing an idea of the embodied experience of a building, of the way it is actually lived in and how it is related to its larger environment (for a building is never a stand-alone construction). Comics also succeed in adding a temporal dimension that is generally missing in architectural sketches or plans, thus heightening the embodied experience of something that may not yet exist as an actual building. At the same time, they also link the experience of the house with that of its material and social context. As van der Hoorn puts it: "Strip artists do not simply adopt architect's designs, but also appear to develop the concepts on which they are based. The largely 'paper' architecture and urban planning are invariably exhibited in conjunction with the everyday hustle in nearby alleyways, and several storylines unfold within this context. In this way, architectural designs come into direct contact with prevailing societal structures, and develop into urban concepts that embrace much more than what architects have ever been able to demonstrate in their drawings and scale models" (2012, 22). It comes as no surprise that *The Obscure Cities* follows these general lines, as far as seen from the comics point of view (it is not too absurd to think, however, that Schuiten's very interest in the medium of comics can be seen as an attempt to continue the profession of his father). The very structure of the series, which complicates the fundamental properties of what a comics series actually is (a point we will analyze in detail in a later chapter), is clearly a fictional reenactment of the dizzying experience of a visit at the Brussels Law Courts—and probably of the experience of living in Brussels as well, a dramatically eclectic and apparently chaotic city. And many fictional and layout elements of *The Obscure Cities* are an almost direct transposition of some of the features of a classic comic page. The fundamental image of the uncontrollably dynamic network, a permanently expanding structure based on the mathematical figure of the cube, is the visual translation of three basic elements. First, the dimensions of the panel (in *Fever in Urbicand*, where this figure first appears): the opening page is composed of a grid of six symmetrical rectangular yet not completely square panels. Second, the figure of the rectangle is

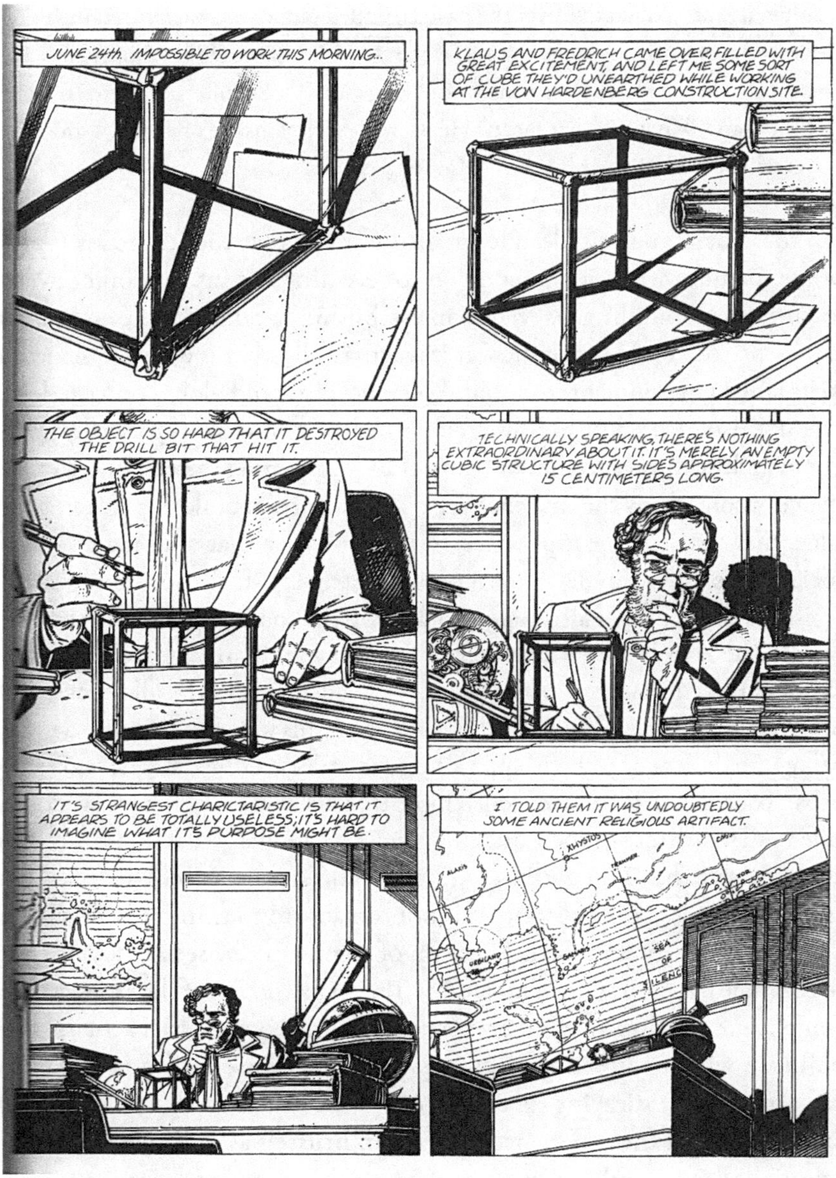

FIG. 2.2 First page of the French version of *Fever in Urbicand*. Excerpt from *Fever in Urbicand*, François Schuiten and Benoît Peeters (© Casterman, with kind permission of the authors and Editions Casterman)

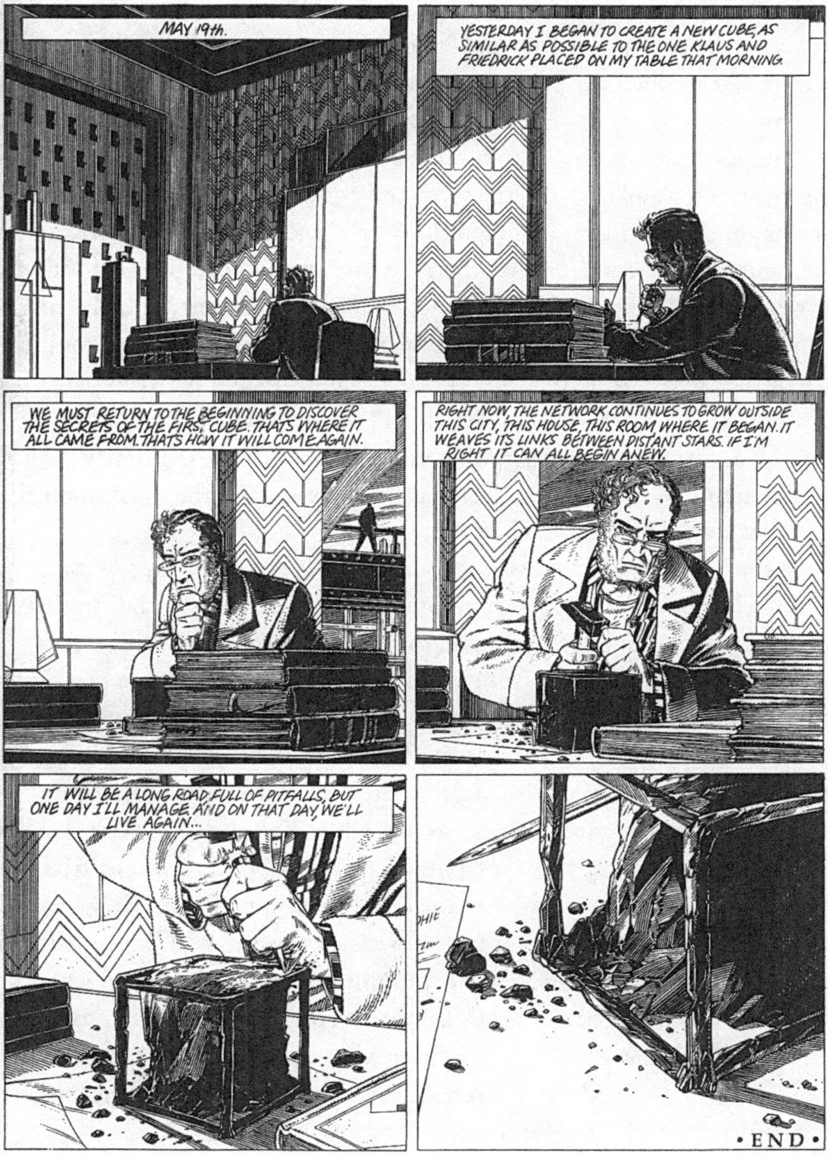

FIG. 2.3 Last page of the French version of *Fever in Urbicand.* Excerpt from *Fever in Urbicand*, François Schuiten and Benoît Peeters (© Casterman, with kind permission of the authors and Editions Casterman)

then, in the fictional world of the comics, translated into the three-dimensional figure of the cube—not Rubik's Cube, one of the fads of the time, but the skeleton of an open cube that at the same time "normalizes" the nonsquare rectangle into the more perfect form of a cube and incorporates certain nodes and bulges that announce the subsequent proliferation of the cubes. Third, the creative tension between the form and position of the layout grid, on the one hand, and the material integration of the figurative elements within the nonfigurative structure, on the other: the page layout is composed of perfectly horizontal units at water level; the fictional cubes are shown in a slanting or oblique position as well, of course, in perspective. The subsequent multiplying of the cube is announced by the material mismatch between panel and content, which at the same time clearly mirror each other—yet not in a smooth or transparent way. Another variation on the cube is given by the general structure of the album, which has six chapters, and the illustration that occupies the first page of each of them.

In their evocation of Brussels, Schuiten and Peeters also pay a lot of attention to the notion of "façadism," that is, the makeover of a building after its almost complete demolishment and the claim to save the past by keeping the façade of the old building. Yet façadism is not only a debatable practice of urban renovation; it is also a good example of the exchanges between referential and nonreferential elements in the debate on comics and architecture. Just as comics can fictionalize material drawing features by projecting them into a 3-D space (the panel becomes a cube, which becomes a network of cubes, which eventually overgrows the city, etc.), the real world can also strip its own 3-D reality in order to reduce it to the two-dimensionality of a drawing, and this is exactly what happens when Brussels city planners and businessmen, instead of tearing down a complete building, leave the façade, which turns the whole city into a flat, almost cardboard setting. This is the fundamental clue of *Samaris*, based on the misreading of a 2-D space as a 3-D space. Other examples of these productive mechanisms, which are typical of the relationship between comics and building, will be given later on.

The question is not, however, whether this way of comics-making distinguishes *The Obscure Cities* from other creators and productions. As soon as one starts studying comics from this angle, examples abound. It would almost be adding insult to injury by recalling here the names of major creators such as Winsor McCay, Seth, or Chris Ware, whose prestigious work is profoundly marked by the convergence of comics and architecture—contemporary architecture in the case of McCay, who reworks not only the "high" art nouveau style of well-to-do New York neighborhoods but also the "low" entertainment

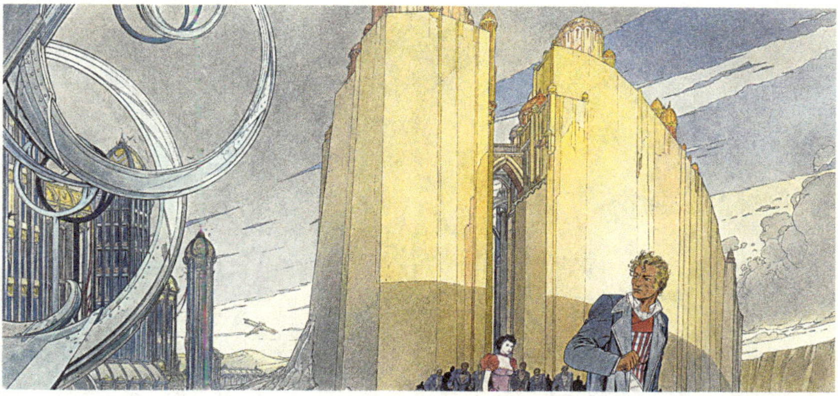

FIG. 2.4 *Samaris*, cover by François Schuiten (© François Schuiten)

architecture of Coney Island (Roeder 2014), and often older and vintage types of architecture in the case of Seth and Ware, whose work has been rapidly introduced in France thanks to the efforts of Benoît Peeters, Jean-Christophe Menu, Thierry Groensteen, and many others (Samson and Peeters 2010). The real question becomes, then, which specific stance *The Obscure Cities* takes in this general context and how it manages to present a different take on comics and architecture during the elaboration of the series. Four elements come to the fore here, none of them per se unique or exclusive to the world invented by Schuiten and Peeters, but the combination of which defines the specific stance of *The Obscure Cities*: (1) the mutual implication of fiction and reality; (2) the open definition of an integral form of architecture; (3) the focus on becoming; and (4) the emphasis on power, discipline, and resistance (three concepts theorized by Michel Foucault in his work on the way in which modern nation-states tend to categorize bodies and make them available for surveillance and control; see Foucault 1995).

Counter-Earth, the global name given to the universe composed by the planet that *The Obscure Cities* progressively discloses, seems at first a fictional universe, an unreal version or transposition of the planet Earth as we know it: not simply a "possible world," as will be discussed in more detail in chapter 3, but a kind of "second Earth" that quotes, changes, and remixes a certain form of life on Earth and human civilization. Yet to identify Earth with reality and Counter-Earth with fiction is precisely what Schuiten and Peeters strongly reject. Instead, they do everything they can to blur the boundaries between both, and the strategy they adopt travels in three directions: the fictionalization of earth, the defictionalization of Counter-Earth, and the building of contact zones between them.

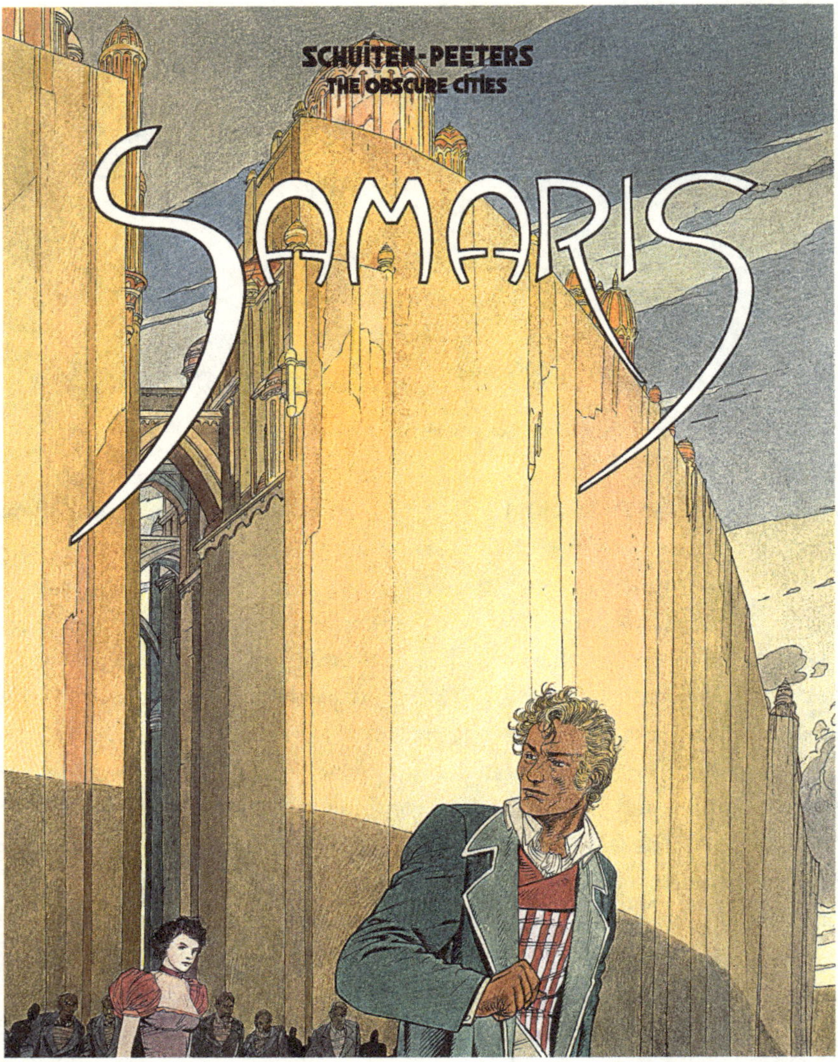

FIG. 2.5 *Samaris*, full cover illustration (© François Schuiten)

True, the world of Counter-Earth definitely refers to "our" world, but it would be a mistake to believe that the countless cultural and historical references and allusions to real-world elements are "pure." Indeed, the world that is being reshaped in Counter-Earth is a world that is already a mix of reality and fiction, as shown, for instance, by the prominence taken by Jules Verne, the great French novelist whose work often presents a sophisticated mix of science, fiction, and science fiction, or figures such as Jorge Luis Borges, Orson Welles, or Nadar (pseudonym of Gaspard-Félix Tournachon), who reappear in a very recognizable way in the Counter-Earth fiction of *The Obscure Cities*. In other words: the real world to which Schuiten and Peeters refer is a reality inhabited by characters whose major contribution to society has been the construction of fictional worlds. The same applies to what is the most visible presence of reality in *The Obscure Cities*, namely, the reinvention of architectural styles, urban ensembles, and a wide range of geographical components. It is impossible not to notice from the very first page of the series that *The Obscure Cities* amorously plays with art nouveau and art deco, that the city map of its invented cities is not without relationships with those of existing cities, and that the living conditions on Counter-Earth are not very different from what we know on Earth. At the same time, however, the underlying idea of real Earth as we can derive it from its reconstruction on Counter-Earth is that of a dramatic mix or hybridization of sometimes very heterogeneous elements, and the noticeable place taken by Brussels—the real city of Brussels—as implicit or explicit generator of the Counter-Earth universe is far from being an accident, given the infamous position of the city as the epitome of architectural chaos, permanent destruction and reconstruction, and urban nonplanning (all elements that also have their charm and do not prevent many people from enjoying the city for exactly this reason). Put differently: the world as *The Obscure Cities* invites us to imagine it is to a certain extent a world that is inflected by fiction and that is definitely unclear, impure, highly hybridized.

On the other hand, the fictional world of *The Obscure Cities* is always presented as a real world. In spite of the apparent implausibility of many of its characteristics, Counter-Earth is systematically described in utterly realistic terms, and the authors take many steps to convince us of the actual existence of this no longer impossible world. Hence, for instance, the importance of the meticulous description of technology and all kinds of machines, on the details of measuring time and space, or the permanent reflection on the possibility or impossibility of what is happening. Counter-Earth exemplifies the stunning realizations of old-fashioned technology, it has its own calendar and uses techniques of mapmaking that are not ours, and it exhibits situations that prove quite surprising. Yet this remains a perfectly rational world, at least in theory, not a world of superpowers or a world that rejects the classic laws of physics or gravity. Counter-Earth differs from Earth the way a zebra differs from a horse, not the way a creature from outer space may differ from the human species—and the same goes for the built and natural environment of *The Obscure Cities*.

The most vital element that produces this overlap of fiction and reality is, however, the fact that both worlds are presented as coexisting yet not mutually visible entities. Both Earth and Counter-Earth share the same space; they are both part of the larger universe as we know and experience it. However, one cannot directly see the other, a situation the authors of the series rationalize in terms of a "mutual eclipse" (*The Obscure Cities*, Integral Edition, vol. 1, p. 11). There exist, nevertheless, zones where the frontiers between Earth and Counter-Earth can be crossed, most of the time unexpectedly and even unwillingly. The city of Brüsel/Brussels is the major example of such a contact zone, often more precisely located in the labyrinth of its Law Courts. The existence of these contact zones and the consequences of the movement back and forth between Earth and Counter-Earth are part of the plot drivers of the series.

A second decisive feature in the relationship between comics and architecture is the location of the act of constructing in the larger set of the built environment objects and practices, ranging from furniture and other domestic machines (including decoration, such as plants) to larger issues of city planning (which may obey floral motifs, for example). Karl Blossfeldt, for instance, a photographer much admired by Walter Benjamin and still well known for his close-up photographs of plants published in 1929 as *Urformen der Kunst* (Art forms in nature), is the inspiring source of the whole city of Blossfeldtstad. In the world of *The Obscure Cities*, to build is a comprehensive activity that entails virtually all aspects of human life. The essential art nouveau reference in the series is a good example of such an overarching approach, since it is a style that covers all possible details, including those not directly related to building, such as fashion design (for instance, people are not allowed to wear "unfitting" clothes when living in these kinds of houses!), while at the same time reflecting the outer world (the key structural motives of this style are borrowed from vegetal life), each building also "bleeding" into a hothouse, a garden, a garden city, and so on. In the case of the art deco builders, the link between architecture and city planning is even stronger, and this link—in practice, this tension—is also a powerful motor for various stories.

The strong link between smaller and larger elements of this man-made world (the authors emphasize the sharp distinction between the urban culture of Counter-Earth and the residual presence of natural spaces, which are hardly inhabited) does, however, not mean that *The Obscure Cities* ignores the tension between part and whole. On the contrary, what makes this world so striking and attractive is its very heterogeneity. It is a joyful mix of styles, periods, and also spaces that at first sight may look like the result of a building experiment gone wrong (or mad). At the same time—and this is a fundamental feature of all things architectural in the series—the accumulation of

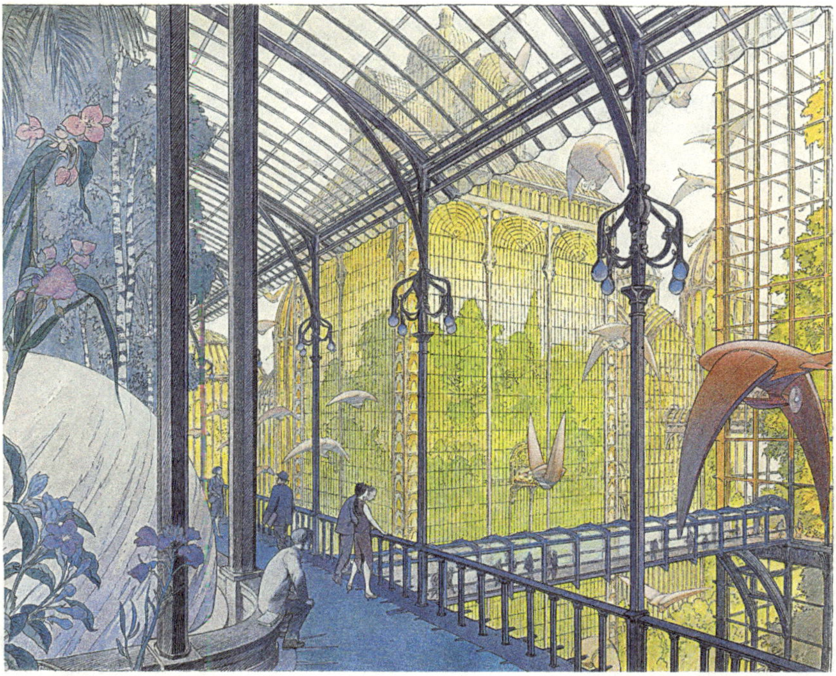

FIG. 2.6 *The City of Calvani*, cover illustration of the Integral Edition, vol. 1 (© Schuiten and Peeters)

building blocks is always experienced in terms of confusion, loss, chaos, bewilderment, and misunderstanding: for those living on Counter-Earth, space is often synonymous with labyrinth, map connotes riddle, left is both left and right and vice versa. In short, the world looks upside-down. This spatial disorientation also has a temporal counterpart: many buildings are not single-period buildings, not only because they present a strong mix of styles, but more importantly because they represent the whole gamut of a building history. They exist simultaneously, that is, in the same physical environment, as plans, as buildings in the making, as finished constructions, as edifices in decay, as ruins, and eventually as legends, uncertain traces of things that perhaps never really existed. The "Tower," for instance, the construction that is at the center (but perhaps also at the periphery?) of the third eponymous volume of *The Obscure Cities*, is a blatant, maddening example of this kind of paradoxical coexistence of past, present, and future, but also of dream and reality. The integral approach of architecture, a practice that swallows virtually everything in the series, is therefore anything but homogeneous. Architecture is always the locus of a conflict, and we will return very soon to this engagement.

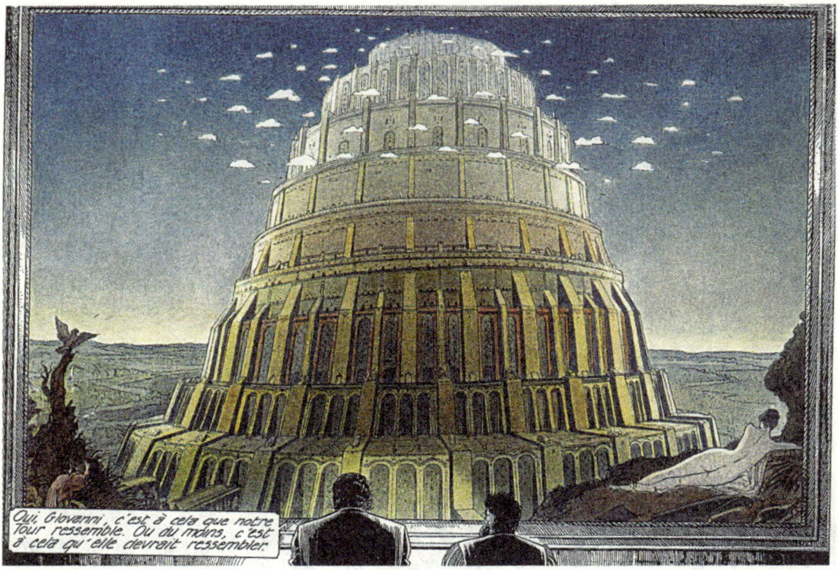

FIG. 2.7 *The Tower*, page 54 in the Integral Edition, vol. 2 (© Casterman, with kind permission of the authors and Editions Casterman)

A third characteristic of the special take on architecture in *The Obscure Cities* has to do with architecture in the making and architecture in the dismantling. Architecture is not only an open structure in *The Obscure Cities*; it also exemplifies the importance of *becoming* instead of being. As already argued by Mélanie van der Hoorn, the comics representation of a building gives rise to the opportunity of presenting access to the embodied experience of it, both by showing how fictional characters live in the building or in the city in question and by offering the readerly equivalent of this trajectory when constructing various paths through the pages of the book. Schuiten and Peeters avail themselves completely of these possibilities. They systematically make indistinct the built space (a room, a house, a city) or the geographical environment (in *The Obscure Cities*, the distance between cities is immense, and the in-between often empty and dangerous) and its actual experience. They always take together the visualization of a space and the trajectory that embodies and at the same time dissimulates its disclosure. In addition, most places are subject to change, a puzzling situation that turns everything into a virtual labyrinth. Hence, of course, the importance of the double theme of transportation and travel. To visit a place means to travel to a place (and from a place that then starts morphing into another place). And the place itself can no longer be distinguished from the transportation system (routes, rivers, railways, airports) whose equally labyrinthine network is superposed on that of the city. The particular names of the cities, which are either direct transpositions of cities on Earth (Brüsel, Pâhry) or indirect evocations of previous, almost mythical civilizations (Xhystos, Alaxis), reinforce the idea of traveling, in this case of interworld transportation.

A fourth and last characteristic refers to the fact that this becoming of places and built spaces is also that of the characters. In a world that conflates object and experience, this transfer is perfectly logical. Characters are attracted to buildings and cities; they try to reach and eventually to inhabit them in order to find their personal selves, as if it were impossible to become oneself outside these spaces. At the same time, however, characters are no less crushed by cities and buildings that they cannot really call theirs. This tension is absolutely fundamental and touches upon the vision of architecture as an instrument of power—in certain cases, even of biopower, literally, power over bodies or, more technically, according to the definition of Michel Foucault, "an explosion of numerous and diverse techniques for achieving the subjugation of bodies and the control of populations" (Foucault 1998, 140). The impact of urban planning on cities like these can be seen as an indirect hint at the simultaneously liberating and totalitarian tendencies of modernist architecture inspired by Le Corbusier's thinking in "The Radiant City."

A simple anecdote may symbolize this dichotomy. In a biographical note reported in the city guide of Brüsel, there is a mention of an architect who has been decorated for never having realized any project (*The Obscure Cities*, Integral Edition, vol. 2, p. 337). What does this praise of inactivity hint at? First of all, it designates ironically the role of the architect and its classic bedfellow, the city planner (the "urbatect," if we follow the neologism popularized by *The Obscure Cities*), as instruments of disciplinarization and the exercise of often very violent power. Architects make buildings, but they also impose a certain way of life, eradicating existing ones or preventing other ways of living. The tragic consequences of this unequal power relationship are shown in all volumes of *The Obscure Cities*: people suffer from the living conditions created by architects and urbatects; they are reduced to wheelworks in the large machine they are required to feed in order to be fed in return by it. They are dominated by an architecture, a transportation system, an organization of city and country, that is not at their service, and this violence hits the socially strong as well as the socially weak. Take for instance "L'Etrange Cas du Dr. Abraham" ("The Strange Case of Dr. Abraham"), one of the short stories comprising the unfinished volume *Les Mystères de Pâhry*,"[4] now all gathered in volume 2 of the Integral Edition. In this story a doctor visiting

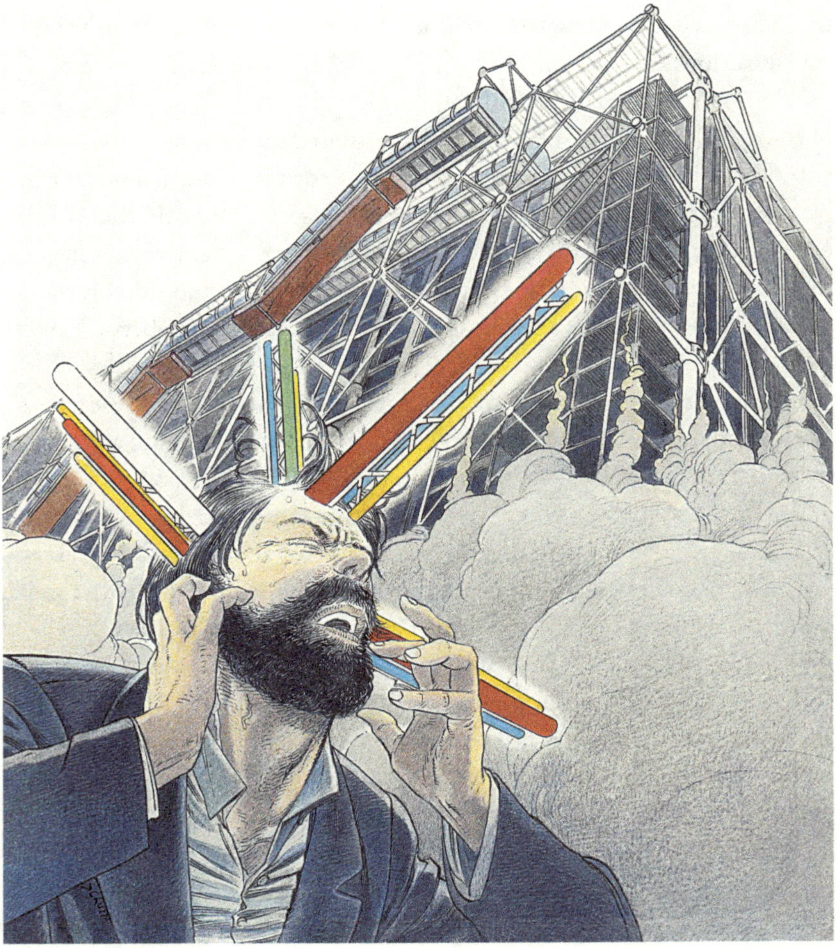

FIG. 2.8 Drawing by François Schuiten for the cover of *The Strange Case of Dr. Abraham* (© François Schuiten)

Pâhry (a clearly recognizable Paris) is suffering from a strange illness that symbolically links the lesion of his body (the idea of extreme headache or brain tumor is visualized by a cluster of colored tubes that spring out of his cranium) and the architectural upheaval of a highly uniform urban environment by a foreign body (in this case the construction of the postmodern center of contemporary arts, Beaubourg, in the middle of a typically nineteenth-century Haussmann-like neighborhood).

What is particularly interesting here is the superposition of architectural violence onto that of the medical sciences. During his stay in Paris,

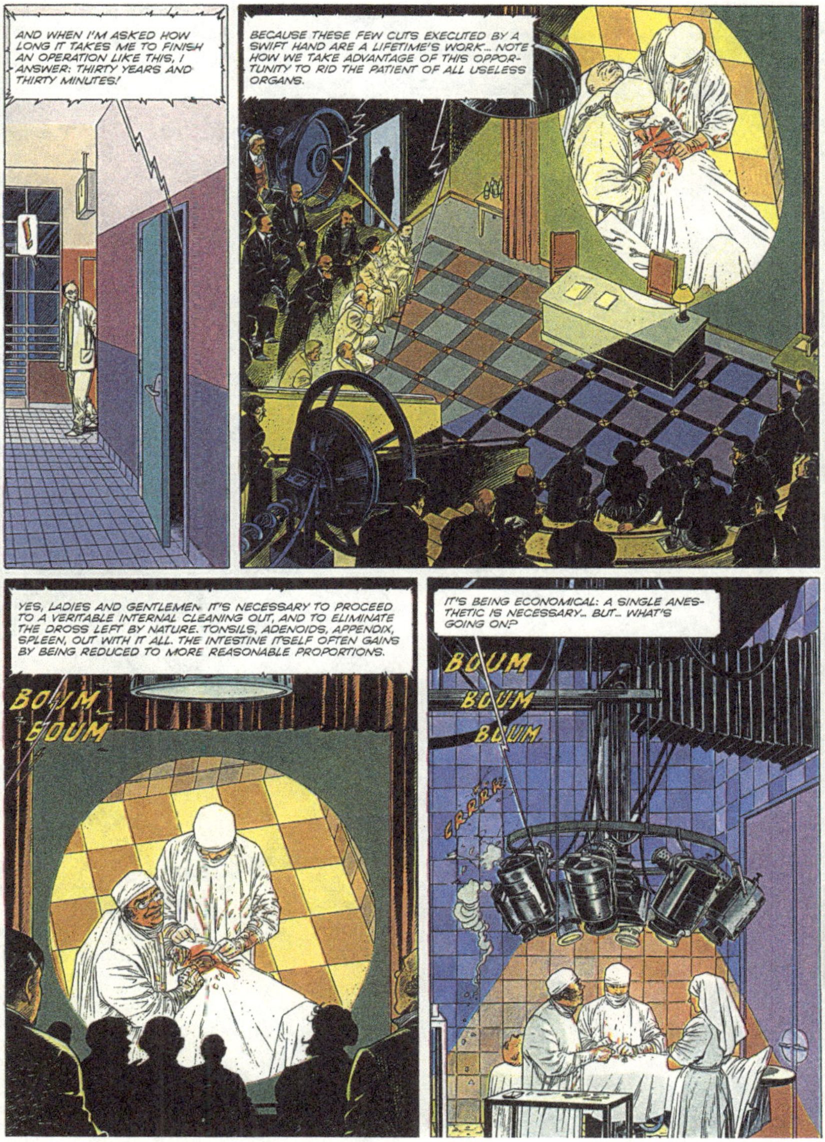

FIG. 2.9 Science and biopower in *Brüsel*, Integral Edition, vol. 2, p. 302. Excerpt from *Brüsel*, François Schuiten and Benoît Peeters (© Casterman, with kind permission of the authors and Editions Casterman)

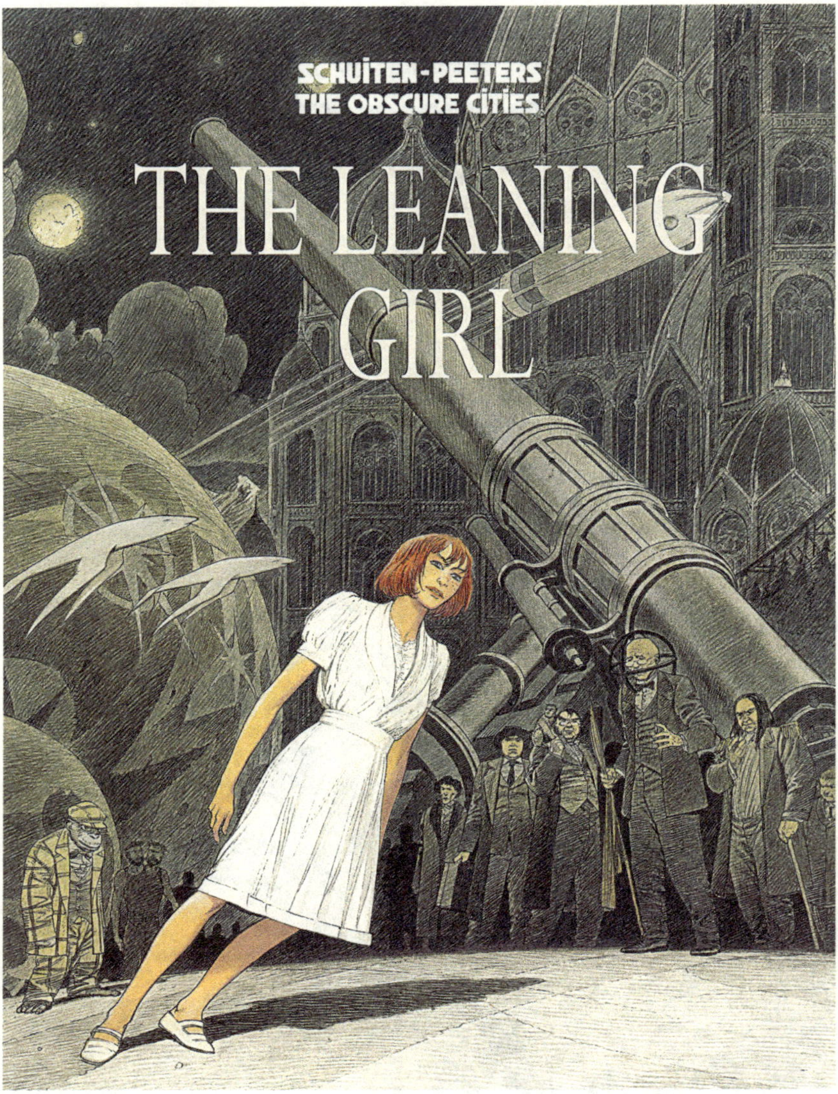

FIG. 2.10 *The Leaning Girl*, cover (© Schuiten and Peeters)

Dr. Abraham, who strangely reminds us of the young Freud, assists one of the legendary classes of Jean-Martin Charcot (the founder of modern neurology, best known for the work with his hysteria patient Louise Augustine Gleizes at the Salpêtrière Hospital in Paris),[5] and *The Obscure Cities* establishes a direct connection between the patient suffering at the hands of the scientist and the doctor suffering from the intrusion of an architectural foreign body: both are victims of a disciplinary power that becomes a biopower in the most literal sense of the word, not just by organizing human groups in categories and thus controlling them, but by infecting their bodies and reducing them to passive objects. The woman hypnotized by the fictional Charcot is the muted victim of all kinds of experiments; the man foreseeing the emergence of Beaubourg is convicted of subversion and eventually executed. Even more direct is the relationship between architecture and medicine as disciplinary forces in *Brüsel*, with the twin plot of the alliance between real estate speculation and medical treatment of recalcitrant individuals and the clandestine grouping of those suffering from both brutal expropriation and even more violent confinement in sinister hospitals. *The Obscure Cities* has many examples of place- and power-induced illnesses, injuries, and dysfunctions, and in a later chapter we will read in more detail the poignant case of the "leaning girl."

Yet, as theorized by Foucault, power and biopower, discipline and control, are never unilateral forces. Any use of power presupposes the possibility of resistance. As a matter of fact, *The Obscure Cities* is equally inhabited by characters—often female ones—who fight the totalitarian aspects of many forms of building and city planning. It is this unending tension between discipline and resistance that defines the world as well as the characters and events of the series.

As we have seen in this chapter, architecture is beyond any doubt the key motif in *The Obscure Cities*. Yet from the very beginning of the series, architecture is a double-faced entity: it refers both to the representational space of the fictional world and to the nonrepresentational or material space of the comics page. *The Obscure Cities* explores this duplicity in various ways, with a special emphasis on elements that are at the same time positive or emancipatory, and negative or repressing. Characters find themselves in their exploration of the built and planned environment, but it also happens that they are crushed by the built environment.

3

More Than a Possible World

In *The Obscure Cities* there is only a small step from building to world making. Architecture is always tightly related to the smallest of tiny ornamental details as well as to the very big features of the mapping of the world known and unknown, including all the zones and spheres in between the utterly small and the very larger than life, from city planning and traveling from city republic to city republic—for that seems to be the political unit that best guarantees the meeting and marriage of microcosm and macrocosm. *The Obscure Cities* and Counter-Earth can therefore be seen as a kind of architecture in the expanded space of the universe. At the same time, however, the part and the whole never seamlessly match or overlap, and for that reason the notion of "world" needs a separate analysis. The universe *The Obscure Cities* hints at cannot be reduced to the sum of what can be said on architecture in the various cities or what can be said on the various cities as architectural constructions.

The gap between part and whole, already referred to in the previous chapter, is not a secondary feature of *The Obscure Cities*. The tension between both levels is a key feature of any real artwork, which resists the confusion of detail and totality and the lack of tension that Theodor W. Adorno and Max Horkheimer considered typical of the cultural industry:

> The conspicuous unity of macrocosm and microcosm confronts human beings with a model of their culture: the false identity of universal and particular.... [The culture industry] crushes equally the whole and the parts. The whole confronts the details in implacable detachment, somewhat like the career of a successful man, in which everything serves to illustrate and demonstrate a success which, in fact[, ... the whole] is no more than the sum of those idiotic events. The so-called leading idea is a filing compartment which creates order, not connections. Lacking both contrast and relatedness, the whole and the detail look alike. Their harmony, guaranteed in advance, mocks the painfully achieved harmony of the great bourgeois works of art. (2002, 95, 99)

The culture industry gives us the illusion that totalities can be grasped. More precisely, it makes us believe that there is such a thing as a totality and that the reduction of a whole to its parts and the subsequent reuse of one of these parts in other contexts do not harm the perception and appreciation of the whole. For example: a symphony is reduced to some famous measures, which are reworked in the musical score of a movie, which is itself nothing else than the faces of its stars. Real art, according to Adorno and Horkheimer, resists this kind of simplification and offers the viewer or reader a confrontation with an irreducible complexity. Instead of reconciling the audience with its own mutilated life through the appealing representation of something that imitates life itself, real art enables its audience to envisage a critical attitude toward life as represented by the work and thus toward the world itself. Such an attitude, Adorno and Horkheimer continue, is both liberating and painful, for there is never a final resolution or reconciliation: "truth"—this is their term throughout the whole essay on the culture industry—is something that can only be found in negative ways, through the never-ending critique of life as it is.

Granted, *The Obscure Cities* should not be interpreted in the first place in light of this devastating critique of the culture industry, but the basic claims by Adorno and Horkheimer certainly help stress the necessity to perform a separate analysis of architecture on the one hand and world making on the other hand. French writer and philosopher Tristan Garcia's essay on *The Obscure Cities* provides an excellent point of departure for the analysis of the world Schuiten and Peeters have built—and continue to do so—in their series. Garcia's reading reveals itself in three steps (Garcia 2013).

First of all, the author underlines the efforts to create a coherent and cohesive universe, which gradually unfolds in permanently altering and always unforeseeable directions, yet never in a purely accumulative, juxtaposing way. Each new item, place, theme, city, character, and so on, that is added to the world is systematically linked to what already exists; and the fact that the number of published volumes remains relatively low, at least in comparison with the proliferation of books in other series or universes, it would seem reasonable to count on the reader's awareness of the totality in the making. The notion of Counter-Earth itself is not something that was already present when the series started, and the elaboration of *The Obscure Cities* does not follow a predetermined order or scheme.

The use of cross-references and the emergence of a global concept are vital in this regard, as happens in the work of all great creators who shift from the publication of a single work to its integration into a larger whole. One finds this mechanism in *Tintin*, but also in Balzac's *Human Comedy* or William Faulkner's Yoknapatawpha County novels, among many other examples. Self-citations and cross-references are countless in *The Obscure Cities* as well. The most radical technique is, however, the decision to reprint all the albums of the series and all other material related to *The Obscure Cities* world as a set of four hardback volumes that reframe the experiments of three and a half decades into a single editorial architecture. Such a presentation does allow an easy and immediate overview of all the building blocks of the Counter-Earth universe. In addition, the inclusion of numerous self-referential documents—authors' comments (but always presented as given by inside witnesses), fictional city guides and encyclopedic entries, pseudo-documentaries, transmedial adaptations (expanding the story world created by Peeters and Schuiten beyond the world of comics in print),[1] testimonies by the characters of the series, archival material from the real world as well as from the *Obscure Cities* world, and so on—reinforces attempts to supersede the idea of *The Obscure Cities* as a mere string of books and adventures taking place in roughly the same world. The importance of this unifying, yet not closing, policy comes even more to the fore if one compares it with the editorial shattering of the individual albums, all purposely published in different series and formats, the material variety of the works being an essential element of the institutional positioning of *The Obscure Cities*, which has always aimed to avoid the stereotypes of the notion of series in comics.

Yet all these world-building procedures and enhancements are also deeply ambivalent, and very different from what can be observed in the case of modern franchised transmedia storytelling enterprises, with their canons and bibles, legally anchored warrants of a unified universe.[2] *The Obscure Cities* obeys another logic, which Garcia examines through the lens of the possible worlds theory. Although this study will not rely on an in-depth discussion of the notion of possible world, initially in philosophy and later also in studies of literary fiction, it is useful to keep in mind the general definition given by one of the leading scholars in the field, Marie-Laure Ryan:

> The foundation of [possible world] theory is the idea that reality—conceived as the sum of the imaginable rather than as the sum of what exists physically—is a universe composed of a plurality of distinct worlds. This universe is hierarchically structured by the opposition of one element, which functions as the center of the system, to all the other members of the set. . . . The central element is known as the "actual" or "real" world . . . while the other members of the system are alternative, or non-actual possible worlds. . . . For a world to be possible, it must be linked to the actual world by a relation of accessibility. The boundaries of the possible depend on the particular interpretation given to this notion of accessibility. The most common interpretation associates possibility with logical laws: every world that respects the principles of non-contradiction and of the excluded middle is a possible world. (Ryan 2013, n.p.)

As stated by Tristan Garcia, the work by Schuiten and Peeters illustrates as well as challenges possible world theory, for it confronts its readers with a universe presenting two parallel worlds, but without giving them strong indications that one of them is the "actual" world while the other one is the "alternative" world. For Garcia, Counter-Earth is not a substitute of our own world the same way as is, for instance, the world of Tolkien's Middle Earth, the *Star Wars* franchise, or any other "possible world." It is definitely a world, and no less definitely an alternative world, dissimilar from ours; but it does not exemplify the technical and philosophical notion of "possible world." A strongly simplifying definition, stripping away the many questions raised by modal logic and other philosophical perspectives, might describe a possible world as an internally and logically coherent universe that functions according to laws that are different from those of the world as we know it. *The Obscure Cities* world does not really follow such a model. Indeed, if each volume of the series presents an aspect of Counter-Earth that matches the possible world definition as given above, the same cannot be said of the complete series. What applies to each part does not apply to the whole: each part may be a possible world, but the whole is certainly not a—that is, one—possible world. As a series, *The Obscure Cities* does not aim at presenting a single unified world, even if each of its fragments may give the impression of doing so. *The Obscure Cities* world has to be envisaged as a cluster of worlds not necessarily compatible, a permanently moving set of variations of a certain world, which is not the world in which we are currently living and perhaps not a state of the world that has existed before, but a certain world as it has imagined and represented itself. This world, if one follows Garcia's analysis, is the second half of nineteenth-century Europe—and to put things even more sharply, a stage of European society and civilization as masterly imagined by Jules Verne and several of his contemporaries, with only occasional references to more recent elements and situations, such as, for instance, in *The Theory of the Grain of Sand* (which it is even now possible to read as a parable on the restitution of looted art works to their countries of origins; see Duplan 2018). These different variations, however, do not result from a single or unique set of properties, which can be used as a benchmark or point of reference for the singularities of the *Obscure Cities* universe. They are instead the effect of a number of idiosyncratic, perfectly ad hoc properties or hypotheses that each book of the series invents from scratch. The physical oddities that appear in *The Shadow of a Man*, where a man rids himself of his nightmares but has to pay a terrible price for this, since his shadow is in color afterward, or in *The Leaning Girl*, where a character starts leaning after a freak accident on a roller coaster, are anything but properties of an alternative possible world. In the first book, other characters keep having "normal," colorless shadows. No one other than the lead character of the second book starts to lean. And these quirks and twists are certainly characteristic of the series as a whole. To paraphrase Adorno and Horkheimer: what is highlighted by Schuiten and Peeters is the gap between the universal and the particular—with priority given to the latter at the expense of the former.

The *Obscure Cities*' view on pre-twentieth-century European history is not pure nostalgia, since the series does not try to restore, embellish, or reboot that specific fragment of the past, but to use it as a springboard to something that is a hybrid of historical fantasy, if not fantasy *tout court*, and a kind of retro–science fiction, that is, a revisit of futurology as it was shaped in the past. At the same time, it is not a kind of counterfactual history either, since the scope of Schuiten and Peeters's inventions is less concerned with time than with space. The idea of *The Obscure Cities* is not to show how things would have evolved if certain historical events had been different from what they actually are, but to explore new aspects and dimensions of a world that reshapes the past—more precisely, the self-imagined past—in unexpected ways. Schuiten and Peeters's endeavor is above all to deepen and broaden the great era of progress represented by European culture in the second half of the nineteenth century—a world far from idyllic but apparently still untouched by the catastrophes that would occur in the following century and that would inevitably cast a disturbing shadow on Europe's self-representation.

The world of *The Obscure Cities* is thus not a world judged according to today's ethical, social, and political criteria, but a truly fictional rather than a truly possible world, which of course does not mean at all that the series adopts an uncritical stance toward the multiple events and situations that it displays. Gender, for instance, is not a general frame that is imposed top-down on the traditionally pre-gender world, so to speak, of *The Obscure Cities,* and the same can be said of issues such as colonialism. This "omission" has a reason, namely, the attempt of Schuiten and Peeters to play ball with fiction, highlighting in almost absolute terms that "anything goes" when one invents new worlds and stories, and avoiding as much as possible the bias of presentism—an almost inescapable temptation in science fiction. (*The Obscure Cities* is much closer to "revisionist history" or "what if" stories than to science fiction as such.) But as we will examine in later chapters, gender and colonial issues are anything but absent (Hansen 2019). They are even all the more noticeable and far-reaching given their contrast with the apparent respect of the nineteenth century's strangeness and distance. Just as there is no place for nostalgia in *The Obscure Cities,* there is also no room for anachronism. The past, here, is literally a foreign country, whose eccentricities are diminished by nostalgia and presentism. Evoking a "confederation of possibles," Tristan Garcia summarizes the world of *The Obscure Cities* as an attempt to preserve the nineteenth century as the birthplace of twentieth-century modernity, nonetheless deprived of the failures of the realization of the former by the latter.

A comic series and the universe it builds are never just ideas. As works of art, they must also shape a material form and thus organize the best possible way to go back and forth between the general idea that governs it and its concrete visual and other forms. In this case, one has to wonder about the creative tension between Counter-Earth as a concept (that of a possible world that turns out to be an open set of sometimes conflicting possibilities) and Counter-Earth as a fictional reality having its own spatial and temporal characteristics.

Tristan Garcia also suggests—and this is the second step of his argumentation—that the organization of Counter-Earth always starts from a "Great Form," a unifying principle that determines the whole fictional world and that is symbolized by a specific type of architecture. This Great Form generally illustrates and exemplifies either the radicalization or the combination of two major mathematical, almost Platonic ideals: that of the straight line and that of the circle. As shown above, the Great Form in question is a universal principle, but not a universal material structure: each volume and each new contribution to the series obey the idea of a Great Form, but the Great Form in question is not necessarily the same in all volumes and shorter contributions. Nevertheless, the Great Form is always making absolute claims: all that is within the fictional word—people, places, habits, ideas—has to follow the concrete rules that embody it, apparently with no way out for anybody or, indeed, anything.

However, this way out is exactly what will be at the heart of all books and shorter units of *The Obscure Cities*: stories of resistance and agency, stories of the overcoming of totalitarian and dictatorial tendencies inherent to the Great Form as well as the political powers that represent it and impose on it in each of the *Obscure Cities*. As we have seen, these totalitarian leanings impact on not only the mind but also the body of those having to live under their rules. The Great Form and its norms as well as those who are in charge of imposing their scrupulous and unconditional respect do not only punish; they also discipline, and as convincingly studied by Foucault, the shift from punishment to discipline—that is, from a system in which the breaking of rules is sanctioned by crude penalties to a system in which the subjects themselves interiorize the rules in order to avoid punishment—is a historical process. As already mentioned, the replacement of punishment by discipline (read: self-discipline) is a defining feature of modernity, just as is the notion of biopower (see chapter 2).

Both elements are repeatedly thematized in *The Obscure Cities*, as for instance in *La Route d'Armilia* (The road to Armilia), a dreamy travelogue, radically separated from the embedding narrative that highlights the situation of enslaved children, radically isolated from the rest of the population and kept in absolute isolation, literally as prisoners, while being plugged through electronic wires into the machines they are forced to feed, allegedly in order to be kept alive and fed by them in return (the embedded story is quite literally an illustration of the evasion offered by reading, the young protagonist trying to escape forced labor by secretly plunging into a book). The result is an authoritative reworking of child labor in savage capitalist conditions that directly reflects the twin notions of biopower and discipline: the children are targeted as useful for a malleable workforce; the power exerted by their adult masters relies on the inculcated belief that it is in their own interest not to aspire to any other form of life than serving the machines.

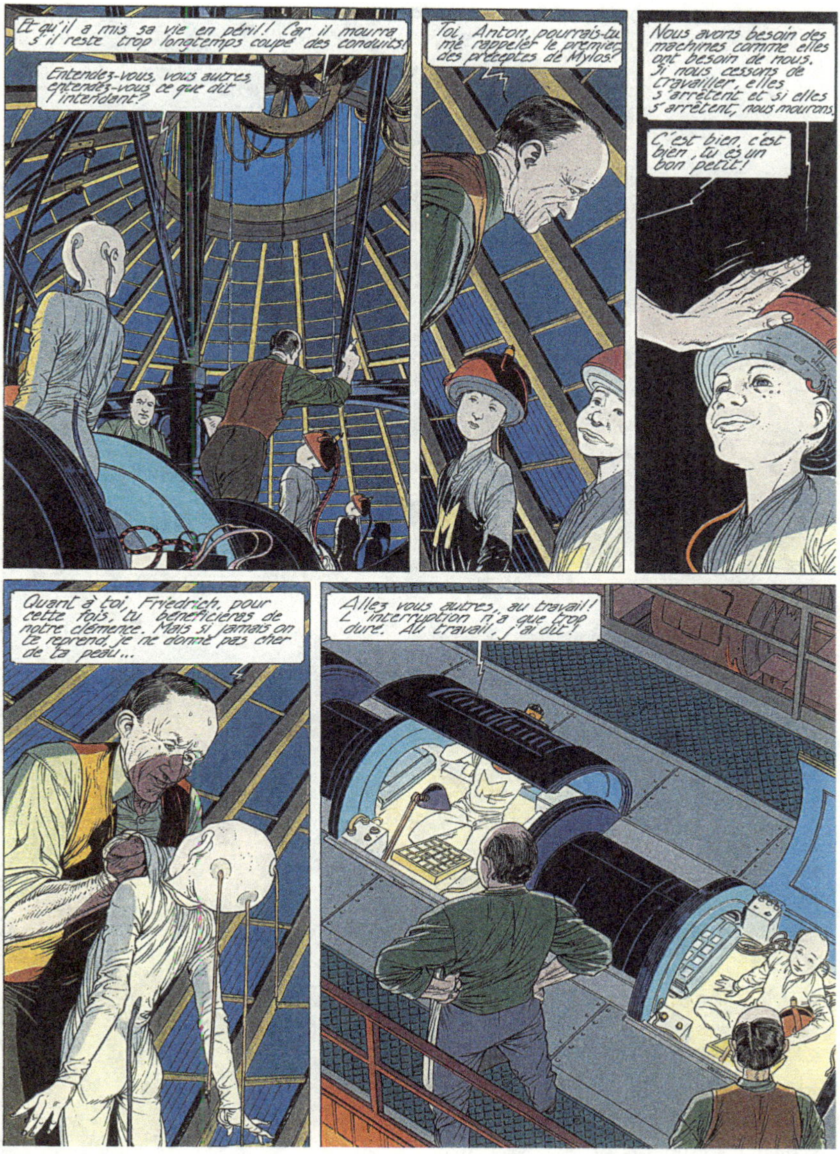

FIG. 3.1 *The Road to Armilia*, page 190. Excerpt from *The Road to Armilia*, François Schuiten and Benoît Peeters (© Casterman, with kind permission of the authors and Editions Casterman)

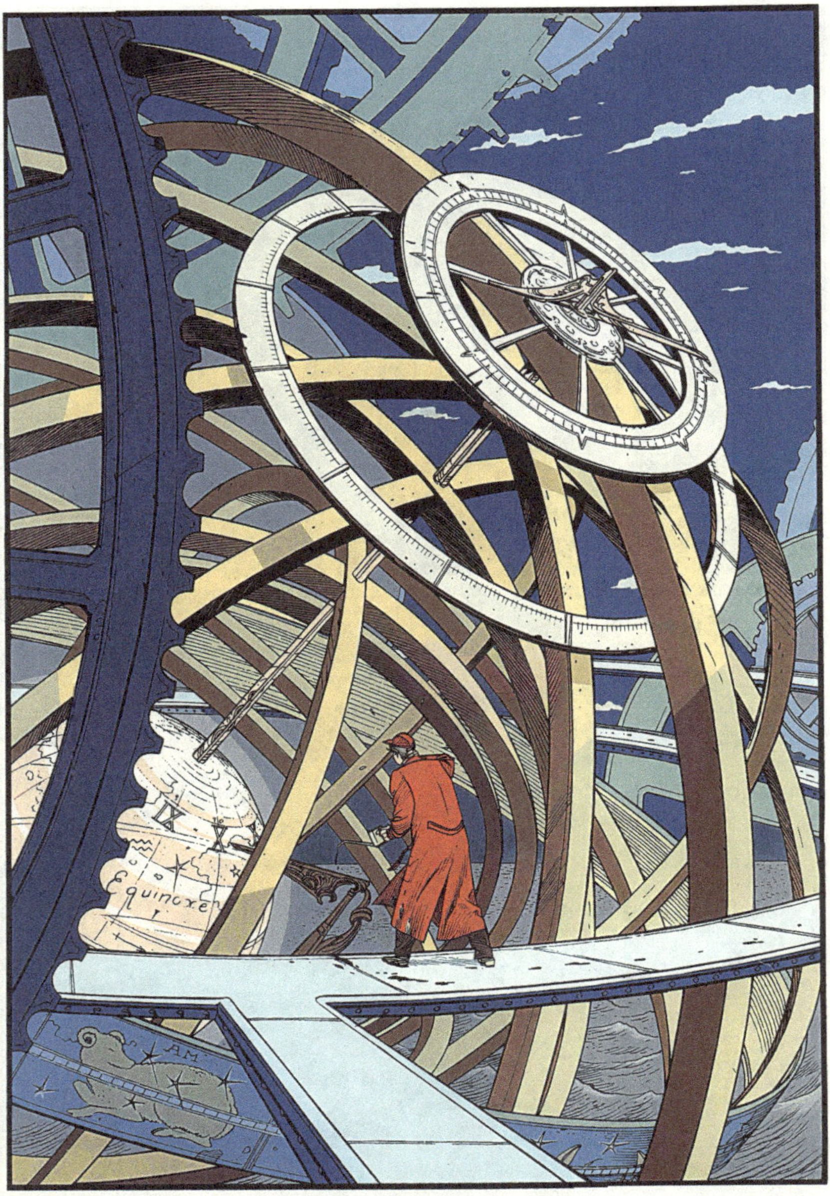

FIG. 3.2 *The Road to Armilia*, serigraphy by François Schuiten (© François Schuiten)

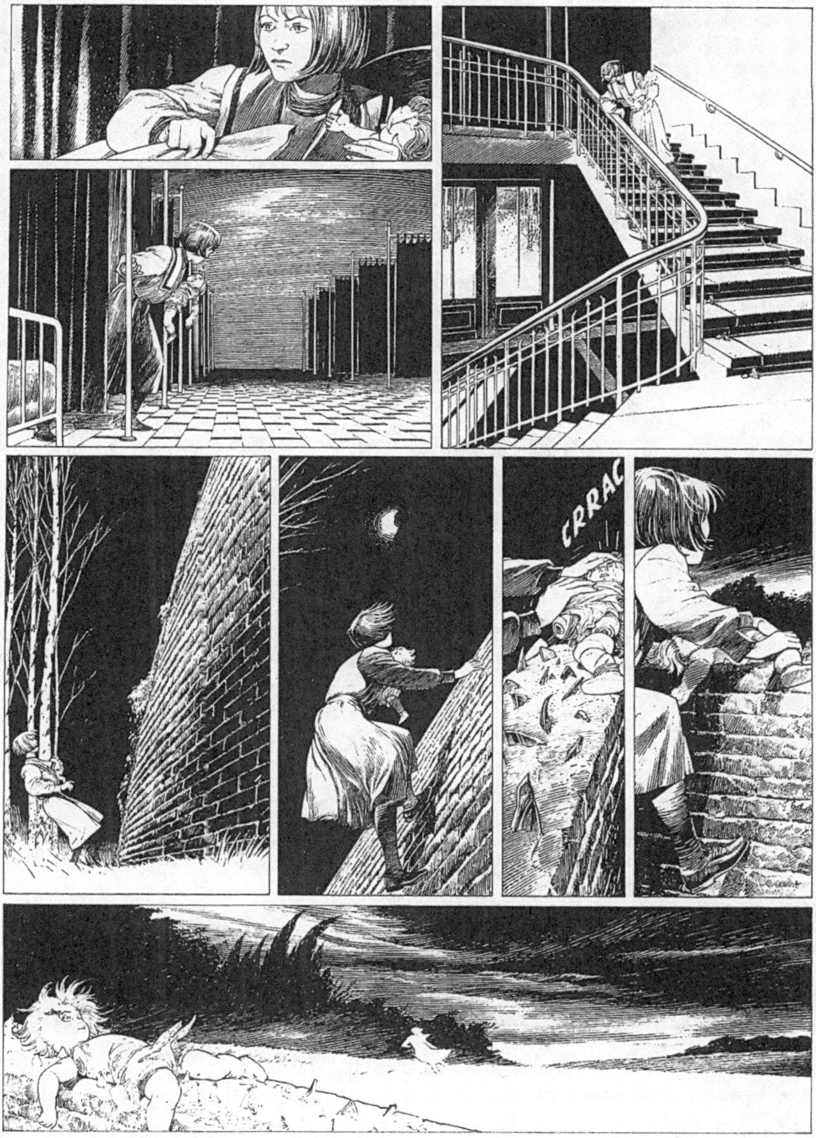

FIG. 3.3 The evasion from the youth detention center in *The Leaning Girl*, page 49. Excerpt from *The Leaning Girl*, François Schuiten and Benoît Peeters (© Casterman, with kind permission of the authors and Editions Casterman)

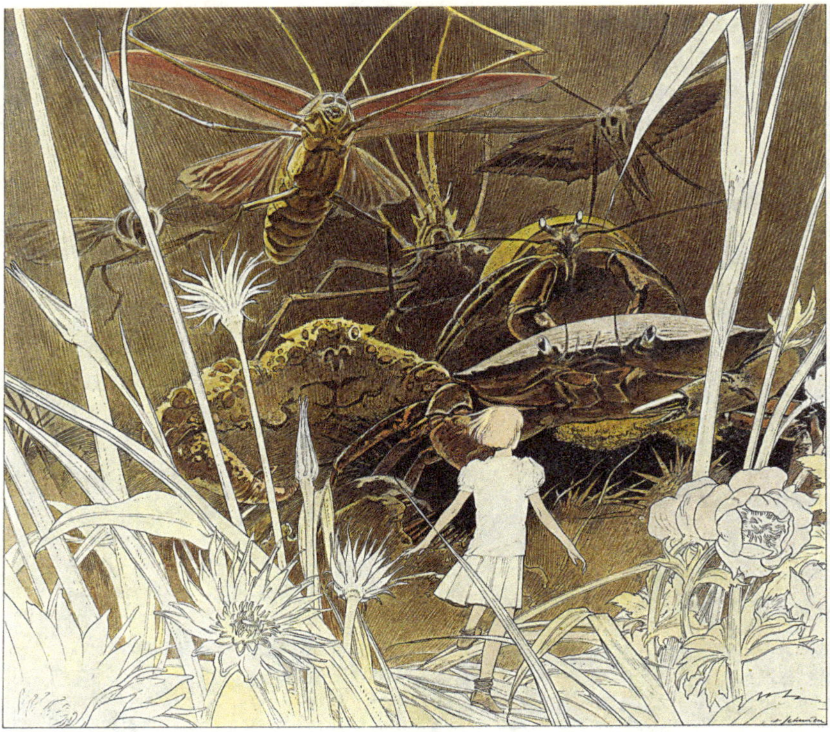

FIG. 3.4 The dream of Mary, in *The Leaning Girl*, drawing by François Schuiten (© François Schuiten)

Power, punishment, discipline, even in their most totalitarian forms, always leave possibilities of "resistance," a term shared by those working in the field of cultural studies (Hall 1993) and by critical theorists who rely on the work by Foucault, whose thinking on the notion of resistance gradually shifted from radical theories on madness and activism to a broader notion of a diffuse but always strongly localized resistance to power. Power, in that sense, however ubiquitous it may be, does not necessarily paralyze (as Adorno and Horkheimer claimed in their pessimistic and seemingly defeatist study of the culture industry, a Moloch that forces its victims to relinquish the very possibility of resistance). Power also opens up a field of tensions where resistance can emerge and grow. This is precisely what is happening in *The Obscure Cities*, even if the outcome of this resistance is not always successful. The protagonist of *Samaris*, for instance, fails to convince the leaders of the capital city, Xhystos, that inexplicable and disquieting things are happening in the faraway frontier zone of Samaris (his final return to Samaris is less an escape from the asphyxiating order of Xhystos than the acknowledgment of a personal failure).

Yet in spite of this gloomy ending—a recurring pattern in several of the volumes that does not correspond to an idealized journey from darkness to light—the very story of *Samaris*—and indeed all other volumes and side stories and documents of the series—performs first a critique and then the ruin of the homogeneous and totalitarian order of the Great From that seems to rule each of the settings and worlds of *The Obscure Cities*. Each story brings in an element that undermines the general rule and whose consequences introduce a slow-to-rapid cracking of the existing order, which is always an order with a capital *O*. For Tristan Garcia, the most visible aspect of this fissure, which he calls the revenge of Life on deadly Order, is the sensuality introduced by attractive and independent heroines, who liberate the doubtful and weak heroes from their own lack of courage. Not all characters prove strong or are self-determined enough to accept this invitation to leave behind the comfort zone of abstract forms and general rules (the hero of *Samaris* abandons his lover in the first pages of the book; the hero of *The Invisible Frontier* is incapable of even recognizing the sensuality of women).

This anecdotal blindness notwithstanding, the plot of all stories is built around the fundamental conflict between the world the characters live in and another world that comes to light through certain experiences. However, the very existence of this tension suffices to dismantle the belief that the possible world in which the characters are living is the only one, while systematically producing a story line that, regardless of its positive or negative denouement, decries the totalitarian assumptions of the initially defined order. Some characters may lose their fight against that order, but their fight puts an end to the uncontested reign of the Great Form.

On Counter-Earth, one of the most striking aspects of this irruption of freedom in the constrained world of order has to do with the search for a pathway to another world. Just as certain "documentary" works made by Schuiten and Peeters on Brussels—the "real" city, the one on Earth—are built around the idea that certain places are a kind of turntable giving access to another world, all *Obscure Cities* stories foreground characters who are looking, be it very consciously or just driven by some vague initial desire, for something else. And in the spatially and architecturally organized world of the series, this "something else" means of course another place, another world, or another way of living and building in known worlds and places. Tristan Garcia is certainly right when defining the experience of the frontier zones they eventually meet in terms of *initiation*, whatever the outcome may be. Certain characters will be crushed by their discovery, or unable to frame or recognize it, while others find there the beginning of a totally new life.

It should be stressed, however, that the antagonism revealed by *The Obscure Cities* is more complex than the opposition between Order and Life, as Garcia names them. On top of this basic tension, or underneath, is also a profound ambiguity and perhaps even weakness of Order itself, which is not just rule-constrained. Various building and planning mechanisms in the series present a double face, and each of these faces is simultaneously active. The monstrously growing network of *Fever in Urbicand* is at the same time something that destroys the totalitarian architecture of the city planners and that proliferates along rules that are as rigid and unbending as the inflexible environment that it dismantles. The network is at the same time "life" and "order." In *The Road to Armilia*, the heavy industry–based system is relying on such a weak basis—child labor, child slavery, child imprisonment and forced labor—that it is impossible to believe that such a system can survive in the long run. In *The Leaning Girl*, the male-governed world of big business grows a child that will try to change the rules of the game. As a matter of fact, both albums refer to the same city, Mylos, the father of Mary being the CEO of the industrial consortium that exploits the children of the Armilia book. In other words: the challenges to order do not come solely from a revolt that expresses an irrepressible energy and freedom of life; they also come from within, as if constraints were capable of producing something else than just the mere reproduction of themselves. These ambivalences actually continue the contradictions and fluctuations at work at the level of building and architecture and cannot be identified with the simple opposition Order versus Life.

At the end of his essay—step three of his argumentation—Tristan Garcia formulates another stimulating yet perplexing hypothesis: the way in which *The Obscure Cities* is organized presents a strong analogy to the fundamental mechanisms of a comic: "un monde et . . . une vie conçus comme la bande dessinée elle-même, où il faut passer de monde en monde, et d'âge en âge, comme le regard d'un lecteur doit toujours passer de case en case" (a world and a . . . life elaborated as comics themselves, where one has to move from world to world, and from era to era, just as the gaze of the reader has to move from panel to panel). The transformation of the rules of a medium into the properties of a fictional universe is a powerful and appealing intuition, which helps Garcia to underline the difference between a series like *The Obscure Cities*, where the key words are plurality and hybridity, and the franchised, canon- and bible-based DC or Marvel universes, which he believes exemplify an attempt to unify and homogenize. I will not discuss this part of Garcia's interpretation—some scholars will certainly disagree with the centripetal stance Garcia places at the heart of the DC and Marvel universes—but instead, I shall focus on an astonishing aspect of his interpretation.

If one can agree with Garcia's claim that *The Obscure Cities* series reflects some fundamental properties of the comics language, it is more problematic to accept the idea that the fictional world that results from this translation is a world that actually predates comics as a historical medium. The world of *The Obscure Cities* is, roughly speaking, an imaginative re-creation of a certain type of late nineteenth-century Europe, but this world is *not*, as Garcia argues, a world "before comics," and thus hardly a world that can treat the language of comics as an "eternal promise," undamaged by later evolutions as the fictional world of *The Obscure Cities* is kept intact from the horrors of the twentieth century. Regardless of the quite strange idea that the more recent forms of comics would have destroyed the optimism and charm of its first, still pre-comic versions, the idea that, historically speaking, the second half of the nineteenth century would have been a more or less comics-free era is strongly open to debate (see, for instance, the pioneering work of David Kunzle [1973] and, more recently, Jared Gardner [2012] and Thierry Smolderen [2014]).

However, the real question lies not in whether the period can be defined as a pre-comic era—after all, *The Obscure Cities* is a work of fiction, not a theoretical essay on comics—but to examine whether the type of comics Schuiten and Peeters are presenting in their series interact with older forms of comics. Once again, the answer is that of profound ambivalence. It is certainly correct to state that the comics of *The Obscure Cities* do not aim at reviving the many types of comics that already existed in the period that seems to be that of their fictional universe.[3] There are no blatant echoes of, for instance, the work of Rodolphe Töpffer (1799–1846), who is generally considered the founding father of Western comics. Nor will one find immediately recognizable references to the spectacular experiments of Gustave Doré in his *History of Holy Russia* (1854) or the cartoon art of Gustave Daumier (1808–1879). Despite the ubiquity of famous nineteenth-century artists such as the all-round creator and inventor Nadar (pseudonym of Gaspard-Félix Tournachon, 1820–1910), who appears in *The Obscure Cities* under the anagram Ardan,[4] comics artists and their work are unmentioned relatively in frequently. Instead Schuiten and Peeters strongly foreground other, non-comic aspects of late nineteenth-century visual culture in their own comics. The drawing style of François Schuiten is clearly influenced by and admiring of the etching style of Gustave Doré's illustrations. Much artwork in *The Obscure Cities* is indeed indebted to the history of illustration, and it is the mutual implication of comics and illustration that particularly characterizes the visual style of the series. The hybridization of these two traditions (first, that of the single "large" images versus that of the spatial and sequential arrangement of smaller pictures; second, that of drawing versus that of storytelling) is what defines the position of *The Obscure Cities* as a singular and actually very new form of comics, that is, not just a pre-comics form that keeps the promises of the emerging medium as open as possible. As a matter of fact, the hybridization is far from being complete. Schuiten and Peeters consciously maintain the specific features of the visual styles that they are mixing, in order to achieve a maximal awareness of the hybridization process itself. Readers do not discover a hybridized format; instead they are witnessing the ongoing and never fully achieved work of mixing various types. Such a hybridization goes further than merely suggesting the comics as promise, as a form to be fully developed in later periods (many aspects of the comics page layout of the series are perfectly recognizable as late twentieth-century comics), but it matches well the general aesthetics of possible worlds as performed by *The Obscure Cities*.

There is, however, next to the comics model, a very different model for the series, which is the book, more precisely the codex form of the book. The image of the world as a book is a very ancient one. We all know, without necessarily acknowledging the source, the famous quote often attributed to Saint Augustine: "The world is a book and those who do not travel read only one page"; but the idea is certainly much older.[5] This deeply rooted cultural metaphor is, however, completely reframed by Schuiten and Peeters, who decide to take it literally. Hence the multiple analogies between the materialities of the book and the features of their fictional world (walls as pages, houses as books, streets as shelves, cities as libraries). Hence also the supplementary layer they add to the almost congenital relationship between comics and architecture, as addressed in the previous chapter. If the link between a comics page and a building is so convincing, it is also because the world itself can be visualized as a codex, a book constructed of a number of sheets of paper or similar materials and bound together between two covers. The number of places, buildings, and other items that are drawn in such a way that they resemble book-like items is innumerable in *The Obscure Cities*, just as are the countless occurrences of reading and writing, not to mention the profound analogy on the one hand between the natural coincidence of 2-D and 3-D in books, with their two-dimensional sheets and three-dimensional containers, and the frequent use of the tension between flatness and depth, between material surfaces and fictional expansion, on the other. The back-and-forth movement between the flatness of lines and paper and the completeness of a real—or allegedly real—world is perhaps the most fundamental narrative structure and metaphor of *The Obscure Cities*, which thus offer an original variation on the age-old problem of illusion and reality. The dichotomy of Earth and Counter-Earth, both of which consider themselves real while taking the other pole for a kind of nonexistent fiction, is another way of expressing this ultimate structure.

Moreover, the image and structure of the book are both fixed and dynamic, exactly in the same order as what can be read into the architecture of *The Obscure Cities* and the fictional world that it built: all these layers and elements are at the same time fixed structures and moving targets. The same applies to the book, not only in the sense that it can be read in countless ways—and in *The Tower*, the return of a character (first introduced in *The Archivist*) in the cameo of Jorge Luis Borges, who is there to make us better understand this vital aspect of all things written—but also in the sense that, as a material object, the book is permanently undergoing an endless chain of transformations, from writing and printing at the beginning of the process through to loss, decay, and unreadability at the end (as is already familiar to the readers of *Fever in Urbicand*, in which each of the six chapters is introduced by an illustration based on the motif of the book as a printed volume). But this is obviously never a dead end, for it relaunches new processes of rereading and interpretation. Book technology is key in the whole series, in the fictional world of *The Obscure Cities* as in the various forms it takes itself throughout the many years of its material existence. Later volumes of the series, which started at a moment when the Internet was still to appear, introduce the tension between print and screen or analog and digital culture without reducing their conflict to the simple supersession of the old by the new (a recent album like *Revoir Paris*, a side project of *The Obscure Cities*, even strongly claims the merits of print culture). We will come back to these material transformations. Let it suffice for now to notice the extreme care that is taken of the currently published "complete version" of the series in four volumes, which clearly demonstrates that the essential place in which the series comes alive is the book, more precisely, a set of books highlighting the tension between 3-D and 2-D (the front covers of the volumes contain a peep-through that blurs the boundaries between the flatness of an abstract surface

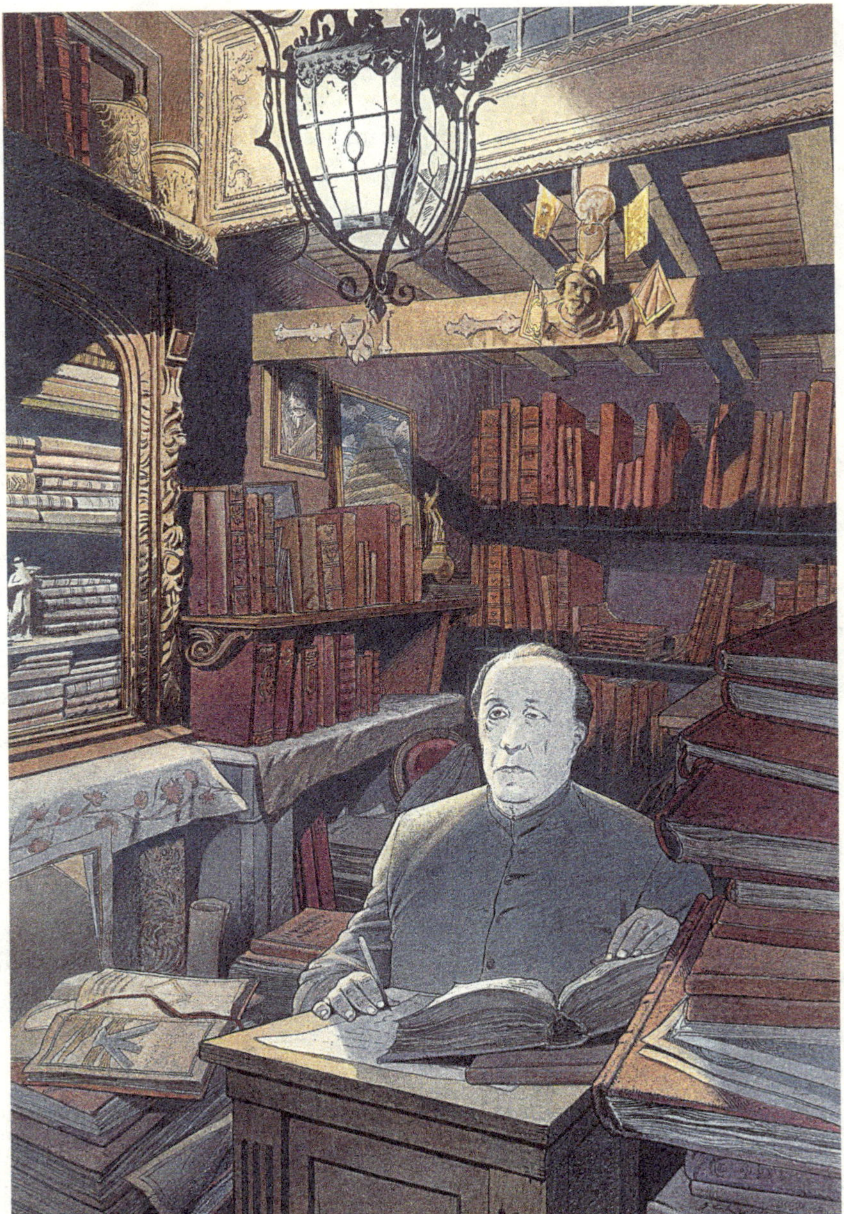

FIG. 3.5 *L'Archiviste*, inspired by Jorge Luis Borges, Integral Edition, vol. 1, p. 325. Excerpt from *The Archivist*, François Schuiten and Benoît Peeters (© Casterman, with kind permission of the authors and Editions Casterman)

and the illusionary depth of the image that appears "below") and offers the reader a collection of units that is simultaneously unified and impossible to streamline.

The Obscure Cities is not a "possible world" in the traditional sense of the world, as often explored in science fiction. As argued by philosopher Tristan Garcia in his powerful discussion of the series as a possible world, one has to view *The Obscure Cities* as a universe of multiple and continuously shifting reinterpretations of a proto-modern world. The essential feature of these worlds is the clash between Order and Life, or, if one prefers, between mechanical and dictatorial repetition, on the one hand, and an ethics of becoming and emancipation that breaks down the aesthetic, political, and ideological underpinnings of the world imposed on the characters, on the other. Garcia's reflection on the form and content of the particular multiverse of the *Obscure Cities* helps foreground a supplementary hypothesis that deepens the links between architecture and comics addressed in the previous chapter. The fictional world of *The Obscure Cities* not only replicates the basic material features of the comics language; it is also inspired by the model of the book as a codex.

4

Between Chapter and Series

Counter-Earth is a multiverse that has not only its own geography but also its own calendar and chronological particularities (the Altaplana website includes a double time line: that of the "Lighted World," our world, and that of the "Obscure World"). This singular rearrangement of what we recognize as the underlying time and space of Earth itself is in line with the mutual reflections and transformations of the different worlds in *The Obscure Cities*. Yes, these characteristic features of time and space concern narrative diegesis in the narrow sense of the word only: they define the spatial and temporal settings in which the other and larger diegesis—that is, that of the plot and the story themselves—takes place. As shown in the previous chapters, the spatiotemporal background of *The Obscure Cities* is that of a kind of pre–twentieth century Europe, and it categorically foregrounds the technological dimensions of this culture. The story itself, however, has its own temporal organization, its spatial structure being that of the spatial and sequential arrangements of the panels on the page, in the book as well as in the series. At first sight, the temporal structure of the *Obscure Cities* stories does not immediately appear as different from the structure on Earth, in "our world." All these stories have a beginning, a middle, and an end, even if not all of them are told in a straightforwardly linear way. In a complex book such as *The Tower*, the first reading may even have some difficulties in recognizing where to localize beginning, middle, and end, but this impression does not last till the end of the work, whose ambition is to complexify story lines, not to put them between brackets.

Yet *The Obscure Cities* tells stories in ways that are quite different from "normal" or "average" stories: content-wise, without any doubt, as shown by the effort to build a counter-universe and even an open set of shifting counter-universes, but also from a properly narrative point of view. The present chapter aims at unpacking some basic features of this nonmainstream storytelling. It will do so by studying storytelling techniques at two levels: First, in general, without taking too much into account the visual characteristics of the stories told; here, stories will be approached as more or less abstract narrative patterns and structures, as they can be described and paraphrased with the help of words. Second, at the medium-specific level of stories, as they are materialized as narratives told in comics format, signifying stories whose narrative organization cannot be separated from the material features of the medium. It should be noticed, however, that in the comics medium, these material features are not necessarily monomedial. Comics not only mix words and images; they can also combine drawings and photographs, handwriting and mechanical letters, and so on. This *multimodality*, currently a hot topic in comics criticism (Pedri 2018), is a key characteristic of *The Obscure Cities*, not only because of the importance of photographic archives during the preparation of the series, but also because of the actual usage, both visually and narratively, of multimodal images and techniques in some of the volumes (see chapter 8 for a close reading of *The Leaning Girl*, which heavily relies on the blurring of boundaries between drawing and photography).

At a general level, the most crucial question raised by *The Obscure Cities* is that of the relationship between story and story world, or, in other words, between the ambition to build a world and that of telling stories that are situated within this world. This distinction may seem somewhat futile or theoretical, since stories generally do both jobs at the same time, but in practice it is a real issue for all those who try to combine the building of a new world, in singular or in plural, and the telling of a story, regardless of the manifold paths these stories can take. There exists indeed a strong tension between these two sides of the same coin, world building and storytelling, not in the sense that they are incompatible, but in the sense that in certain cases both may compete for attention at the center of the work's hierarchy. Some works tend to prioritize the building of a world, which reduces the actual stories to a secondary position, while other works favor storytelling at the expense of their spatiotemporal background. In many transmedial franchises, for instance, the building of a story world and the establishment of a list of characters are at least as important as storytelling. In transmedia theory, stories and storytelling are generally defined in relationship to the notion of *story world*, which appears to always have top priority. As Henry Jenkins puts it: "Most often, transmedia stories are based not on individual characters or specific plots but rather complex fictional worlds which can sustain multiple interrelated characters and their stories. This process of world-building encourages an encyclopedic impulse in both readers and writers" (2007, n.p.). Or as a recent handbook states, reinforcing the structural dissociation of world building and storytelling:

> *Collaborative Worldbuilding for Writers and Gamers* shows how writers can co-create vast worlds for use as common settings for their own stories. Using the worlds of *Star Wars*, *Lord of the Rings*, *A Game of Thrones*, and *Dungeons & Dragons* as models, this book guides readers through a step-by-step process of building sprawling fictional worlds complete with competing social forces that have complex histories and yet are always evolving. It also shows readers how to populate a catalogue with hundreds of unique people, places, and things that grow organically from their world, which become a rich repository of story-making potential. (Hergenrader 2018, blurb)

Transmedia franchises generally have a detailed scriptwriters' "bible" describing these worlds and their characters. Such a conceptual framework allows for an allegedly clear-cut distinction between "canonical" and "non-canonical" productions. Moreover, storytelling in these transmedia universes is often more at the service of the story world than of storytelling: what is told is less the story itself than a certain way to display and exploit a generally predefined story world. The superiority of the story world, which reduces the stories to a simple tool of continued world making, is not really astonishing in this context: since transmedia structures are based on the possibility to easily move from one medium to another, it is important to foreground those elements that are easy to transfer, such as a certain spatiotemporal setting and a set of characters, and to be careful with story lines that may be difficult to be lifted intermedially or transmedially. In transmedia storytelling, medium specificity does harm.

In Jenkins's quote, the key concept is probably "encyclopedic impulse." What such an impulse is triggering is definitely something else than storytelling. An encyclopedia may tell stories, but does so within a larger framework that is not narrative, but descriptive. Whatever form its organization may take, an encyclopedia is *more a list than a story*. Of course, stories can contain lists, just as lists can trigger stories, as theorized, for instance, by Lev Manovich in his defense of "database narrative" as the new type of nonchronological narrative that appears with the digital era (Manovich 2001). Yet this possibility of a fruitful exchange between list and story does not mean that both types of arrangements have the same weight. True, certain works manage to create a perfect balance between both: Milorad Pavic's *The Khazar Dictionary* (1984), a book that tells the history of the former Yugoslavia through the competing entries of three cross-referenced encyclopedias (one Christian, one Jewish, one Muslim), is a wonderful example of such an alliance. But most of the time, lists and stories have a different logic and a different agenda.

In *The Obscure Cities*, this tension is made dramatically visible. Certain albums adopt a strongly encyclopedic format—for example, *L'Echo des cités* (1993), a large album that reproduces select pages from a famous newspaper of the Obscure World, from its first issue to its last—whereas others turn the general narrative frame in an encyclopedic direction. In *The Road to Armilia*, the travelogue genre is used as a pretext for a more encompassing nonnarrative project.

Since the notion of nonnarrative is key to the project, it may be useful to specify without further delay in which sense this term will be used in this analysis. Nonnarrative does not have the critical or negative connotation of a concept such as antinarrative, which refers to all kinds of techniques and strategies that prevent the reader from doing what is actually at the very core of *The Obscure Cities*, namely, building a fictional universe capable of hosting a certain number of plots, stories, characters, events, and places. There is nothing antinarrative in the general purpose of Schuiten and Peeters, who have repeatedly emphasized the pleasure of storytelling. Yet in the relationship between story and story world, the authors clearly prioritize the latter, not the former. What Schuiten and Peeters try to do is to use stories, which are different in each album and which do not constitute a coherent whole, in order to shape a complex fictional universe, also open to permanent change but nevertheless much more stable—although ambivalent if not paradoxical—than the individual story lines. Nonnarrative thus refers to the various methods and strategies that are implemented to assemble and reinforce the story world. The systematic use of these elements, such as for instance the detailed visual description of places, puts the narrative impulse "on hold," and this interruption or delay is what the notion of nonnarrative is mainly hinting at. It is, if one prefers, a way of showing without telling (but not in such a way that the telling is completely put between brackets).

The Obscure Cities' "City Guide" (*Le Guide des cités*) logically elaborates on the encyclopedic and documentary dimension of the work and combines it with an unusual vertical format. In addition, Schuiten and Peeters have developed from the very beginning of the series a wide array of side projects and complementary realizations, some of them in print, others in multimedia and nonbook format, that highlight world building rather than storytelling. Finally, the gathering up of all the *Obscure Cities*–related material into an integral edition of four volumes pays as much attention to the encyclopedic as to the narrative aspects of the series, both from a quantitative and a qualitative point of view. The complementary documents one finds in the Integral Edition are not page-fillers or bonuses for the die-hard fans desperate over having missed the initial special editions. On the contrary, the analogous treatment of encyclopedic and narrative material functions as a kind of reader's manual or instruction guide on how to make sense of the unusual montage, in each of the four volumes, of highly diverse works and items. At the same time, however, the ordering of the major albums generally follows the original publication order, which helps maintain the links between the old and the new presentation, a logical decision in a project in permanent expansion and rebuilding.

The gathering of all available materials in print that explore or document the *Obscure Cities* universe is a very complex and ambivalent sign. On the one hand, it certainly stresses the world-building dimension of the project. The fact that "everything," that is, all elements available in print format, is brought together underlines the desire to finally showcase the multiverse in its (impossible) totality. In this perspective, the stories of the albums become something like side projects within a larger program, whose main objective is less storytelling than world building. The stories are there to enhance the world on display and to enable the reader to experience it in different ways. On the other hand, the *Obscure Cities* universe is not the materialization of an underlying bible, and it would be absurd to envisage the Integral Edition as the final word of an equally nonexisting canon. The *Obscure Cities* world remains full of gaps, questions, contradictions, unforeseen and unforeseeable transformations. As a matter of fact, the new presentation foregrounds the encyclopedic dimension of the narrative albums, which mirror the accompanying documents specifying the manifold material and cultural components of the *Obscure Cities* world. Such an intertwining of fictional stories and nonfictional documents has a double effect: it blurs the boundaries between fiction and nonfiction. The fictional stories are read in light of the nonfictional documentation that accompanies the albums; the nonfictional items are displayed as the starting point of the fictional stories. The double effect also conflates the regimes of encyclopedia and narrative. The stories appear as a narrative disguise of parts of the *Obscure Cities* encyclopedia, while the encyclopedic essays that surround the stories are read as nonnarrative rearrangements of the material offered by the albums.

The resulting composition is much more radical than what one finds in, for instance, *Watchmen*, a work that equally tries to offer a twofold fictional and nonfictional structure, each chapter of the ongoing story being complemented with documentary information on a specific aspect of the narrative. Yet in *Watchmen*, there is only one story, cut up into twelve installments, and the documentary material mainly serves to provide background information that deepens the story but which is clearly not essential to its understanding. At the risk of scandalizing the *Watchmen* fans (I am one of them!), it seems reasonable to think that the nonfictional pages that complement the chapters are unnecessary. Although reading *Watchmen* while skipping the nonfictional bonus of each chapter is not recommended, such an omission does not really harm the understanding of the story itself. Totally different is the construction of the Integral Edition of *The Obscure Cities*, which deconstructs the very difference between fictional albums and accompanying documents: first, by refusing to distinguish between them in the table of contents, where the documentary parts are presented exactly the same way as the fictional items; second, by sticking to a similar treatment of both fictional and nonfictional parts, much more visually homogeneous than in *Watchmen*.

At the same time, the more or less equal handling of world building and storytelling confirms the nuanced "flank-guard" position of *The Obscure Cities* in the larger history of comics. Just as Schuiten and Peeters succeed in radically innovating within the tradition—a posture that seems contradictory, but that summarizes very well the historical position of their work—they also manage to find a midway position between storytelling and world building, not by scaling down each of these strategies in order to merge them, but by sharpening them in such a way that they eventually prove capable of including their opposite.

But what to think of *The Obscure Cities* stories when it comes down to analyzing them as comics stories, *stories told in comics format*? Narrative analysis unfortunately lacks the lexical distinction visual studies has introduced between "image" and "picture," the former being the idea of a visual representation, the latter being a material object, the thing itself, as it were; or as art historian Hans Belting synthetically puts it, "a picture is an image with a medium" (2014). The same applies to stories: one can study them either as general structures, deprived of any reference to a specific medium, or as medium-specific structures, shaped by a given medium, with its own affordances and restrictions.

In the case of *The Obscure Cities*, the notion of medium can be used in various ways. It certainly refers to issues of drawing and page layout (and these elements have already been touched upon in previous chapters), but it certainly has to do as well with aspects of the work's material support: namely, the host medium of print (magazines, albums, other types of publication). Schuiten and Peeters do not use the structures of these print formats as neutral carriers; they instead rely upon them as an inspiring constraint on the composition and elaboration of their work. Storytelling, for them, is not storytelling "as such," but "a way of telling" that actively takes into account three key features of the host medium in comics: first of all, the fact that stories can be organized either as independent elements or as series—a distinction often made to distinguish between one-shot graphic novels and serialized comics; second, the fact that these stories are often initially published in magazine format, which raises questions on the internal organization of each story, be it a one-shot or a serial work; and third, the fact that stories can continue outside the various print formats or even be initiated outside the book in totally different media formats, as a film or an exhibition, for instance. In the following pages, we will examine the *Obscure Cities* treatment of print-related issues; subsequently, I will return to some transmedial extensions of the work by Schuiten and Peeters.

As already sketched, *The Obscure Cities* appears at a turning point in the medial history of Franco-Belgian comics. After the shift from newspaper and magazine comics to comics in album format, either original stories or stories that were a reprint of short daily and weekly installments, the comics industry of the mid-1970s reinvented the magazine format, giving a special agency to the singular properties of a new medium, the "literary" comics monthly as chiefly represented by *(À Suivre)*. As far as storytelling elements are concerned, the novelty of this magazine can be summarized with the help of two vital changes, which it is necessary to discuss in more detail: first, the introduction of the "chapter," which accompanies the literary turn of serious comics; second, the renewed use of seriality, which involves an even more radical disruption of traditional storytelling techniques.

By introducing the notion of "chapter," a completely new feature in comics narratives emerges, and so too arises an original yet very logical answer to the classic problem that is raised by the reissue of previously serialized segments in the album with the complete story. In the classic way of writing and reading, cliffhangers were an almost universal and often very cleverly used technique (Peeters 2018). The daily strip or the weekly page or double spread was organized in such a way that it both started with a recapitulation of what preceded and open-ended with a question or suspense effect that would be addressed the day or the week after. In album format, however, this complex composition becomes pointless, as shown ably by the reissue in book form of an adventure strip such as *Terry and the Pirates*, whose daily strips generally take off with an almost literal repetition of the last panel of the previous installment and no less often end with a strong cliffhanger. This may be the best possible way to proceed in the newspaper strip, which was actually the only format in which *Terry and the Pirates* was initially meant to appear, but it becomes highly problematic at the moment, decades later, when these daily strips are republished in book format. The overlap of final and initial panel strip after strip is then very dull, and the cliffhangers lose their meaning in a reading process that is no longer based upon the systematic stop-and-go alternation of suspense and denouement. The *(À Suivre)* serializations the various installments are no longer artificially isolated strips or pages of a unified story, but independent chapters of a work in the making. In other words, instead of first writing a story, which was then divided into short segments having a strong triadic structure—each time with a beginning, a middle, and an end: first the summary of what came before; second, a new development; third, a cliffhanger (all that in no more than four panels, a terrific achievement!)—the storyteller[1] now develops a longer whole (an average of ten to twenty pages) that will eventually become part of an album, structured like a novel composed of distinct chapters, even when one does not know how the story will end—an openness that creates a new type of suspense, very different from that of the cliffhanger. In the case of the cliffhanger, what comes next is always a direct continuation of what came before; in the case of the chapter structure, anything can happen in the following chapter.

This dramatic change in storytelling techniques is not just the result of the craving for a more "literary" form of comics, although there certainly is a direct link between the adoption of the chapter structure and the upwardly mobile move toward new types of literature-inspired narrative (Dürrenmatt 2013). At least as important is the impact of another change, more particularly a medium change, in this case the new approach of the comics magazine, which ceases to be a mere prepublication format in order to become the laboratory of a narrative *as it unfolds* (on the importance of the process, see

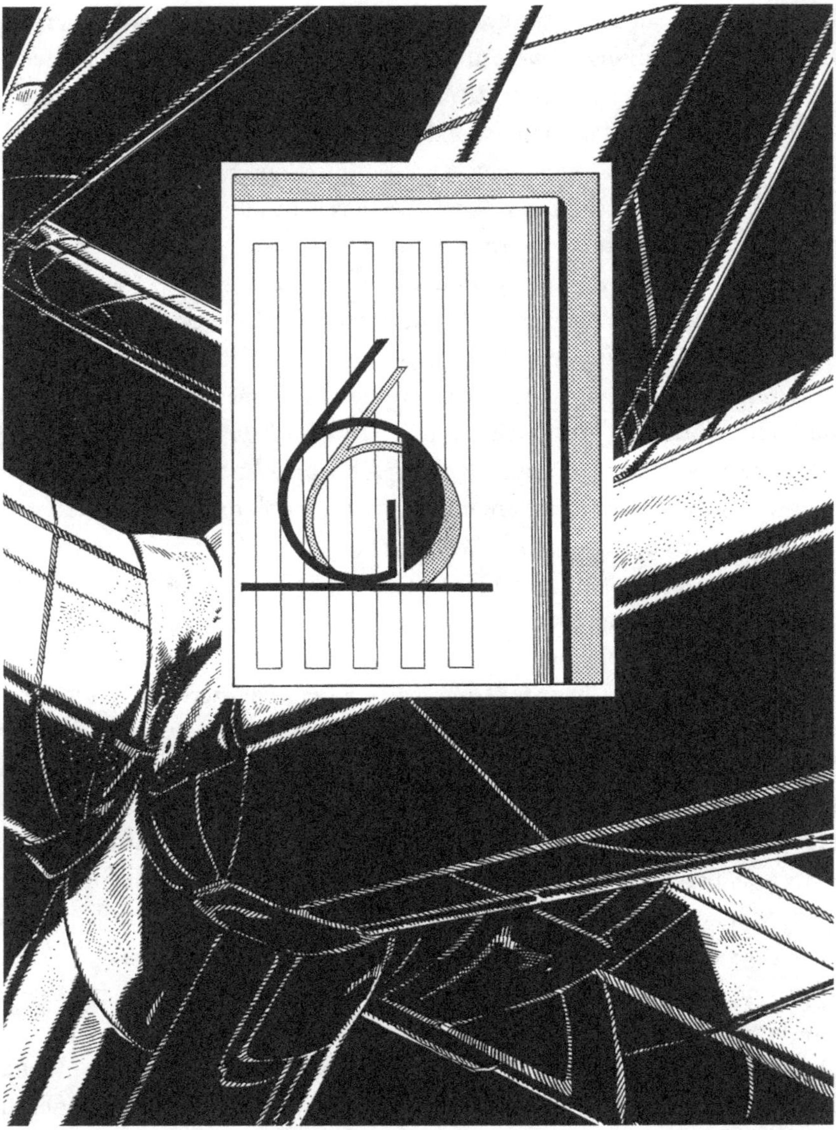

FIG. 4.1 Opening page of chapter 6 of *Fever in Urbicand*. Excerpt from *Fever in Urbicand*, François Schuiten and Benoît Peeters (© Casterman, with kind permission of the authors and Editions Casterman)

Baroni 2011a and Baroni and Revaz 2015). This new freedom does not come, however, without a price. In exchange for the possibility of inventing the story while making it up (instead of cutting up an already existing one into short fragments) and the freedom to build larger and autonomous chapters (instead of having to stick to the daily strip of the weekly single- or double-page format), the authors have to work in black and white, color still being excessively expensive for these kinds of long works in these years. For many of them this proved a real sacrifice. *The Obscure Cities* albums are a good example of these new practices, since they start in color, accepting in exchange a drastic reduction of page numbers. The first edition of *Samaris* follows the forty-eight pages norm; the next album, the long *Fever in Urbicand*, is in black and white; color will be reintroduced with great caution and never as a default option. In addition, one feels that between the first and the second volume of the series, there is a dramatic change in the treatment of the chapter structure. In the beginning, there is still an attempt to mix the old (cliffhanger) with the new (chapter), but very soon the authors abandon the classic cliffhanger and opt for the new chapter structure.

In both cases, we can see how Schuiten and Peeters learn on the job: the progressive abandonment of the cliffhanger and the strategic reinsertion of color are clearly marks of a process that slowly discovers the new rules of fame. Let us compare once again the first two volumes of the series, *Samaris* and *Fever in Urbicand*. In the former, Schuiten and Peeters are progressively dropping the cliffhanger technique, while not yet stressing the chapter structure. In the latter, the chapter autonomy is dramatically enhanced by the addition of a powerful paratextual apparatus with heavily illustrated and blown-up chapter numbers. The partial reworking of the first volume, *Samaris*, whose initial development left the authors somewhat unsatisfied and pushed them to rapidly publish a revised edition,[2] is equally a trace of the general move from the old paradigm to an unknown one. There are no real breaks in the series, which at the same time offers new surprises at every new publication.

The second major change, relatively independent from the new magazine format imposing the chapter structure, is a new relationship between album and series, more precisely the arrival of a new type of series that radically redefines the interaction between single volume and open-ended series. Contrary to what happens at the level of the chapter structure, where *The Obscure Cities* takes part in a collective trial-and-error experiment, the work by Schuiten and Peeters is unique at this level.

A cultural-industrial medium, comics as a whole are clearly part of popular culture. Within this field, seriality was a decisive feature for over a century. Seriality is much more than just a matter of seasons and sequels, the repetitive logic of media formats and concerns about return on investment. It is a creative and productive feature that deserves to be studied without the stereotypes that traditional views of culture hold up against everything that does not correspond to the notion of a highly original, unique work,

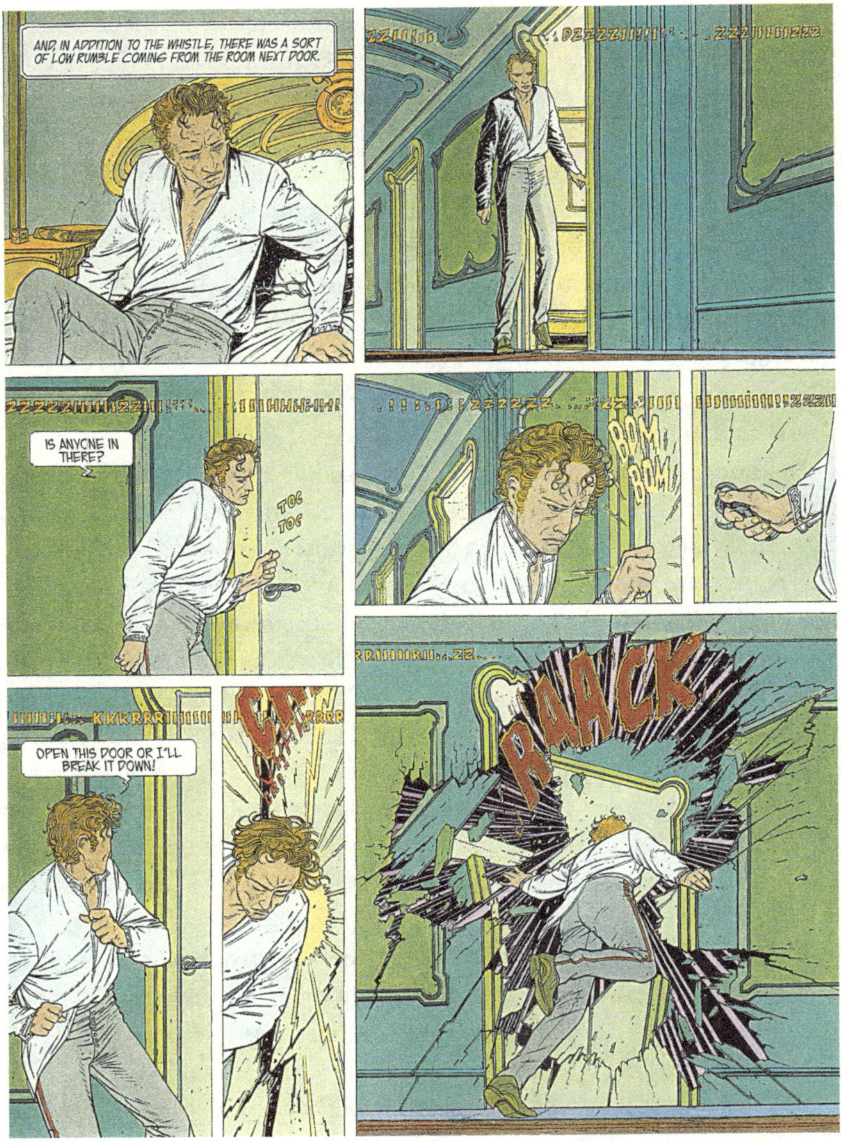

FIG. 4.2 A trace of the old cliffhanger technique in *Samaris*, Integral Edition, vol. 1, p. 69. Excerpt from *Samaris*, François Schuiten and Benoît Peeters (© Casterman, with kind permission of the authors and Editions Casterman)

intentionally produced by an exceptional artist and addressing universal audiences outside of any specific cultural context. Scholarly research on seriality has been conducted, mainly in the field of narratology, for at least four decades now (in the following pages and later in the book we will mainly rely on Kelleter 2017a and Letourneux 2017). In addition, recent scholarship has powerfully underlined the strong relationship between the mechanisms of serialization and the technical transformation of media structures (Allen and van den Berg 2014). As argued by Shane Denson: "Seriality, accordingly, is tied to mediality in transition, offering itself as a form of medial self-observation at times of media change and as a means of negotiating a medium's place within a changing media landscape" (2014, 69).

In a remarkable synthesis on popular seriality, Frank Kelleter (2017b) has listed a number of general features that help frame the difference between conventional forms of serialization—to crudely simplify: the cutting-up of existing stories into smaller installments—and more creative and open forms, as illustrated today by many television series. As one easily imagines, the distinction between conventional and creative forms is not to be read in chronological terms; there have always been creative forms of seriality, and conventional forms have certainly not gone away. According to Kelleter, serial structures, which he globally defines as the opposite of one-shot or stand-alone productions, are characterized by, among other elements, a feedback loop of production and reception and thus a recursive progression. Series are not first made and then watched: they are watched while being made, and this overlap "allows serial audiences to become involved in a narrative's progress" (2017a, 13). Recipients can thus operate as "*agents of narrative continuation*," for instance through their remarks and comments on the way the story unfolds, but even when they just watch the producers will "make inferences about their behavior as *customers*" (13). The progression of the story thus becomes recursive, and the writers will do anything they can to keep the possibilities of readjustments as open as possible. In addition—and this is another basic feature of these creative serials—the telling of the story may be accompanied by a proliferation of "amateur and reader productions," which tend to generate "*authorization conflicts*" (17; author's emphasis). Indeed, not all audience expansions, which capitalist serial production encourages, as it implies a greater audience involvement, will be considered legally or artistically acceptable.

(À Suivre) is a very special case in this regard, since it mixes in dramatically new ways the conflicting aesthetics of stand-alone and serial production and reception methods, on the one hand, while also exploring the limits of

an auteur approach of a traditional culture industry with strong editorial interventions and commercial horizons, on the other. Since the magazine was a monthly, and the making of each chapter always a race against time—all historical witnesses agree on this point—there was certainly a feedback loop between writers and readers. At the same time, none of the artists was willing to trade the newly obtained creative freedom for a stricter obedience to market expectations. *(À Suivre)* appeared in a moment where serious comics were booming and comics artists had the possibility to make a living by combining magazine publication and publication in book format. In many cases, their ambition was less to permanently revise their story lines in order to include audience expectations or ongoing fan discussions, as may be the case today, than to challenge the audience as much as possible and to write against the grain of these expectations. To a great extent it is reasonable to suppose that this was also what the curious and demanding audience was asking for: not to become a coproducer of the work, but to be amazed month after month.

Yet what *The Obscure Cities* is exploring in its making is once again at the same time more radical and in dialogue with existing formats and formulas. As already mentioned, classic cliffhanger endings are not automatically rejected, and in comparison with other trendsetting works such as Jacques Tardi and Jean-Claude Forest's *Ici-Même* (astonishingly still unavailable in English) or Moebius's *The Airtight Garage*, narrative continuity and the construction of well-built story arcs are very present in Schuiten and Peeters, without being as traditionally conventional as in Pratt's *Corto Maltese* (in fact a rather old-fashioned series, in spite of its charming hero, quite untypical of the type of avant-garde work *(À Suivre)* was actively promoting). But what they are doing with the very notion of series is extremely innovative.

The most important change brought about by *The Obscure Cities* is the far-reaching deconstruction of the opposition between one-shot and series. In the work by Schuiten and Peeters, the relationship between part and whole is made almost indistinguishable. Granted, the various albums, short stories, and other side projects are all part of the *Obscure Cities* universe, but each of them occupies a position that is both totally indebted to the series and resistant to its seamless integration in it. On the one hand, all works are clearly fragments of the series as it gradually develops. Yet on the other, none of them is limited to the unveiling or the expansion of a fixed totality. With each new contribution, the whole series changes: the characteristics of *The Obscure Cities* already known to the readers are redefined in each new album, and despite the relative stability of time and space and the return of many characters, each new work searches for different ways of storytelling as demonstrated, for instance, in the difficulty of actually defining the "genre" of these stories (a point to which I will return in the next chapter). Similar observations apply to questions of rhythm, length, visual style, and of course the question of fiction and nonfiction, which all further complicate the play with genre labels and conventions in *The Obscure Cities*. If all the *Obscure Cities*–catalogued works are structurally dependent on the larger whole, the relationship between these works and the larger series is often so different that it becomes difficult, if not impossible, to maintain the classic hierarchy between the whole and its parts, since each part builds a specific relationship to the whole, and the whole does not simply function as the general umbrella that helps to cover and unify the various parts. It is as if *The Obscure Cities* was a whole with no stable center, with certain parts claiming to represent such a central position. Very typical in this regard is the multiplying of encyclopedia-like fragments that are no simple addenda or ornaments but that can be seen in the new context of the Integral Edition as the breeding ground for the stories themselves. And if one accepts, as the series frequently suggests, that the relationship between Earth and Counter-Earth can be symbolized as a Möbius strip, there are good reasons to think that the situation of serial structures and stand-alone productions in *The Obscure Cities* is not very different: each part partially tends to be promoted as the center of a never-ending and permanently reconstructed universe (Duplan 2018).

Once again, this very radical reshaping of the dialectics of part and whole is not the result of a frontal attack against the traditional structures of series and works. *The Obscure Cities* remains a *real* series; its various parts remain *real* parts of this series. At the same time, the difficulty of making a logical or chronological ordering of the parts—the lack of a fixed "bible"—transforms the whole series into a kind of mobile: everything is tightly put together, but it is not possible to determine once and for all the relative positions of the parts, and thus to stabilize the global structure of the series. The reunion of all available elements in the four-volume complete edition increases this structural ambivalence. The whole story world and all the stories are here gathered and comfortably made available to any reader. Yet the way in which this is done maintains the uncanny relationships between the whole and its parts. The new edition does not follow a genre-based organization—for instance, one that groups the major types of album-length stories, shorter narratives, documentary side projects, and editorial and critical comments—but mixes them with the help of alternating montage techniques that at the same time stress and partially undermine the publication history of *The Obscure Cities*. While the chronology of the album releases is globally respected, their

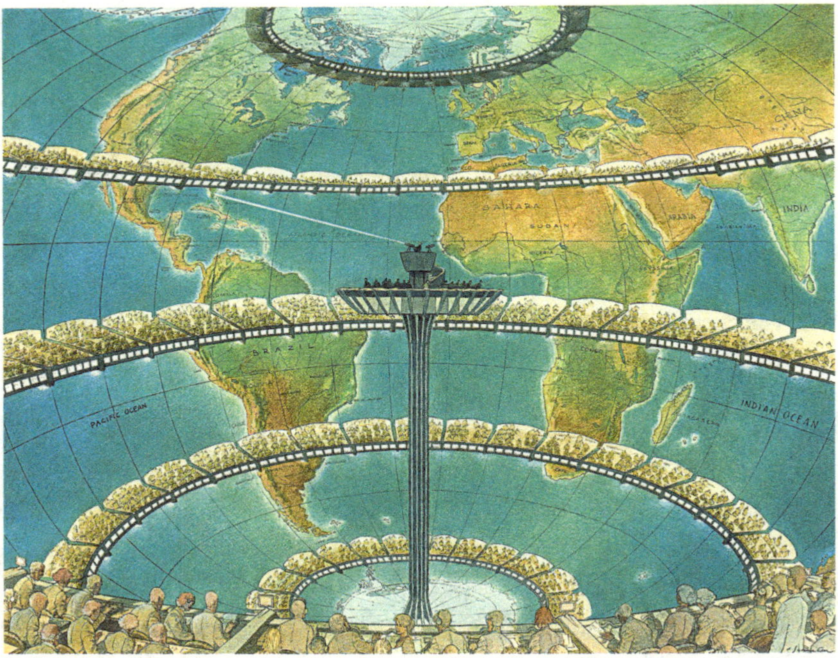

FIG. 4.3 The "Moebius theme" in a serigraphy by François Schuiten: "Listening to the World" (© François Schuiten)

sequential arrangement makes visible how the works' fictional chronology remains open to future revisions. The stylistic convergences, in texts and images alike, between albums, short stories, documents, and comments, makes this way of reading almost inescapable.

In short, analyzing the stories and storytelling techniques of *The Obscure Cities* addresses first of all the relationship between world building and storytelling. These two tendencies are conflicting in many fantasy and transmedia contexts, which emphasize world building and character building at the expense of plot and storytelling. Yet in spite of the vital importance of world building in the work of Schuiten and Peeters, storytelling proves no less paramount a reconciliation that confirms their careful blending of tradition with innovation. In the second step, the narrative analysis of the series also involves a radical medium-specific approach. Storytelling in *The Obscure Cities* cannot be separated from the materiality of the publication formats of the series, which appeared at a moment of great change in the comics magazine business. The introduction of chapters and the challenging of the classic distinction between one-shots and series are less the consequences of the literary turn of serious comics in the 1980s than the result of the introduction of a new type of publication format: the monthly comics magazine with multipage installments. But even here, the possibility of changes and revisions remains a vital aspect of Schuiten and Peeters's work, since the published albums are not simple reprints or gatherings of the monthly serializations. The albums are new and independent items, which introduce smaller or larger changes in comparison with the initial publication format.

5

A New Fantastic

In the previous chapters, the work by Schuiten and Peeters has been analyzed in terms of world building and storytelling as well as in terms of visual style, media formats, and publication history. The notion of genre was, however, hardly mentioned. In the context of comics—which is of course not a *genre*, but a *medium*—this relative absence should have come as a surprise, given the dramatic impact and importance of genre labels in the production and reception of popular culture. In popular media culture, genre is not simply an option, it is a necessity. Together with, for instance, the use of series instead of stand-alone volumes and the use of highly recognizable characters with which the general public can identify, genre is one of the elements that compensate for the commercial risk that accompanies any cultural production whatsoever (Hesmondhalgh 2012). There is no domain where the uncertainty principle rules as ruthlessly as culture: nobody knows whether something new or the continuation of something old will achieve success, even if everybody claims the contrary—hence the categorical imperative to protect oneself as much as possible against the indifference or hostility of the audience, for instance with the help of genre structures.

Genres are useful when it comes down to streamlining not only the production but also the reception of works. Without genre labels, it is more difficult for creators to present works that can be identified as being both part of a given tradition and capable of promoting a novelty effect—two necessary conditions to survive in the extremely competitive market of popular culture. Granted, some works appear as "genre mavericks," but in general popular culture is quite reluctant to leave too much room for maneuver. In this regard, the contrast with high or elite culture is very striking, for this field of cultural production is characterized by a strong distrust of so-called genre fiction, that is, works that fit into strongly preformatted genre protocols. High or elite culture displays a huge discrepancy between genre fiction and genreless fiction, with a strong preference for the latter, whereas popular culture has often no other choice than to accept the existing genre rules and classifications. One should stress, however, that the acceptance of genre labels and conventions is far from excluding creativity and originality. Many popular authors and productions do not slavishly follow genre protocols but succeed in subverting or displacing them. A number of successful genre fictions in popular culture are genre fictions with a certain twist, since the craving for novelty is as strong as the longing for immediate and automatic identification and positioning.

The Obscure Cities plays ball with the expectations of the cultural industry of comics, even in the age of the emerging graphic novel culture, often highly critical of the existing genre classifications and restrictive genre formats. In many cases, certainly in the United States, this suspicion takes the form of a critique of classic comics genres such as superhero fiction. Alan Moore and Dave Gibbons's *Watchmen* is a frontal attack against the ideology of the hooded superhero and his or her magic powers, but the distance between "real people" and imagined superhero alter egos is also very visible in the work of Chris Ware, Charles Burns, and Daniel Clowes. In the case of the European *(À Suivre)*, the distrust of older genres and formats is blatant in both parodic subversion and the effort to tell stories that evade the usual classifications.

Schuiten and Peeters have taken up the gauntlet of expanding their initial volume, *Samaris*, into a real series—the basic gesture of all art that seeks to enter the domain of popular cultural production at large. By doing so they have inevitably been confronted with the question of the genre as a key instrument in the consolidation of a series. Before examining this problem in *The Obscure Cities* it may be interesting, however, to remind ourselves of some very general principles of genre theory and analysis (see Altman 1999 for a pragmatic, multilayered, and highly contextualizing approach to genre labels). First of all, *genres are not texts*. The former are an abstract category; the latter designate concrete works that are always more—or something else than—the materialization or exemplification of abstract categories. Second, *genres are better defined in prototypical than in essential terms*. Genres do not coincide with a fixed and transhistoric set of genre features. Formal and semantic characteristics of genres change in time and space, and they should be seen as open clusters of more or less systematically present aspects that creators as well as readers or viewers can rely upon to produce or to make sense of a given work. Not all of these features are to be present in all works, just as all works are always open to elements that are not part of the core definition of the genre prototype. Third, *there is never an automatic one-to-one correspondence between works and genres*. Many works are identified as belonging to more than one genre, in varying degrees of course, while genres can inspire or generate more than just one text. Even in those cases where there is only one known example of a given genre, the very acknowledgment of a genre structure allows for the production or reception of other works that belong to the same genre. Until now, for instance, there is nothing that resembles a work like Chris Ware's *Building Stories*, fourteen printed works—clothbound books, newspapers, broadsheets, and a flip book packaged in a boxed set—which has "invented" a new genre, but it is easy to imagine that within a couple of years there will be many more examples of these kinds of comics.

In order to stress the fundamental openness of genres, to genre theory has been introduced the concept of "genericity" (Baroni 2011b); that is, the possibility of works to refer to one or more genres, a mechanism that leaves room for impurity and combination of genre features and aspects—even in those cases where a single genre label is narrowly applied to a given work. Hitchcock's *Rear Window* is undoubtedly a thriller, but it is no less a romance story. *The Wire* is crime fiction, but it is also a sociological research report—and according to the makers even a modern Shakespearean tragedy.

But what are we to think of *The Obscure Cities* as a genre-related series? The great originality of the fictional world invented by Schuiten and Peeters, whose eclectic treatment of fin de siècle images was immediately recognizable to the larger audience, far beyond the more specialized circles of graphic novel readers, and the persistent focus on world building through storytelling is such that the series is commonly labeled as "architecture comics," a new and unique yet not eccentric genre tag. Other genre markers seem to play a smaller role—a regrettable lacuna since, in the work by Schuiten and Peeters, world building is never done at the expense of storytelling.

There are, however, other and more significant reasons that enlighten the absence of strong discussions on genre in *The Obscure Cities*. First of all, most of the albums and short stories of the series follow different genre models. A non-exhaustive overview would easily unravel into a listing of stories sharing affinities with travel literature (*The Road to Armilia*), time travel (*The*

Leaning Girl), dystopic fiction (*Fever in Urbicand*), historical novels (*The Tower*), the artist novel (*Le Musée A. Desombres*), coming of age stories (*The Leaning Girl*), documentaries (*L'Echo des cités*) and fake documentaries (*Le Dossier B* and the many variations on this theme), science fiction (mainly of the Jules Verne type, although it is difficult not to acknowledge certain echoes of a Philip K. Dick paranoia in works such as *The Shadow of a Man* or *The Theory of the Grain of Sand*), and of course fantasy, more exactly the fantastic, probably the most ubiquitous genre reference, to which I will shortly have to return. All these elements are clearly present in the whole series, often blended in individual works, but at first sight their weight is minimized by the strong impact of the *Obscure Cities* universe as a whole. This world is instead systematically foregrounded through the fact that Schuiten and Peeters not only tell stories but also make illustrations, standalone nonnarrative variations on their universe, both outside the books and the series, including in the "real world," and within the books and short stories themselves (see chapter 7). The tension between story and illustration is always there. One can easily read it as the visual transposition of the age-old intertwinement, sometimes peaceful, sometimes conflictual, of *narrative* and *description* in storytelling. At the micro level, *The Obscure Cities* goes back and forth between narrative genre impulses and nonnarrative illustrative predispositions. At the macro level, the series oscillates between storytelling and world building. And the symmetry between micro and macro levels is always very visible.

Yet there is more than this balance between the narrative and the nonnarrative or between storytelling and visuality. If genre labels appear less important, it is because the very position of genres as overarching structural principles is challenged in *The Obscure Cities* by a totally different mechanism, namely, the idea of "constraint" or "constrained writing." In literary theory, constraints can be defined as self-chosen and systematically followed generative principles that aim at producing works that no longer rely on notions of inspiration, expression, or representation but rather on the generative power of formal or semantic structures, as exemplarily shown by Georges Perec's 1969 lipogrammatic novel without the letter *e*, *A Void* (Motte 1986; Mathews and Brotchie 2005).

Comics have always been extremely active and inventive in constrained writing. Contemporary U.S. examples can be found in the work by Matt Madden, whose *99 Ways to Tell a Story* (2005) is a series of engrossing one-page comics that tell the same story ninety-nine different ways. Inspired by Raymond Queneau's 1947 *Exercises in Style*, a mainstay of creative writing

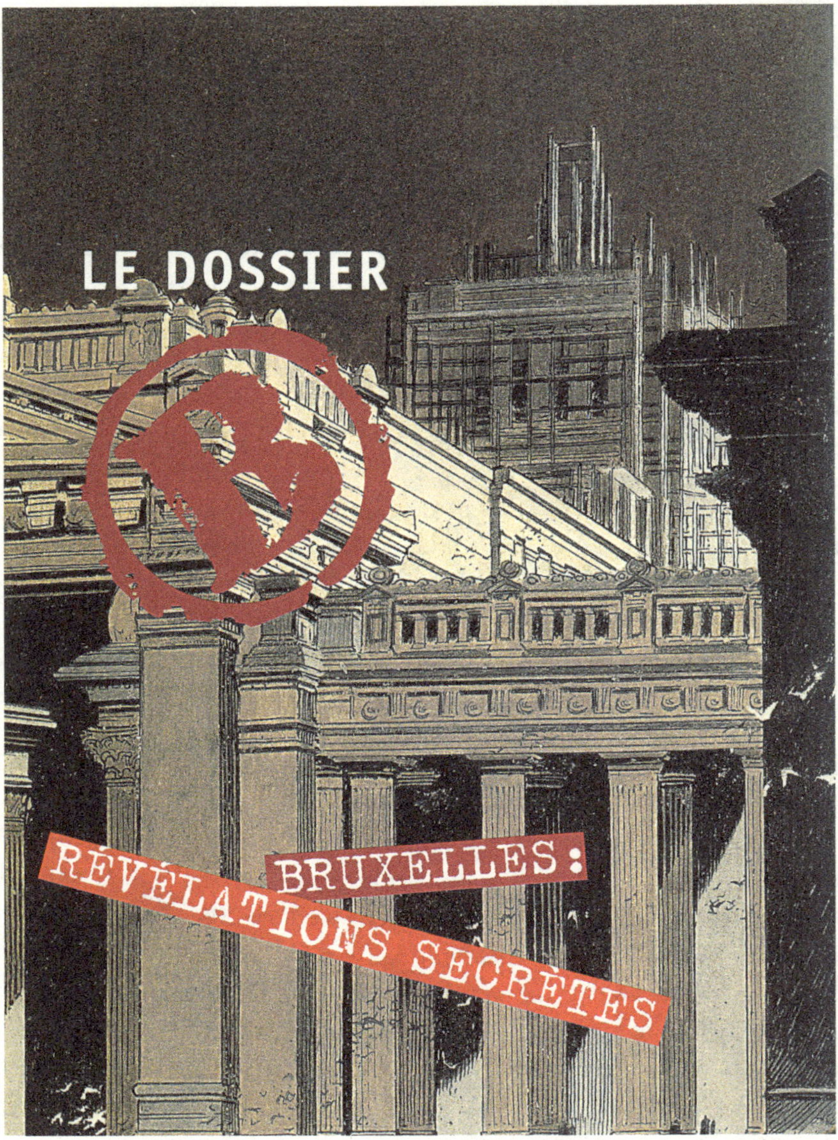

FIG. 5.1 A fake documentary on a Brussels contact zone: *Le Dossier B* ("The B File"), cover of the DVD (© Benoît Peeters)

courses, Madden's book has proved a watershed moment in the U.S. recognition of this way of inventing comics. The constrained writing tradition in comics is long-standing, as shown for instance in the pioneering work of Gustave Verbeek. His weekly *The Upside Downs of Little Lady Lovekins and Old*

Man Muffaroo (1903–1905) was a six-panel comic strip in which the first half of the story was illustrated and captioned right side up, then the reader would turn the page upside down, and the inverted illustrations with additional captions told the second half of the story, for a total of twelve panels.

In *The Obscure Cities*, constrained writing can be linked with the concept of "productive" page layout and, more generally, "productive" medium use in the technical sense coined by Benoît Peeters himself. In a much-quoted essay on the language of comics, Peeters (2007) has developed the idea that the relationship between narrative form and narrative content, to put things as simply as possible, can go in either of two directions: either the form is chosen in such a way that it reinforces the story elements one wants to communicate (the appearance of a huge skyscraper may determine the shift from horizontal strips to vertical panels, for instance); or the formal features of the works are used in order to trigger the story units themselves (in this case, the use of vertical panels will spark the idea of a skyscraper). In Peeters's terminology, the former is the *rhetorical* use of page and medium, while the latter is the *productive* use of it. The first one is more or less the default option for all those who want to do something with the creative tension between form and content. The second one, although rarer and not always easy to acknowledge by readers used to the rhetorical frame, is, however, crucial in comics history, as shown by various plates of *Little Nemo in Slumberland* that demonstrate a clear impact of the page layout on the very content of the young boy's dream.

A series that invents a new dynamism between tradition and innovation, *The Obscure Cities* relies on countless rhetorical techniques, but it would be a mistake not to highlight the vital presence of the productive use of the medium, which makes the series a further example of constrained writing. Some examples: the format of the rectangular 2-D panel bleeds into the fictional motif of the proliferating cube; the tension between fixed drawn images and their dynamic sequential arrangements engenders multiple variations on the trompe l'oeil theme; the closeness of fact and fiction in the case of authors who fictionally reshape real-world experiences translates into the exchanges between Earth and Counter-Earth and the narrative paths of initiation and transgression; the mirror effect of the double spread and the possibility to expand it to the dimensions of a whole book constitute the central principle of the fascinating side project by François Schuiten and his brother Luc in *Nogegon* (1990), a palindromic title that hints at the basic structure of the *Obscure Cities*–related universe: a world of total and therefore dictatorial symmetry that will be opened up and disrupted by the anarchic power of an unconventional protagonist (whose female gender is far from being a detail, as a later chapter of this book will examine).

The Obscure Cities displays a well-crafted balance between the rival forces of narrative invention and constrained writing, rhetorical and productive uses of the medium, stories and images, dreams and formulas—and this impacts upon the perception of the genre patterns, both very present and relatively secondary for the reader, who does not cease to focus on other overarching structures. But constrained writing, medium awareness, and the enduring fluctuation between stories and images are of course not the only transversal elements of the series. No less important is the visual and thematic cross-fertilization of styles and historical periods, all glued together by the stylistic idiosyncrasies established by François Schuiten. The world the series has been building is a mosaic of numerous influences and references, perhaps implausible if not impossible on Earth, in the real world, but which ceases to be a conflict of the self-contradictory in the *Obscure Cities* multiverse. From this point of view, the genre label of the fantastic (as defined by Tzvetan Todorov as the genre that produces a hesitation of characters and readers when presented with questions about reality; see Todorov 1973) is the first that springs to mind when trying to cope with the dizzying diversity of objects, people, styles, motifs, and story logics. The smooth integration of a broad range of sometimes heteroclite units and themes creates a world that would be in danger of disintegration without the umbrella term of the fantastic. In comparison, the scope of a label such as "fantasy," often associated with dungeons and dragons or medieval fantasy à la *Lord of the Rings*, is much narrower and much more stereotypically circumscribed than that of the fantastic. The mix of documentary and fiction, science and pure imagination, or history and poetry is easily managed by the fantastic, which is more a tone and a mode than a real genre, contrary to fantasy, which has more difficulties in exceeding its own genre boundaries.

When discussing fantastic literature, it must be made clear that its current prestige is rather low, due to the endless output of run-of-the-mill fantasy works, the increasing success of nonfiction, and the frequent links with other typical genre fiction productions such as horror and gothic. Yet the historic importance of the fantastic in comics culture in general and its impact on the emergence of the European graphic novel in particular, with authors such as Moebius (*The Airtight Garage*) and Tardi and Forest (*Ici-Même*), but also Rivière and Floch (*Le Rendez-vous de Sevenoaks*), make it a very logical reference for contemporary creators eager to reinvent the tradition instead of rejecting it. In the case of *The Obscure Cities*, it is possible to claim that both authors aim to rethink the status of the fantastic, rather than simply innovating or transforming the fantastic. Schuiten and Peeters construct this project as part of a larger attempt to question the very notion of genre itself in order to induce new forms of the fantastic. Such a policy is much more in harmony with the general line of their series, which does not prioritize identifiable genre conventions, but rather reveals the will of certain authors—one may think of Borges or Cortázar but also James or Kafka—in order to establish new forms and a new canon of the fantastic. In the creative enterprise of Schuiten and Peeters, the revival of the fantastic is the result of a more all-encompassing approach to genre and storytelling themselves. More concretely, *The Obscure Cities* series explores various aspects of high-literary creation, such as for instance the narrative technique of metalepsis or the conflation of levels that are *ontologically different* (Genette 1983, 234, who gives the example of a Julio Cortázar story in which a man is assassinated by one of the characters in the book he is reading). Moreover, the series also pays a lot of attention to the techniques of constrained writing, in order to invent a form of fantastic literature that is radically transgenre while also blurring the boundaries between the notions of time and space, as articulated in the chronotope, and character, as traditional carrier of the story. In other words, the reflection on the fantastic morphs into a larger approach of playing with narrative and fictional mechanisms beyond genre boundaries. This is exactly what Schuiten and Peeters do in their use of the fantastic. They do not make the a priori choice of the "new" genres that appear within the burgeoning field of the graphic novel—autobiography and historical nonfiction, via the model of U.S. alternative *comix* or audacious literary interpretations, as inspired by European or Latin American examples. Instead, they turn to the more traditional framework of the fantastic as a broad umbrella as a means to rethink and question the hierarchy of genre fiction and fiction in general, as well as between fiction and nonfiction, or realistic and fake documentary elements in writing and drawing.

But what constitutes the fantastic in *The Obscure Cities*? The most straightforward answer would be, of course, in the foregrounding of the place and role of Counter-Earth, the parallel universe whose relationship with Earth we know pervades all smaller and larger elements of the series. A more detailed description will foreground other aspects, which all hint at a kind of fantastic that is no longer *essential*, nor one that is linked with the presence of a nonrealistic entity such as Counter-Earth, but *induced*, that is, resulting from the specific treatment of certain narrative or thematic building blocks.

Nothing in *The Obscure Cities* is fantastic per se, but everything is capable of becoming fantastic, as soon as one realizes that the fictional world on display is not the visual and narrative translation of an idea, but the result of a certain number of transformations that can be applied to virtually anything in the series. Just as the proliferating network of tubular-sided cubes in *Fever in Urbicand* is not only the materialized form of the nightmarish delusions of a wild city planner, but the logical consequence of a "productive" reading of the medium, the exuberant floral motifs that appear in Blossfeldtstad (indeed throughout the *whole* series) are not only an art-historical nod at the typical Jugendstil elements of fin de siècle architecture but also the symbol of what challenges the ideal yet dystopic order or the Platonic line, triangle, or circle of which all architects and city planners of the series dream.

These kinds of transformations—a panel becoming a fictional labyrinth or a theme of ideological resistance taking the form of an ornamental paradigm, for instance—can rightly be called fantastic. The shift from 2-D to 3-D or from idea to material form is not something mechanical, but a strategy that casts new light on the fictional world, always capable of exuding unforeseen materializations on the one hand while, on the other, no less capable of being trapped the other way round by the awareness of the mechanism that moves between various ontological spheres. In *The Obscure Cities*, the fundamental thematic element of the passage from Earth to Counter-Earth and vice versa, which at first sight founds the fantastic character of the series, is not the starting point of a fantastic voyage between different spheres of the real and the unreal, but the consequence of the productive play with the comics medium, a play with the illusionistic reading of 2-D drawings and the animation through montage and reading of fixed images. What *The Obscure Cities* suggests is that in actuality all comics are open to a reading in terms of the fantastic. Furthermore, the series puts forward that possibility becomes a reality in this series where the very mechanism of the oscillation between strictly formal elements and their thematic and narrative interpretations is, first, systematically highlighted and, second, thematically represented via the recurrent motif of boundary crossing (between regions, either on Earth or Counter-Earth, but also and more crucially between Earth and Counter-Earth themselves). Such a fantastic does not precede the actual making of the work but is a dimension that accompanies the making of it as its shadow, hence the concept of "induced" fantastic.

The example of *The Tower* demonstrates how much this induction also relies on the treatment of specific comics features, in addition to the general aspects (2-D vs. 3-D, static vs. dynamic) already mentioned. In this album, the sudden and unforeseen transition from one universe to another is prompted by a chromatic event, which is itself prepared by a narrative incident. In the pivotal scene of the work, the protagonist, who is looking at a painting, notices that the character represented in the painting "comes alive"—a characteristic device of French avant-garde narrative in the 1960s and 1970s, where "immobile" characters such as statues could suddenly morph into "real" and thus moving characters or the other way round (Ricardou 1975, 118–121)—while at the same time the black-and-white drawings of the album start shifting to color, first only within the limits of the painting's frame, later also in the world that surrounds the frame. The observing character, that is, the protagonist of the fictional world, is clasped by the fictional world—he will shrink and climb over the edge of the painting in order to enter another reality—and here as well the general principle of induced fantastic is crystal clear: what the protagonist is doing is triggered by a thematic element—he feels seduced by the woman in the painting, who addresses him in order to make him enter her world—but this mechanism both reveals and disguises the shift from one universe to another by which the whole series is structured. In the present case, one can even argue that climbing into a picture replicates at the level of the reading of the work what we have already seen at the level of its making: to be seduced by what one sees or reads and to be psychologically absorbed by this reading or viewing is the readerly equivalent of the productive interpretation of the medium, which shows what happens when "living" fictional characters are totally absorbed by "nonliving" fictional representations.

Technically speaking, what happens here is called metalepsis. One should realize, however, that in *The Obscure Cities* metalepsis is not only the most important mechanism of all stories, for in all albums characters are looking for or confronted with the contact zones between Earth and Counter-Earth; it is above all the result, the logical consequence, of ways of writing and reading that are rooted in the wavering between ontologically different spheres: the material features of comics, the thematic transposition of these features in a fictional universe based on the encounter of dissimilar worlds. In the example of *The Tower*, the combination of a shift in the color code and a disruption of the usual distinction between immobile and mobile characters is less the mechanism that underlines or highlights the metaleptic event than the formal mechanism that actually produces it. Crossing the boundaries between different worlds is not the initial idea that is rhetorically marked with the help of certain technical devices. Ontological border-crossing is instead one of the things that happen when the authors of *The Obscure Cities* make a productive use of the affordances of their medium. Any comics element can

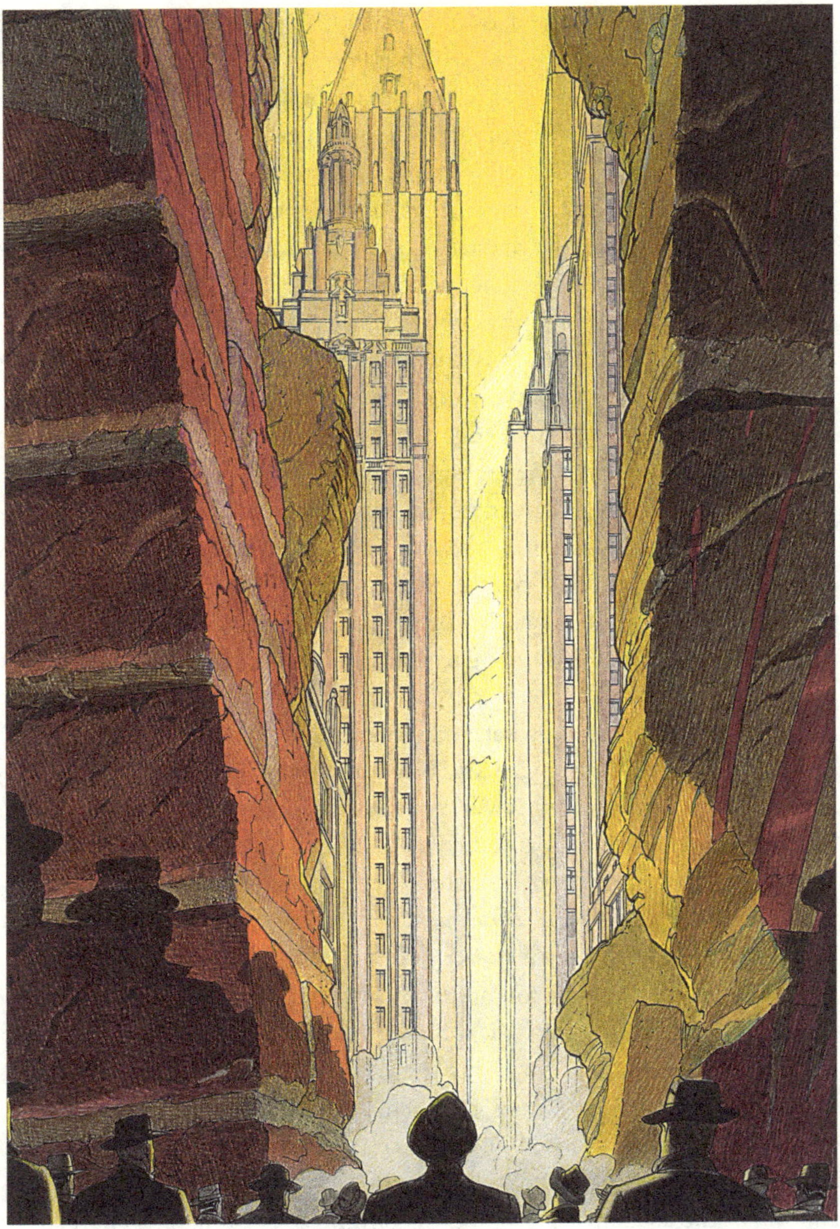

FIG. 5.2 An example of a "contact zone," drawing by François Schuiten for the poster of the Grenoble 1989 Detective Story Festival (© François Schuiten)

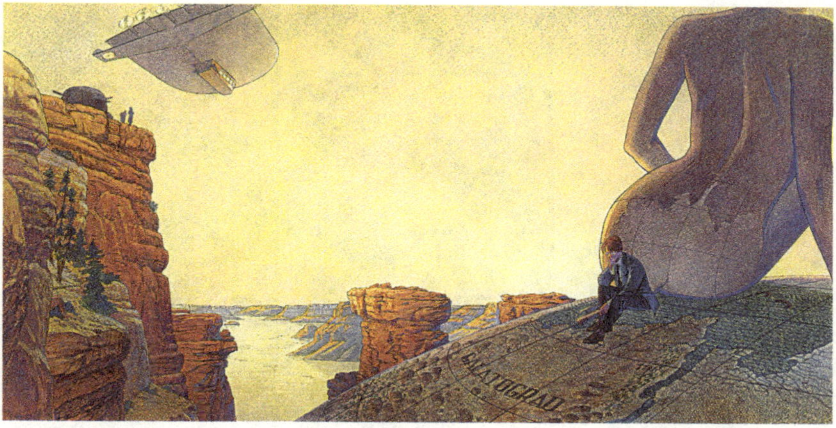

FIG. 5.3 Another example of a contact zone, cover illustration by François Schuiten for *The Invisible Frontier* (© François Schuiten)

become the springboard of a thematic and fictional development that the reading community will generically frame as "fantastic," an appropriate and utterly useful label that helps keep together very different themes and forms while allowing their smooth integration in larger narrative arcs. The latter is crucial, given the refusal of Schuiten and Peeters to do away with the power and pleasure of pure storytelling.

Next to *The Tower*, another excellent illustration of the links between the narrative device of metalepsis, the use of medium-specific comics elements, and the general thematic frame of interpenetrating worlds—the combination of which constitutes the typical fantastic of *The Obscure Cities*—can be found in *The Leaning Girl*, a touching variation on the theme of adolescence and puberty and a book I will come back to in detail in chapter 8. In this book, the circulation between ontologically separate universes relies on a visual metamorphosis: drawn images turn into photographs and vice versa.

In so doing, Schuiten and Peeters address the most fundamental material feature of their medium, namely, drawing. Their amalgamation of drawings and pictures does not aim at revealing two different points of view. Nor does it want to make distinctions between two types of sequences—as occurs for instance in *The Photographer*, the "comic-cum-photographs" trilogy by Emmanuel Guibert and Didier Lefèvre on the work of French Doctors of the World in Soviet-occupied Afghanistan—but to make use of this shift and eventual blend of materialities to produce a fictional move in time and space. *Changing media and changing places go hand in hand*. From a more anecdotal point of view, the blending of fictional and nonfictional characters points in

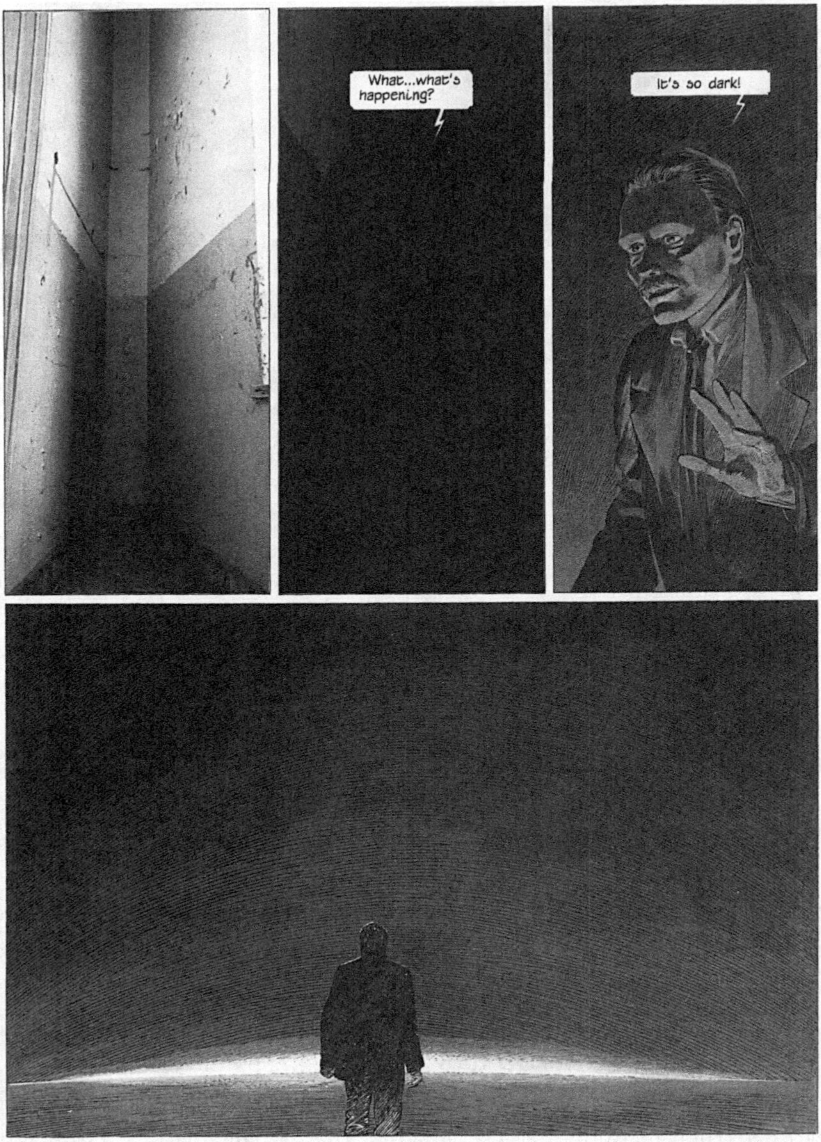

FIG. 5.4 The morphing of photographs into drawings, *The Leaning Girl*, Integral Edition, vol. 3, p. 145. Excerpt from *The Leaning Girl*, François Schuiten and Benoît Peeters (© Casterman, with kind permission of the authors and Editions Casterman)

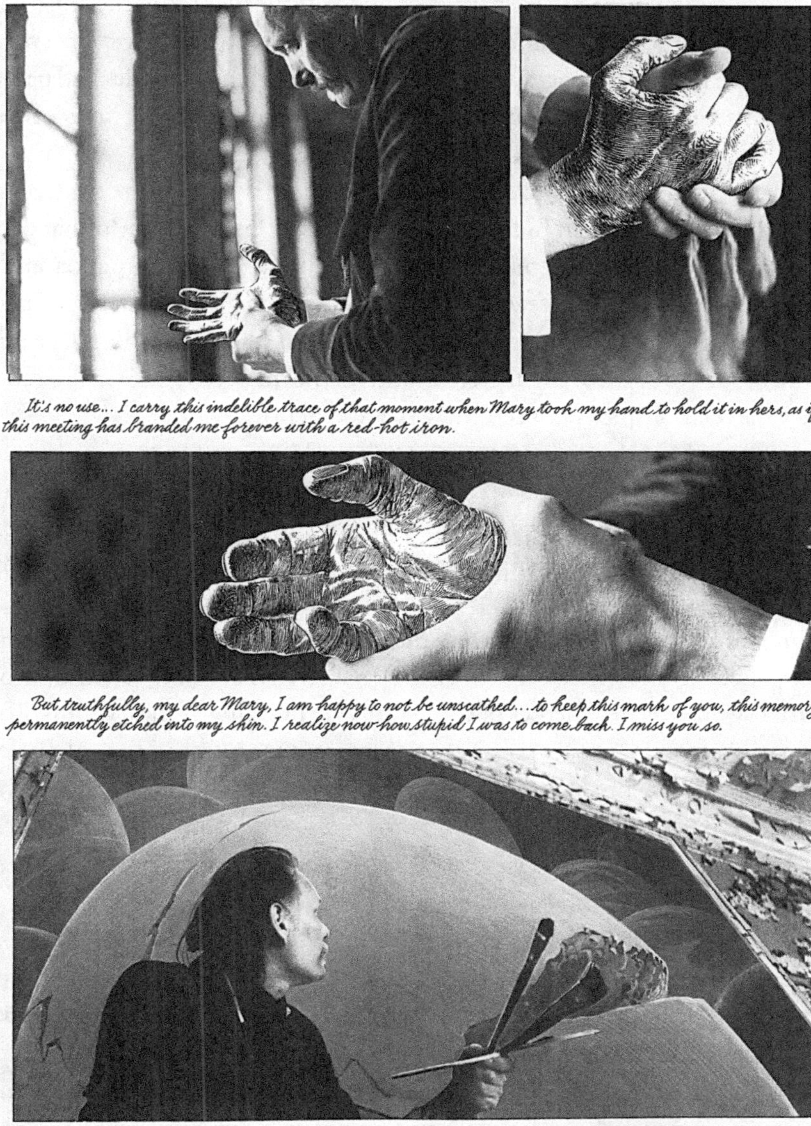

FIG. 5.5 The return from drawings to photographs, *The Leaning Girl*, Integral Edition, vol. 3, p. 171. Excerpt from *The Leaning Girl*, François Schuiten and Benoît Peeters (© Casterman, with kind permission of the authors and Editions Casterman)

the same direction: the characters of *The Leaning Girl*, some of them already known from previous albums of the series, meet representatives of several major arts: Nadar (photography) or Martin Vaughn-James (comics and painting; he is the only one to appear also in the photography sections of the book).

Yet the work by Schuiten and Peeters does more than redefine the fantastic in the direction of an induced fantastic—not a fantastic world that conceptually precedes its materialization in comics form, but an apparently plausible although quite exotic world that becomes a fantastic interplay between Earth and Counter-Earth via the singular use of medium-specific elements of the comics language. In addition, the induced fantastic also redefines the relationships between character and fictional world.

In fantastic works, place is never a detail, and its importance is heightened by the tight interaction with plot elements as theorized in the Bakhtinian chronotope. No cave or crypt without horror story, no Gotham City without adventures of masked superheroes, no secret garden without initiation rites. *The Obscure Cities* follows this canonical chronotopical path; it also adds a singular feature to it. As shown in previous chapters, Schuiten and Peeters create fictions in which the role of the character is actually taken over by spatial agents: the real heroes of the albums are buildings, cities, worlds. The human characters are part of this spatial environment, whose gradual disclosure and permanent changes and surprises constitute the true center of the series. Despite the subtly constructed intrigues and attractive human figures, the protagonist of the series is not a character but a chronotope, or, if one prefers, a chronotope complemented with a set of characters. Is it an exaggeration to imagine that *The Obscure Cities* might function, even story-wise, as actions without human characters? Certain volumes and certain sequences in any volume of the series strongly evoke the narrative transfer of a certain landscape tradition in painting, where the main role of the human characters visible on the canvas is to give an idea of the spatial dimensions of the setting (a tourist and a camel next to a pyramid, a shepherd next to a tree, etc.). In a similar way, Schuiten and Peeters use characters in order to make us aware of the material properties of the world they explore, at least in the first half of the series, for once this paradigm is clearly established, the authors can then move to other questions and frontiers.

In terms of the fantastic, such an approach signifies a real paradigm shift. In *The Obscure Cities*, the world becomes fantastic, but what changes even more is the dynamic relationship between human actions and the worldly environment. In *The Leaning Girl*, Mary suddenly falls prey to the attraction

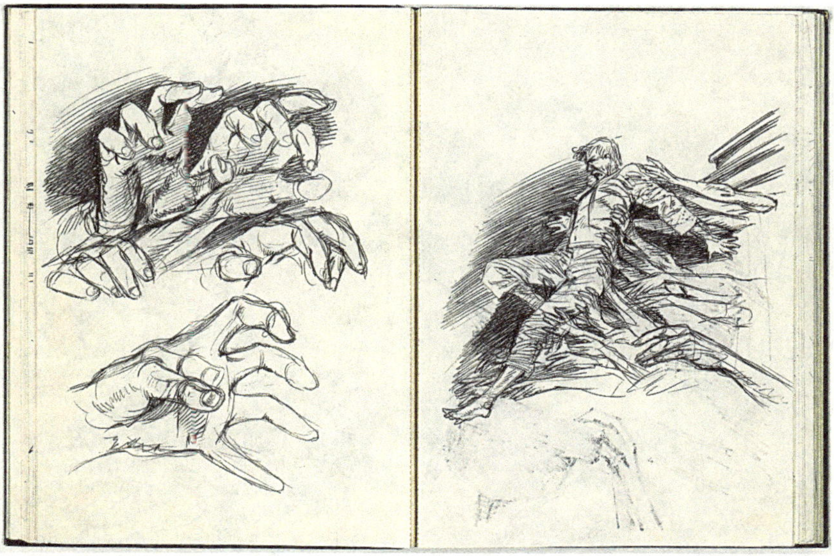

FIG. 5.6 *The Shadow of a Man*, sketches (© François Schuiten)

of an invisible planet, and the disruptive power of this change transforms the whole Counter-Earth universe, for instance by giving credit to the very existence of this invisible planet and thus by pushing certain characters to leave Counter-Earth to get in touch with Earth. In *The Shadow of a Man*, the protagonist of the story, Albert Chamisso, is abruptly confronted with the transparency of his own body, and the impact of this discovery has concentric effects on a whole society.

The central concern of the passage between worlds, characters moving from Counter-Earth to Earth and vice versa, resides not only in the core of a fantastic adventure; it is above all the perfectly logical consequence of a world building whose strange particularities are the visual and fictional translation of the particularities of the comics medium. Hence the "clarity" of what happens when a contact between worlds is established: in all cases, it is accompanied if not directly induced by a special treatment of medium. Typical elements of traditional fantastic plots and genres, such as studied in "unnatural narratives" that "[violate] physical laws, logical principles, or standard anthropomorphic limitations of knowledge by representing storytelling scenarios, narrators, characters, temporalities, or spaces that could not exist in the actual world" (Alber 2013), are often absent. Framing *The Obscure Cities* as unnatural narratives therefore would miss the essential point, which has to do with the relationship between world building and comics-making and

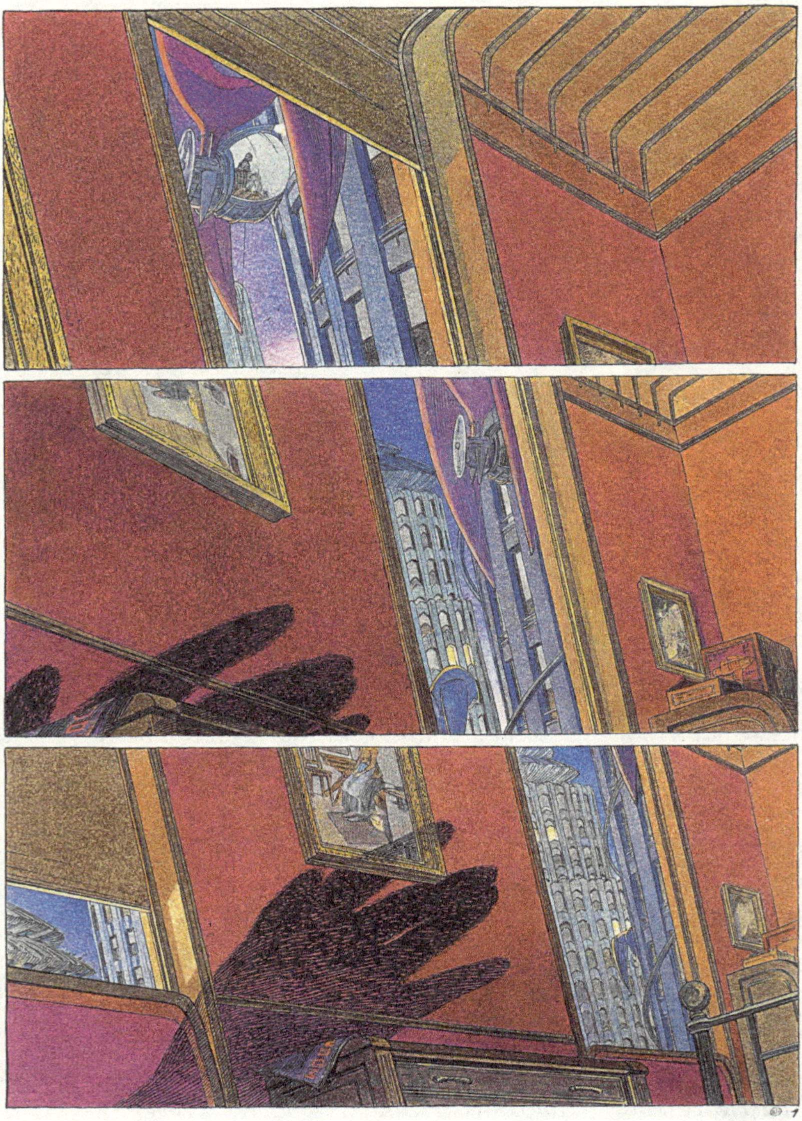

FIG. 5.7 *The Shadow of a Man*, page 1. Excerpt from *The Shadow of a Man*, François Schuiten and Benoît Peeters (© Casterman, with kind permission of the authors and Editions Casterman)

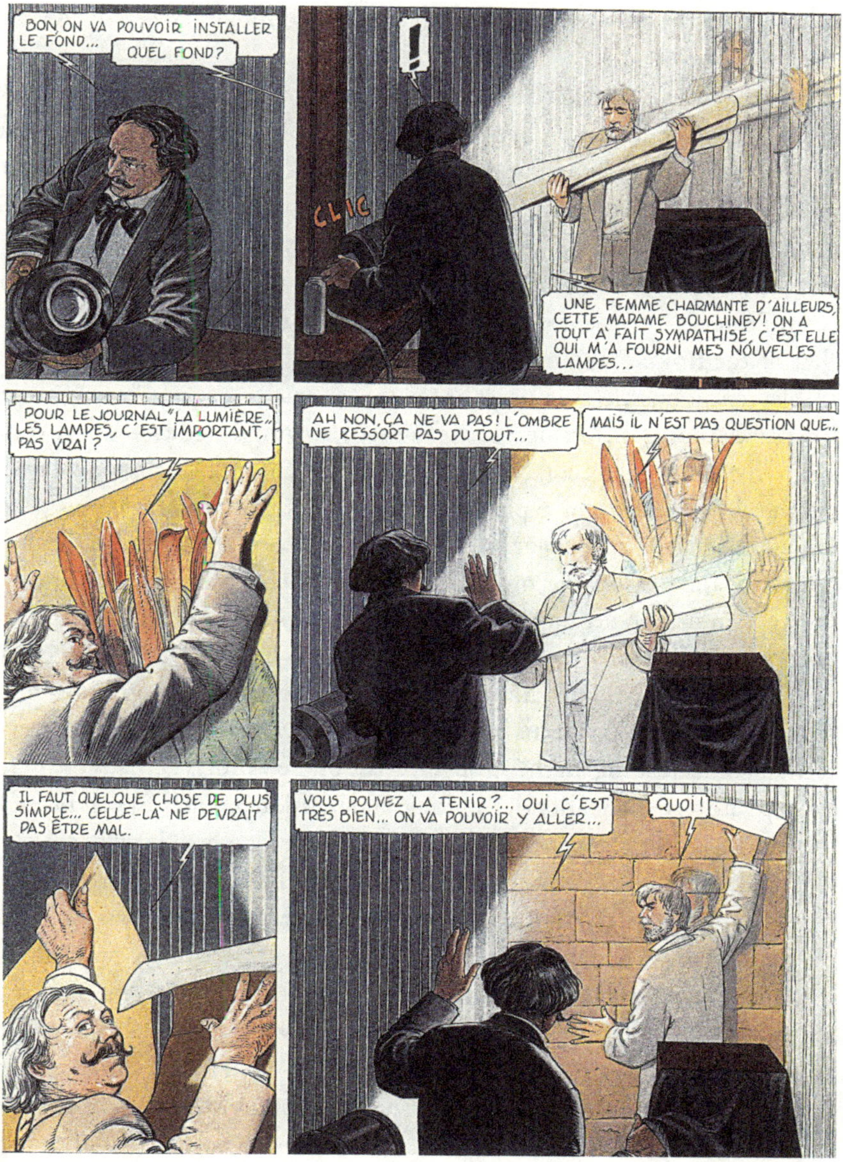

FIG. 5.8 *The Shadow of a Man*, Integral Edition, vol. 3, p. 368. Excerpt from *The Shadow of a Man,* François Schuiten and Benoît Peeters (© Casterman, with kind permission of the authors and Editions Casterman)

reading, not the relationship between logical and illogical elements within the fictional world.

What Schuiten and Peeters are interested in is less the fantastic as a genre or metagenre, therefore, than the possibilities it offers to further explore the movements back and forth between the microtextual treatment of medium features and the macrotextual constructions of worlds and stories. In *The Obscure Cities*, the enigma that all mystery tales want their readers to unravel exceeds the limits of the plot—even if this element is far from being neglected, given Peeters's love of classic storytelling. The real enigma to disentangle is that of the link among medium, plot, world, and character. Finding the answer to this question can never be reduced to cracking a code, having a one-time revelation, deciphering a secret message, solving a riddle—even if, once again, these elements are far from absent in *The Obscure Cities*, for instance via the appropriation of typical plot patterns in the work by Jules Verne, undoubtedly one of the major intertextual references of the series. The reader's desire to understand the mysteries of Counter-Earth and its intriguing presence in its parallel universe called Earth does not end with the stories' denouements. All answers trigger new questions, and this openness engenders a reading that is both linear (from mystery to solution) and translinear (each new solution invites us to reread the totality of what has already been read). Parallel reading, in the strongest sense of the word, is perhaps the most appropriate term to qualify the multiple and multidirectional aspects of reading, always on the move, never sure where to look for which kind of clues.

Yet if *The Obscure Cities* encourages this type of infinite reading, the stories do not do it in a paranoiac way—paranoid interpretation being the result of suspicious readers who believe that "everything" is virtually meaningful but who do not manage to identify textual clues that help them to find real answers (Andrews 2009). Next to the humor, always helpful when it comes down to refraining from overzealous elucidations, there is the similar treatment of story logic and series logic. True, the albums of *The Obscure Cities* are all genuinely connected, and the unity as well as homogeneity of the series cannot be denied. At the same time, each album or short story also manages to be an independent territory. The underlying visual model of *The Obscure Cities* is not that of the jigsaw puzzle, which presupposes an existing totality and the possibility to achieve a complete view of it, but that of the mobile, more particularly that of an incomplete or multiplying mobile, which constitutes a different canvas for the reading of the fantastic. The fantastic according to Schuiten and Peeters is not previously disclosed; it is another way of labeling the multiple adventures of making and reading comics.

6

In and Out the Medium

Much has been written on the fictional reworking of late nineteenth- and early twentieth-century architecture and city planning by Schuiten and Peeters as well as on the place of nostalgic techno-utopia in their work. As in the field of building history, there is only a thin line between fiction and reality in *The Obscure Cities*. When walking by certain buildings in Brussels, one can suddenly see and almost touch, but alas not always visit, some of the settings of the series. The same goes for the strand of technology in the books. A visit to the Paris Musée des Arts et Métiers is illuminating in this regard. The museum's self-presentation already sounds like a shortcut of what readers may discover in drawings by François Schuiten: "Founded in 1794 by Henri Grégoire, the Conservatoire national des arts et métiers, 'a store of new and useful inventions,' is a museum of technological innovation. The Musée des arts et métiers was refurbished in 2000, and now exhibits over 2,400 inventions. They are split into seven collections: Scientific instruments, Materials, Energy, Mechanics, Construction, Communication and Transport" (MAM—Musée des Arts et Métiers, Paris 2018).[1] A walk through the rooms of the museum, created in the post-Revolutionary years as a technological counterpart to the Louvre Fine Arts Museum, immediately confronts the visitor with some key elements and motifs of *The Obscure Cities*, all creatively but recognizably reimagined by François Schuiten. Clément Adler's aircraft prototype resembling an enormous bat made of linen and wood, with a fifteen-meter (forty-eight-foot) wingspan? Definitely a model for some of the old-looking flying machines invented by Schuiten (his other model is of course the balloon, from the post-Montgolfière types tested by Nadar to the Zeppelin-inspired planes that connect one Obscure City to the other).The automate collection of the Paris Museum, with its eighteenth- and nineteenth-century masterpieces combining fixed and animated representations as well as 2-D and 3-D settings? Undoubtedly a source of inspiration for the simulation of a real city and its living inhabitants with the help of cardboard surfaces in *Samaris*, the cradle of the whole series. And the alignments of transportation engines, steam machines, and measurement tools? They are ubiquitous in every page of *The Obscure Cities.*

Yet the importance of the Arts et Métiers Museum cannot be reduced to that of a real-life repository for the series' research, a display of authentic props open to fictional reappropriation. What Schuiten and Peeters find in the museum is less a collection of inventions and techniques that are contemporary of the historical period crucial to *The Obscure Cities* than an incentive to reflect upon the possible remediation of their work outside the conventional form of book and print. *The Obscure Cities* is then less a creative copy of the museum—a narrativization of inanimate objects, if one prefers—than a signpost for what can be done with the series once the drawings have been made public in a journal or an album. The exchanges between comics and industrial heritage and, more generally, fictional and nonfictional worlds are not representative of one-way traffic. Schuiten and Peeters acquire their inspiration from authentic sources while at the same time establishing a powerful feedback loop. The fictional series becomes the origin of a number of realizations outside the universe of print culture.

Before discussing some examples of this feedback loop, it is crucial to recall the role and place of the classic comics host medium in *The Obscure Cities* as well as the possibilities offered by the subsequent exploration of first, serialization and second, book publication. This programmed remediation allows for many novelties, but its liberties also come at a price, for instance the impossibility of using color in works of greater length. Yet what makes *The Obscure Cities* so exceptional is that Schuiten and Peeters have severed all essential or supposed natural ties between series, journal, and album. Although their work is considered the flagship series of the magazine *(À Suivre)*, both authors have, from the very beginning, elaborated their world in different directions, using different media, addressing different audiences, exploring different types of narrative and/or illustration. The uniqueness of *The Obscure Cities*

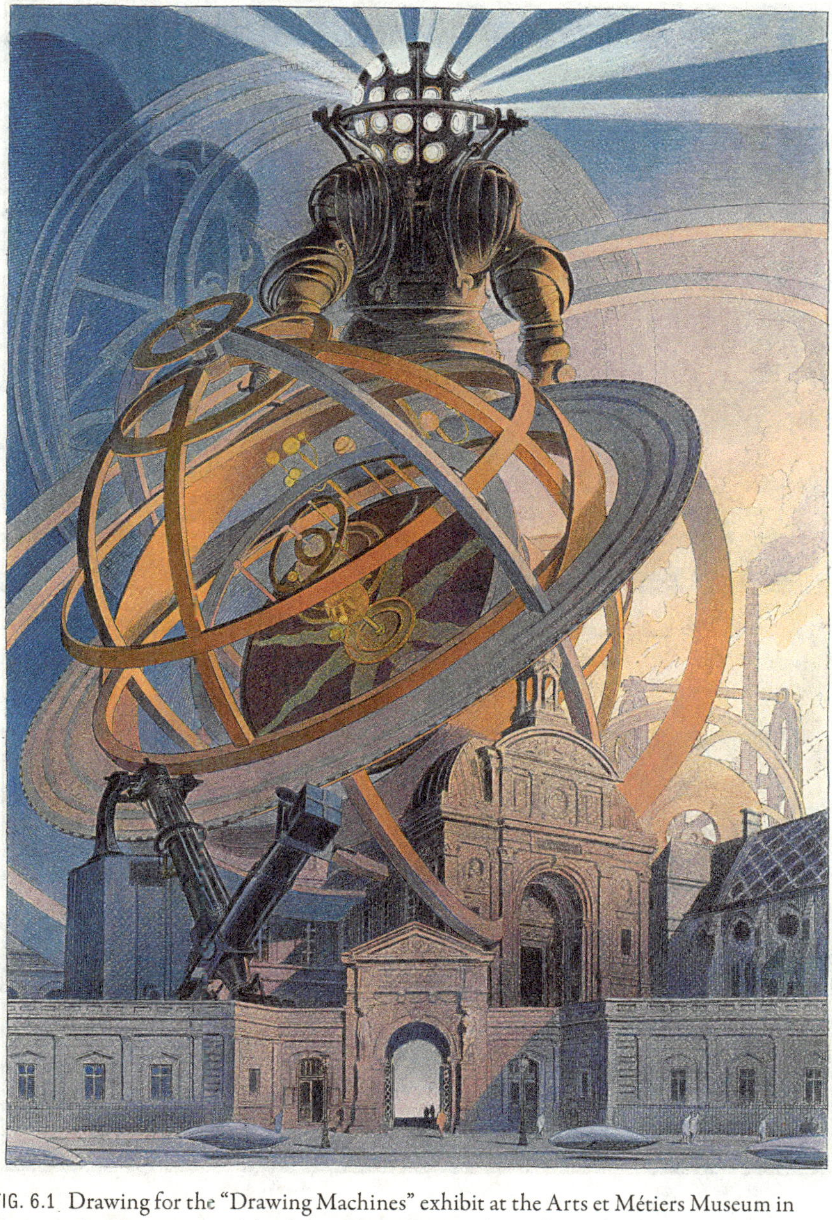

FIG. 6.1 Drawing for the "Drawing Machines" exhibit at the Arts et Métiers Museum in Paris, 25 October 2016–26 March 2017 (© François Schuiten)

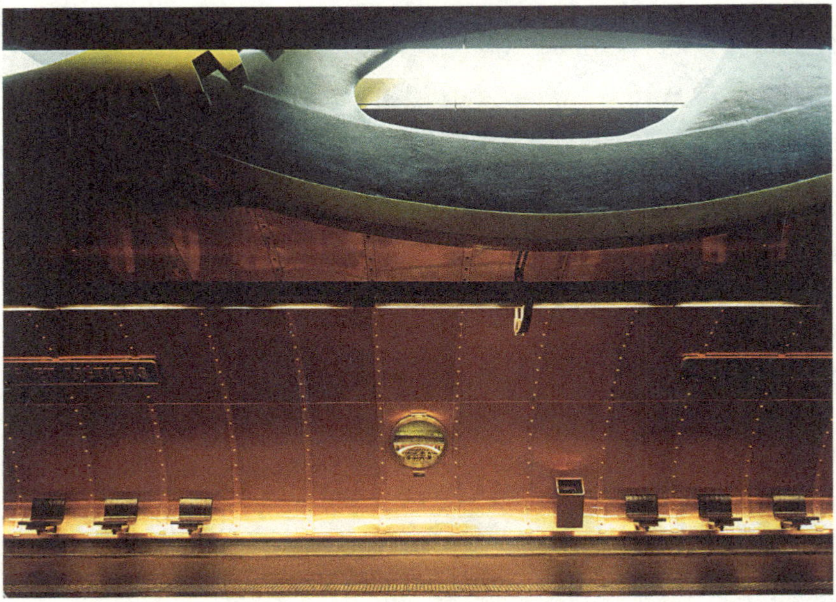

FIG. 6.2 The Arts et Métiers subway station in Paris, photography by Marie-Françoise Plissart (© Marie-Françoise Plissart)

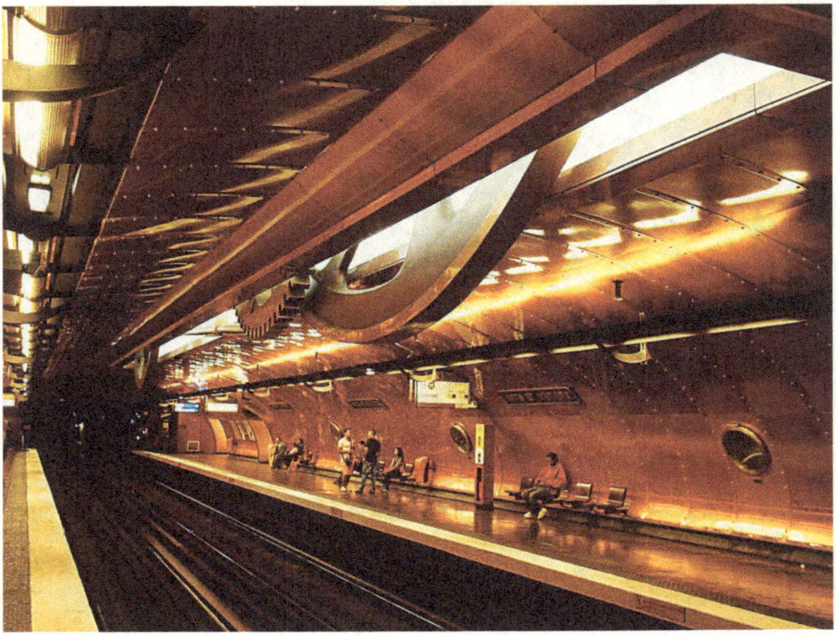

FIG. 6.3 The Arts et Métiers subway station in Paris, photography by Marie-Françoise Plissart (© Marie-Françoise Plissart)

in this regard has been acknowledged almost from the start (Groensteen 1994; see chapter 1). At first sight, it may seem relevant to qualify such a policy as an example of transmedia storytelling, as coined and then theorized by Henry Jenkins (see chapters 1 and 4). However, this generic pigeonholing would dissimulate what is so singular about the medium policy of *The Obscure Cities* as a cross-platform and multimedia project, since various basic parameters of Schuiten and Peeters's work do not fit into the prototypical transmedia storytelling format as sketched by Jenkins. The principal divergences can be listed in the following way:

- Genealogically speaking, the building of a transmedia universe was not part of the initial moment of the series. It was only later on that the first book evolved into a series, and eventually into a real network of variously linked products and activities.
- In *The Obscure Cities* world, the notion of a "bible" describing the various aspects of the universe (characters, places, settings, events, chronology) and its prototypical plot structures (having to do for instance with genre conventions, commercial formats, merchandising developments) is completely absent. The *Obscure Cities* universe is not only open; it also changes with each new item that is added to the series.
- What is also lacking is the attempt to gather, even if only in retrospect, the various adventures, characters, places, and objects that appear within the series. On the one hand, there is no lead element, such as a character or a place, that gives the series its internal unity or cohesion (each new item has other protagonists and is situated in a different place). On the other hand, all elements are permanently changing: characters may reappear in successive volumes or different contexts, but they are not necessarily completely the same, even if the general geographical and chronological landmarks of the work are remarkably stable—a stability that is imperative if one wants to make clear the fundamental openness of the series: changes are revisions, not disruptions, reboots, or new starts from scratch. The map of *The Obscure Cities* world is always an ad hoc document; new cities may be added, for instance, and the same goes for the chronology, well summarized in the opening pages of volume 4 of the Integral Edition.
- Just as there is no bible, there is also no traditional copyright management system. Granted, *The Obscure Cities* is a copyrighted work, with clearly defined stakeholders, but the application of intellectual property rights is rather loose. The audience is invited to co-create

certain aspects or elements of the work, as demonstrated for instance by the decision to interpret "fair use" in a rather liberal way[2] and to eventually hand over the management of the series' official website, Altaplana, named after the "archive city" in the *Obscure Cities* universe, to unofficial authors, in this case serious and dedicated fans. Altaplana is not the initial website of the series designed by its original authors, but an expansion of it that has organically grown from the fans' involvement in the constant updating and expanding of previous authorized versions. From 1996 on, Schuiten and Peeters were among the first authors to launch their own site, Urbicande.be, but for practical reasons they prefer to hand it over to a different webmaster, Eilko Bronsema, who, with the help of many equally benevolent readers, animates the exceptionally rich trilingual Altaplana website (several thousands of well-structured and permanently updated pages).

- The association with readers can flow over to real-life situations, which have nothing to do with the stereotypical forms of dialogue and appropriation, as for instance in cosplay and fan fiction—and even less to do with pathological mirroring situations between Stephen King's fictional characters and real-life killers. Schuiten and Peeters have thus been exchanging for nearly two decades a number of snail mail and e-mail messages with the "real" Mary von Rathen, a key character of the series (see chapter 8), who started a correspondence with them, making comments on both the series and the way in which she was represented in it, and eager to meet them in person to discuss some troubling interferences between fiction and reality. Claiming to be the "real" character of the fiction and thus to have access to special contact zones between Counter-Earth and Earth, Mary von Rathen, whose very existence continues to be a complete mystery, even published a limited book edition of her letters (*Correspondances*), the answers by Peeters, and some complementary letters by friends (fans and collectors of the *Obscure Cities* world). All efforts to identify or meet the "real" Mary von Rathen were unsuccessful, however, and still today the authors do not know if such a person actually exists. But whatever the truth behind this amazing story (a hoax? a tribute? an appropriation?), it superbly illustrates the essential question raised in *The Obscure Cities*.[3]
- As far as the media policy of the series is concerned, one notices the paradoxical combination of two different strategies: one that pursues

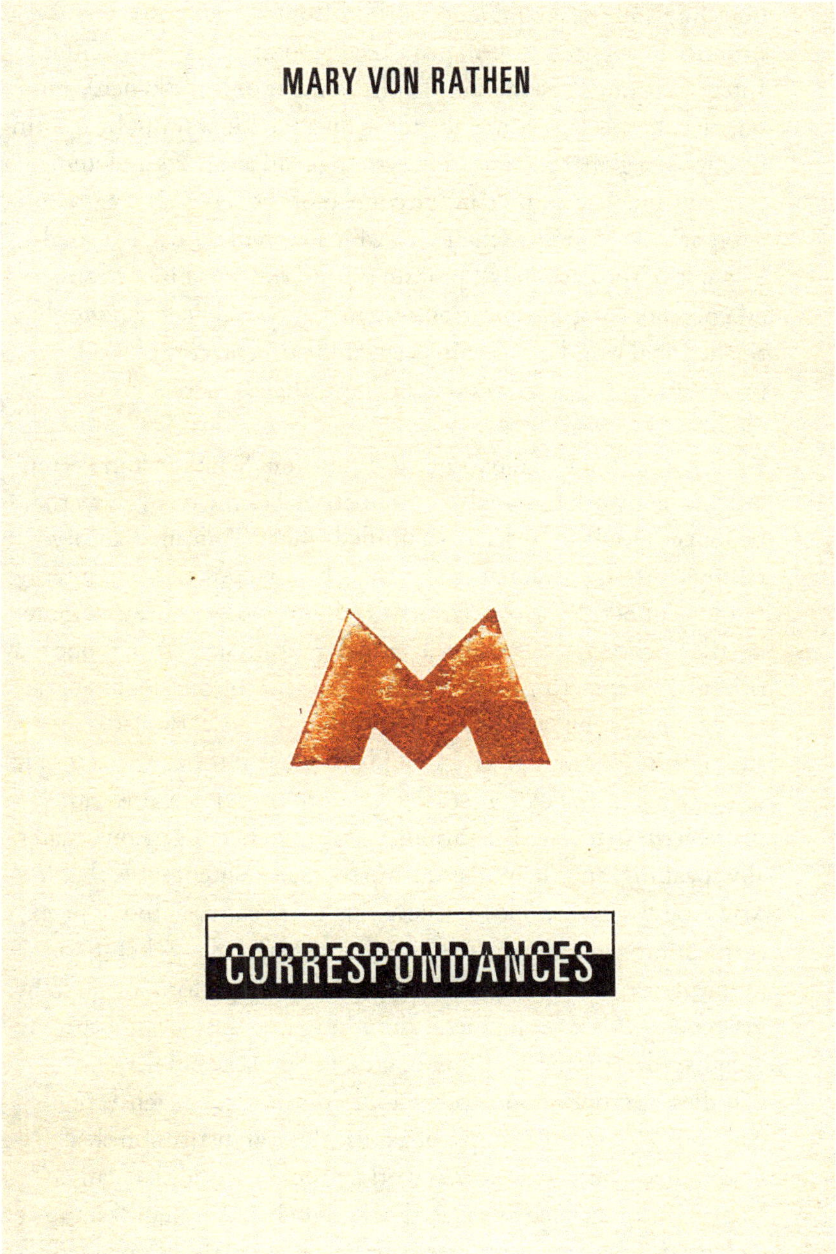

FIG. 6.4 Mary von Rathen, *Correspondances*, private collection (© Benoît Peeters)

- branding and tries to maintain or build an internal unity, for instance by republishing all print-related matter in a four-volume Integral Edition (for the time being available only in French), and one that simply lets things go, not in an anarchic way but by refusing to impose a global classification system on all the parts and items that continuously pop up in the context of the series. The parodic approach of the archive theme, to which we will return, is a good example of the authors' skepticism toward the possibility of an all-encompassing classification system, which is reflected not only in the fictional world but also in the real-life decentering of works, productions, and activities that are nevertheless marked by the *Obscure Cities* seal.
- Finally, and this a vital part of the discussion: Schuiten and Peeters mix in their work fictional and nonfictional elements in a way that is no longer meant to be seen as a unified whole. Transmedia storytelling tends to promote the idea that the juxtaposition and intertwinement of the various narratives will disclose a richer and more detailed fictional universe, and perhaps even to suggest that one may risk missing something when certain elements of the global puzzle are missing, even if the lack of this or that strand of the cross-media and multiplatform narrative should not prevent the enjoyment of its separate parts. *The Obscure Cities* is a work that clearly does not function in that way. The various parts are so heterogeneous, materially speaking, and their relationship so open, content-wise, that it would be absurd for one to believe that there exists a kind of preexisting or progressively unveiled master narrative that is being communicated via different channels. The lectures, performances, shows, master classes, scenographies, exhibitions, illustrations, site-specific designs, advertisements, films, operas, radio plays, fan fictions, parodies, appropriations, and real-life continuations such as the Autrique House, an example of a museological institution that materializes the *Obscure Cities* world, unfold a world that can no longer be experienced as a closed paradigm but that manifests a creative dynamics that progressively becomes partly independent from its origins. The Autrique House plays an important role in *The Theory of the Grain of Sand*, but it is also an existing Jugendstil building in Brussels that can be visited outside any reference to the *Obscure Cities* world. This peculiarity is another illustration of the profound ambivalence of the world built by Schuiten and Peeters.

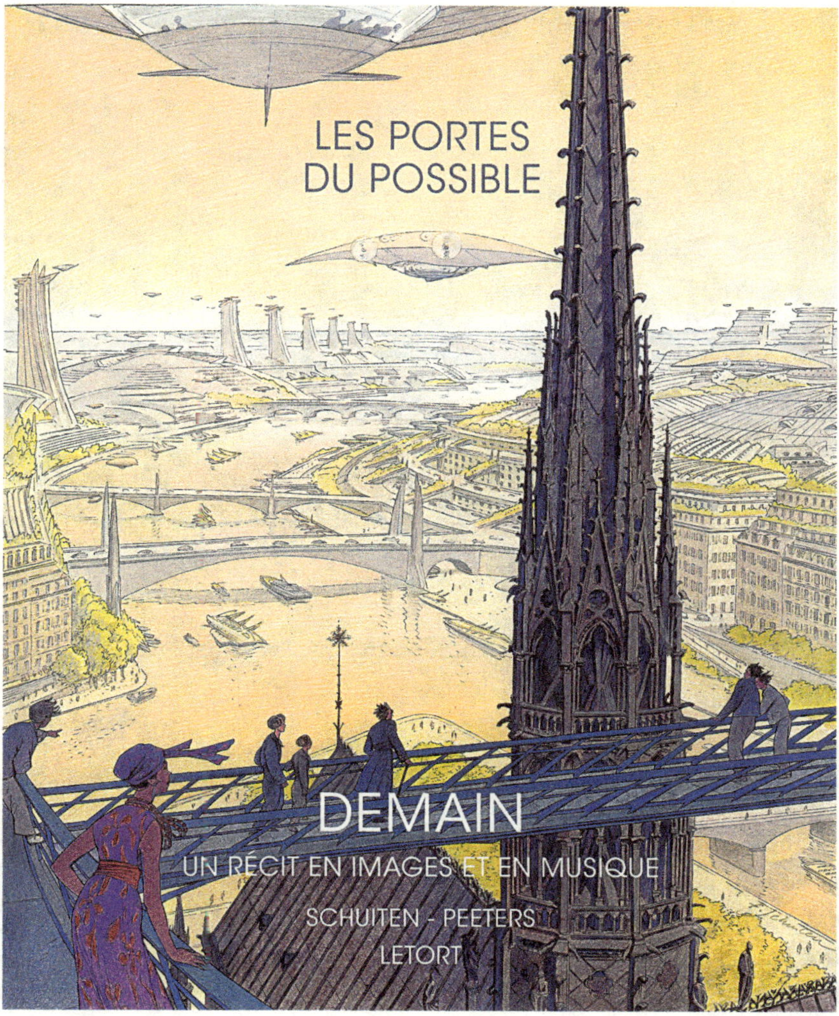

FIG. 6.5 Drawing for the lecture "Demain: Les Portes du possible," a story in pictures and music by François Schuiten, Benoît Peeters, and Bruno Letort, performed 14 April 2013 at the Théâtre Marni in Brussels and in March 2013 at La Bibliothèque de Toulouse (© François Schuiten)

- The shift from the classic merchandising policy that accompanies all known transmedia universes to a gift economy that includes the active withdrawal from the most valuable material from the market sphere is a decisive argument in this regard. Unlike many comics authors, François Schuiten has chosen to donate most of his original plates to the National Libraries of France and Belgium. And as we will see, the Autrique House is not exactly a theme park.

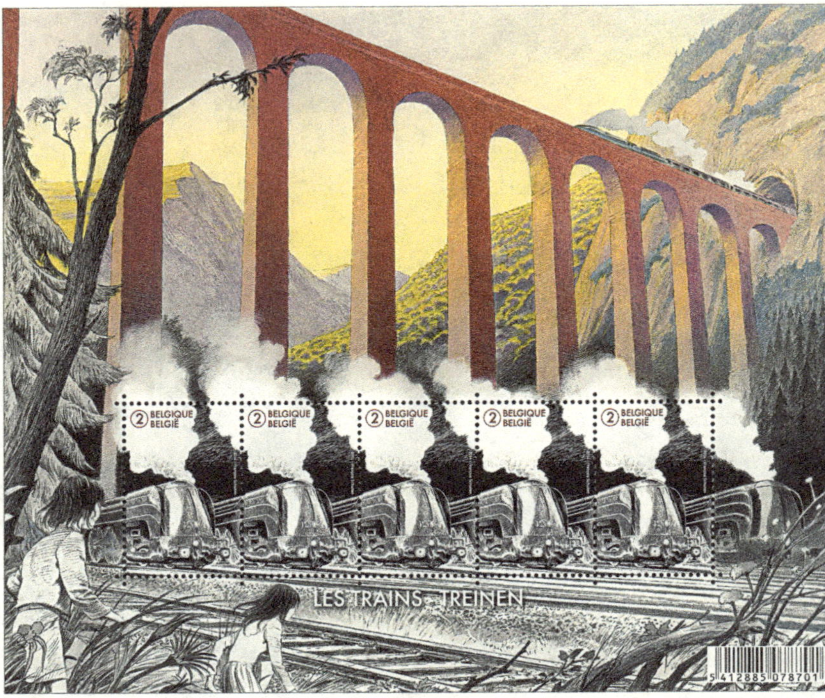

FIG. 6.6 Drawing for a special stamp design by François Schuiten (© François Schuiten)

The attitude toward the archive, as a fictional theme, and digitization, as part of the permanently updated media policy of Schuiten and Peeters, is an enlightening illustration of the singularity of *The Obscure Cities* in the emerging era of transmedia storytelling. Archiving and documenting are key motifs in the albums, and their intertext is very rich, ranging from the work of Jorge Luis Borges and his speculations on the world as library, to the historical figure of Paul Otlet (1868–1944), a Belgian author, entrepreneur, visionary, lawyer, and peace activist, but also one of the fathers of information science, or "documentation," as he called it. Creator of the Universal Decimal Classification, Otlet is nowadays seen as a visionary prophet of the Internet. His own archive, the Mundaneum (literally, World Museum), partially reconstructed in a museum hosted by the Belgian city of Mons, is taken for a kind of physical anticipation of Google and Wikipedia (Otlet's biography has been written by Françoise Levie [2006]).[4] The world of *The Obscure Cities* is full of archives and archivists, which frequently mix the imaginary representations of Borges's conceptual Library of Babel and Otlet's half-scientific, half-junk repository of everything that had ever appeared in print.

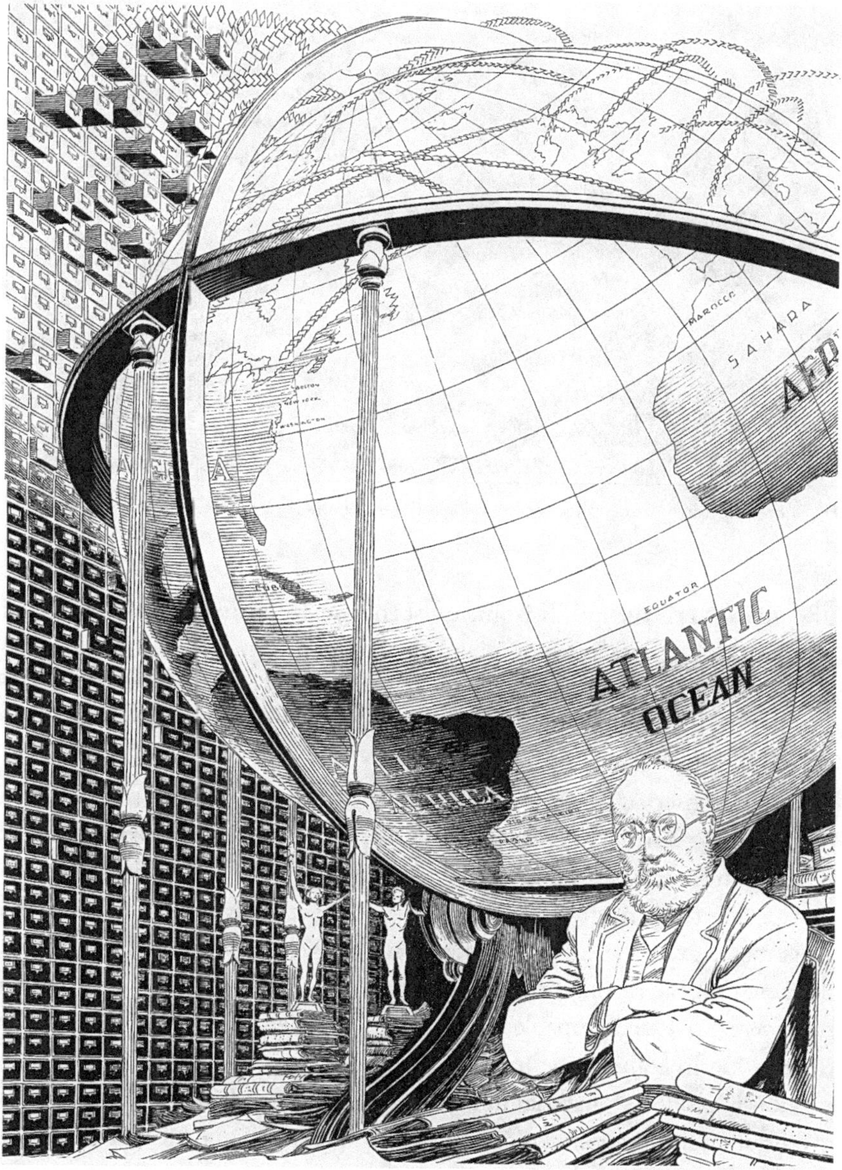

FIG. 6.7 A portrait of Paul Otlet by François Schuiten (© François Schuiten)

(As an aside, both Borges and Otlet appear as cameos in the series.)[5] The Altaplana city is a nod to Otlet's interwar and World War II dreams of building a "world city," initially to be designed by Le Corbusier (!), which, like a permanent universal exhibition, would bring together all the leading institutions of the world. The archival impulse of many characters and institutions is

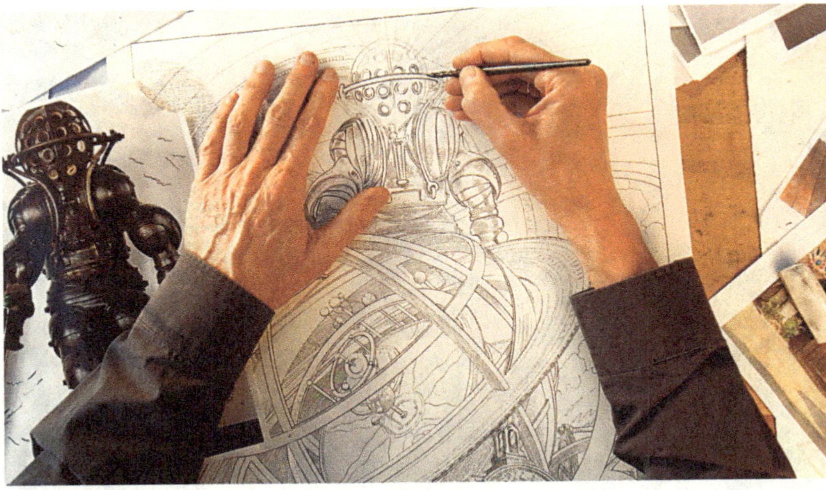

FIG. 6.8 Schuiten's hands, photograph by Vladimir Peeters (© Vladimir Peeters)

undeniable, as is the mildly ironic twist that Schuiten and Peeters give to this theme. The universalizing utopia of the archival system is kept at a safe distance, but never ridiculed, given also the very physical link between archives and books, the book being the key referent to Schuiten and Peeters's vision of building and living.

Similar observations can be made in the field of digitization. The digital turn is often seen as a potent reinforcement of transmedia tendencies that are not new in themselves, but that suddenly became a hot topic with the spread of the Internet, both positively and negatively: digitization stimulated cross-media expansions and continuations, but was also used as a way of making new profits that old media, seriously challenged by the "all for free" Internet, were no longer capable of generating. When addressing the issue of digitization in comics, one has to make a distinction between digitization of previously produced material in print, on the one hand, and on the other the invention or exploration of digital-born work. It is well known that the comics field has proven particularly resistant to the digital wave, most creators proving unwilling to shift from print to screen (Groensteen 2013; Crucifix and Dozo 2018). The position of Schuiten and Peeters will prove to be very different from the mainstream as well as the utopian approach toward the digital turn.

As convincingly argued by Julien Baudry in a landmark study (2018), digital comics are not entities that can be studied regardless of linguistic borders and economic environments (as a matter of fact, both are inextricably linked, and their conjunction severely opposes the idea that digital culture is a purely "global" phenomenon). In the French context, these limitations explain the difficulties of creating a market for digital-born works: the investors of the 1990s rapidly realized that this was not the right way for media conglomerates to establish a dialogue with the comics world, while it took more than two decades before the artists, eager to develop their own online comics, could come up with a new technical standard acceptable to audiences of print-based media. The format in question appeared to be the interactive slide show, sufficiently dissimilar to the classic grid structure of print works, but also very different from the multimedia experiments of the 1990s, including the "infinite string" model as dreamed of by Scott McCloud (2000), a clearly non-medium-specific translation of his sequential "panel-to-panel" approach to comics in general.

Baudry rightly underlines the pioneering role of Schuiten and Peeters in the debate on digital comics. Their book *L'Aventure des images* (Schuiten and Peeters 1997, partially reworked in Peeters 2008), was the first serious attempt, at least in French, to address the many challenges of digital comics. No less rightly, Baudry also stresses the open and cautious positions taken by the authors of *The Obscure Cities*. On the one hand, Schuiten and Peeters acknowledged and even welcomed the changes to come, both in the field of digitized print works and in that of digital-born creations. On the other hand, they admit the many obstacles ahead. In other words: they try to anticipate the future without any elitist bias while at the same time using the awareness of these hurdles to prevent themselves from engaging in head-over-heels experimentations. Practically speaking, this open and pragmatic line brought them to focus on the elaboration of complementary online material, as much a memory as laboratory of a work and series in constant transformation. The creation and reshaping of the digital environment is simultaneously a digital supplement—and thus not a mere copy of the existing material—and a digital-born work that does not aim at competing with or superseding the albums and other works in print. Their role remains structurally modest, in spite of the rapid growth of the available texts and images. Here as well, the exchanges go two ways: the works in print feed the website, which rapidly adopts the open policy of the series so that in turn the digital environment, which does not function as a "meta-site" imposing some kind of unity on the *Obscure Cities* world, can become a source of inspiration for new albums and works in print, for instance via the ongoing dialogue with readers.

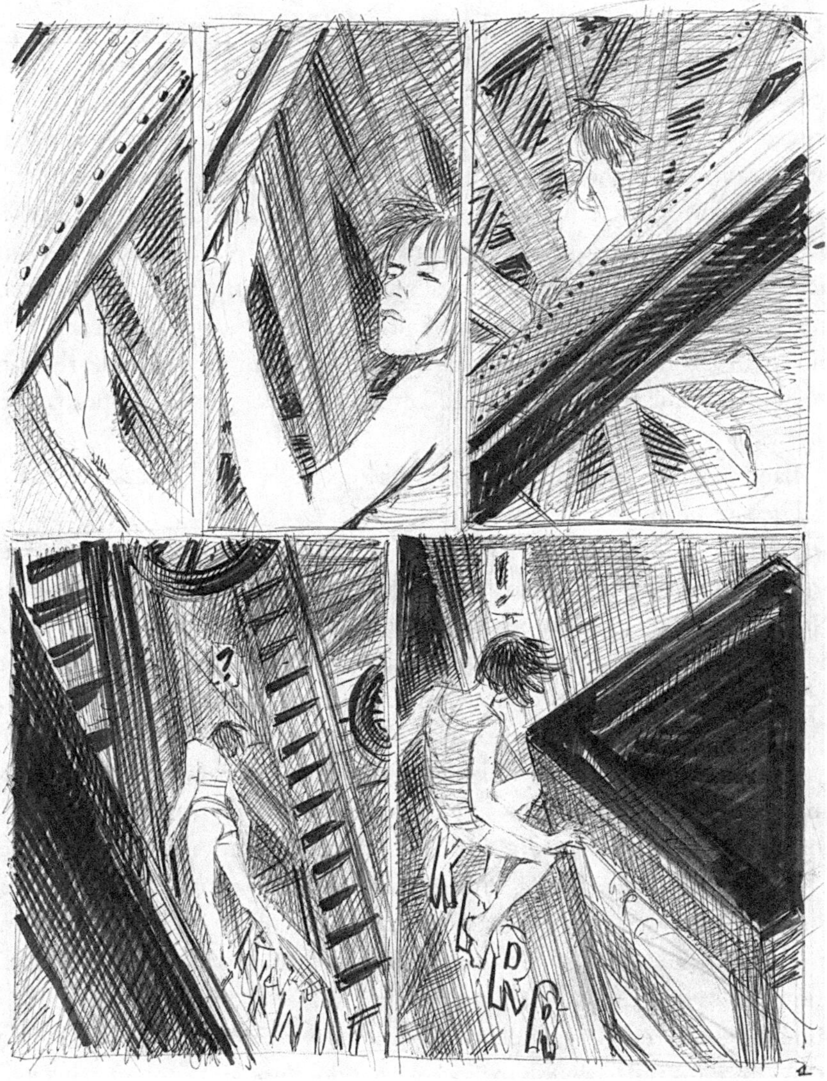

FIG. 6.9 Excerpt from the storyboard of "Back to Paris" (© François Schuiten and Benoît Peeters)

This back-and-forth movement between print and digital is not limited to the *Obscure Cities* chronicles, but extends to the whole joint production by Schuiten and Peeters, as demonstrated by *Revoir Paris* (Back to Paris, 2018), a book in print that gives shape to the typical digital experience of immersion.

The decision to "translate" immersion in a print medium is the opposite of what many authors prefers nowadays, but it is an audacious, not a reactionary, move. Contrary to most comics authors, who either resist the screen as a communicative tool or abandon the book in favor of digital-based productions, Schuiten and Peeters do not approach the relationship between print and screen in terms of conflict and supersession. Hence their capacity to go back from the allegedly typical digital phenomenon of immersion (with glasses, headphones, gloves, etc.) to the traditional host medium of paper (which proves no less capable of producing strong immersive effects—after all, let's not forget that the novel that founded the Western canon, *Don Quixote*, is the story of a knight too genuinely immersed in his readings!).

Such a way of working is deeply political, and it can be linked to Schuiten and Peeters's commitment to a socially just as well economically and ecologically sustainable form of architectural and urban heritage and planning. As we have seen, the common denominator of their action is the repudiation of blind modernization, which reduces humans to mere subjects of disciplinary mechanization. The spirit of *The Obscure Cities* is, however, anything but Luddite, since one feels throughout the whole series a profound affection for inventors, machines, communication systems, and both past and future technologies (and as already hinted at before, the *Fever in Urbicand* network, although elaborated in the first half of the 1980s, can be seen as a clear anticipation of the Internet). In this regard, there exists a strong analogy with the authors' take on digital technology. The latter is, just like architecture, urban planning, or mechanical production, never essentialized, but always used with caution and made relevant to specific aims and projects—and here the difference with certain excesses of individual urbatects or insensible city councils is very clear.

The major particularity of predigital and digital technology, however, is that it is consistently applied to the very host medium of the series, which is always multiple and evolving. *The Obscure Cities* is published in album format, but furthermore in many different formats, and this diversity gives the work by Schuiten and Peeters a special place in the move toward new forms of comics, which progressively exceed first, the world of daily and weekly publications in print; second, the world of comic book and album; and third, the ongoing experiments with comics in 3-D format. The latter is a rather recent but thriving phenomenon that affects the book as well as the nonbook. Chris Ware's famous *Building Stories*, his 2012 unconventional work made up of fourteen printed works—clothbound books, newspapers, broadsheets, and flip books—packaged in a boxed set not unlike the box of a Monopoly game, spectacularly illustrates the tendency that structures the whole history of comics: the desire to move from strip to page, from page to book, and from book as sequential arrangement of pages to book as sculpture. Yet more and more comics artists also try to achieve the tridimensional turn of their artwork by leaving the world of the book. As studied by Jean-Christophe Menu, one of the founders in 1990 of the influential avant-garde publishing house L'Association, modern comics are no longer necessarily bound to the classic technologies of print and the book. In his 2011 treatise, *La Bande dessinée et son double* (Comics and its double; a clear allusion to Antonin Artaud's attack on theatrical conventions and the subjugation of physical experience to the rationality and disciplinary power of the word), Menu argues that the visual and narrative revolution brought about by independent comics since the 1990s will necessarily translate into similar transformations of the host medium, no longer the book but the 3-D environment of private and public spaces, not as "comics on the wall," as in the brief but intense encounter between comics and pop art in the 1960s (Beaty 2012; Frey and Baetens 2019), but as in situ installations.

As a matter of fact, the work by Schuiten and Peeters, from a visual and narrative point of view, stays far away from the extremism of certain independents and indeed goes much farther than their attack on print and book formats. Rather than rejecting older formats, the progressive construction of *The Obscure Cities* series works toward the permanent exchanges between as many host media as possible, but also between as many types of material realization as possible. A key "work" in this regard is the restoration project of the Maison Autrique by Victor Horta (1861–1946), a milestone in Brussels architectural heritage. Built in 1893, this house represents an essential step in the evolution of the greatest of Belgian architects. In *The Obscure Cities*, whose opening page is a synthesis of everything Horta's art nouveau (Jugendstil) stands for, the house plays a crucial role as the principal setting of *The Theory of the Grain of Sand* and, more importantly, as one of the principal "doors" or contact zones between Counter-Earth and Earth, allowing the passage from Brüsel to Brussels. Confronted with the decay of this manor house at the end of the twentieth century, the fate of so many Brussels art nouveau houses that were abandoned in order to be replaced by more functional and profitable constructions, the authors of *The Obscure Cities* successfully launched a campaign to restore the Maison Autrique according to the best possible scientific criteria and to transform its function from private dwelling into a small museum (Peeters, Schuiten, and Plissart 2004). This restoration, however, entails much more than the salvation of an endangered building and its opening to the public. Saved through the "sprawling" of the *Obscure*

Cities universe, which was vital in pushing through the burden of responsibility felt by the public authorities to fund the restoration project, the Autrique House became indeed part of the world that helped revive it. The house was decorated in the style of the albums, with furniture, props, and ornaments that had been seen in the series or that were promised a new life in albums and other works to come. In addition, museological scenography included many audiovisual elements and fragments that staged characters and situations of *The Obscure Cities*. Last but not least, the house also hosts smaller rotating exhibitions that all stress the cultural and historical embedding of the Maison Autrique as well as of the series by Schuiten and Peeters. Each show aims to be a supplementary demonstration of the porosity between fiction and nonfiction, between historical sources of inspiration and contemporary creation.

7

Doing Politics in Comics

A political reading of *The Obscure Cities*? In light of many themes, motives, and events as well as the conflictual relationships between characters, haves and have-nots, victims and perpetrators, agents and patients, die-hard mainstreamers and unworldly solitaries, there are certainly good reasons to inspect the series through a political lens and see how individuals and society interact and how this interaction is organized by rules, laws, and conventions on Counter-Earth. In addition, the series contains many allusions to local and less local abuses, some of them legible to an international audience. It is not imperative, for instance, to know who the actual politicians and businessmen are when portrayed in the roman à clef that is *Brüsel* in order to make a political reading of it. It is clear for any reader that this a book about urban speculation and the ruthless selling-out of cultural heritage, the subsequent disruption of the daily life of the inhabitants, the dehumanizing stubbornness of the bureaucratic class and all those who benefit from being part of it, the helplessness of those who are left behind in changing times. It is even clearer if one takes into account the many intertextual references that foster this type of reading, as for instance in the repeated hints at Fritz Lang's *Metropolis* (1927) when it comes down to portraying the misery of factory life in the big industrial city. And it is also clear that the representation of these situations is not ordained by a pure spirit or a drawing machine. The authors evidently take sides, and their side is that of the victims, the mavericks, the resisting individuals.

At the same time, however, there are also excellent reasons to stay away from this approach, which may be an overinterpretation, if not a blatant misreading, of *The Obscure Cities*, certainly if compared with other inventions of Schuiten and Peeters in the public sphere (or even with other comics by the same authors, such as for instance François Schuiten's collaboration with his brother Luc, a well-known defender of sustainable architecture, in the already mentioned *Nogegon*). First of all, it should be mentioned that the political dimension is not always present in the series. As noted by Thierry Groensteen (1994), the initial volume is almost totally lacking in any political dimension, unless one takes post-teenage existential boredom as a marker of political discontent, which may stretch the notion of politics perhaps a little too far. In later volumes and other expansions of the series, the political sensibility of the work should also be called less systematic than intermittent. Certain episodes are very political, others not at all. Moreover, the presence of political themes is not simply progressively growing; it is more something that comes and goes.

As a matter of fact, the approach of Schuiten and Peeters always refrains from militant or simplified positions, deconstructing the facile oppositions of good and evil. In the satirical attack on speculation and money gain that is *Brüsel*, the principal victim of the story is partly complicit in the larger catastrophe that is destroying his traditional neighborhood, since he presents himself as the defender of the replacement of real plants and flowers by their plastic copies. A similar argument can be made of the fact that characters who have a strong political dimension in a certain album do not maintain that aspect of their psychology and action when they return in other albums. Mary von Rathen, the marginalized youth who will eventually prove a social reformer in *The Leaning Girl*, is quite a different character in *The Theory of the Grain of Sand*, a story that leans much more than other albums of the series toward the fantastic *pur sang*. Moreover, Mary does not exactly return in this album as the same person: she is now much older and has a different social status and profession, and the same goes for the protagonist of the story, Constant Abeels, who is no longer the same person as in *Brüsel*. This kind of metamorphosis partially weakens the political reading of more politicized sections of the series, but they clearly lend to the series an exceptional dynamic. The transition from one album or one story to the next one is full of gaps and ellipses, and it is the role of the reader to imagine what might have happened between them. Readers may be helped by attempts to give a biography of the

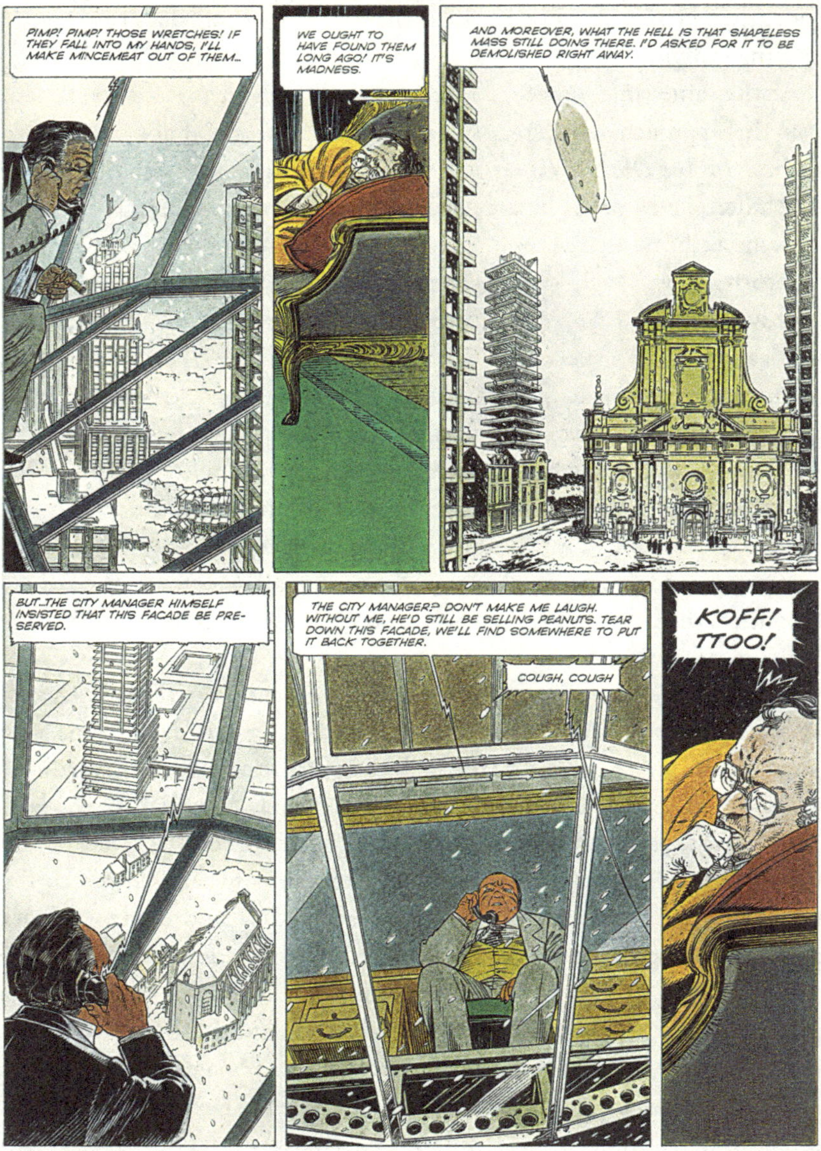

FIG. 7.1 The destruction of architectural heritage in *Brüsel*, Integral Edition, vol. 3, p. 287. Excerpt from *Brüsel*, François Schuiten and Benoît Peeters (© Casterman, with kind permission of the authors and Editions Casterman)

main characters, as summarized in the last pages of volume 4 of the Integral Edition, but these biographies are not to be read in the sense of a "bible," that is, of a document fixing the limits within which a character is allowed to move.

A second reason that should warn us against too rapid and too direct a political reading of *The Obscure Cities* is the rather depoliticized self-representation of its own fictional universe. Even in the more politically inspired albums, there remains a strong emphasis on other themes and dimensions, while the many complementary essays and archival documents are gathered in the four-volume Integral Edition. Counter-Earth is a world that is generally pacified and that seems to have left behind most of the factors of dissension and political struggle that define recent and current history, such as for instance religion, ideological beliefs, or the cleavage between country and city and all that it entails. The partially destroyed Counter-Earth civilization that one discovers at the beginning of *The Invisible Frontier* is more the result of a series of natural catastrophes than of a war of the cities, although this album introduces more than one virtually peace-threatening element, such as the political use of cartography and the dream of a "great Sodrovni."

When reading the introductory notes to the world of Counter-Earth in volume 1 of the Integral Edition (and one should not forget that the first publication of these notes goes back to the first steps of the series, which immediately engendered a large number of side publications), one has the impression that this is one of the possible forms taken by the utopian world "imagined" by John Lennon in his eponymous song. The pacification of Counter-Earth, which of course will have to be nuanced by more than one album of the series, can be inferred from a wide range of elements. Politically speaking, Counter-Earth is not a divided continent—and the fact that its universe has only one continent is already a strong hint in that direction. This continent is surrounded by a sea as well as larger and smaller islands, but at its core is one single mainland whose civilization is almost completely urban, without any major conflict between them. The various cities cannot be compared to nations in the traditional sense of the word, and the large distances between them as well as the almost complete emptiness of the areas that separate them explain the absence of great tensions between political units that all have their own government, once again with the major exception in *The Invisible Frontier* of Sodrovno-Voldachia, a region with clear imperialist ambitions that all Tintin readers will easily recognize as a reconfiguration of the imaginary countries of Syldavia and Borduria. The *Obscure Cities* world is correspondingly characterized by a strong degree of unity in other regards: linguistically speaking, most inhabitants speak a somewhat traditional French; ethnically speaking, almost everybody is Caucasian (among the rare exceptions—but they seem to become increasingly important as the series unfolds—we should mention Boulachistan in *The Theory of the Grain of Sand* and the Neo-Voldachian woman in *The Invisible Frontier*); and from a cultural point of view, this world celebrates books and print, and it possesses a common historical as well as mythical point of departure, the construction of the Tower. The message is clear: Counter-Earth does not claim to be a mirror of the world as we know it.

This exceptional unity is not a mere curiosity or a whim of the authors. It is instead the logical consequence of the underlying historical reference of the whole series, whose fictional world reworks the positive and optimistic take on culture typical of late nineteenth-century European society and civilization as imagined by Jules Verne and others (see chapter 3). As masterfully described by Markus Krajewski (2014), the craving for global information systems and subsequent political and ideological unification was already a major feature of Western culture around 1900. Many revolutionary thinkers were deeply committed to overcoming the divide of languages, media, currencies, disciplines, and national frontiers. Pacifism was certainly one of the basic motivations for their subsequent action, the horizon of their supersession efforts not being the destruction of the existing order—as was the case with the equally important anarchist tendencies of the era—but the integration of groups and nations into a new and totally integrated world order. Politically and institutionally speaking, most of these thinkers were not very successful, even if many of their ideas and projects laid the foundations of achievements that we still live with today, such as the A4 format or artificial fertilizer. They often worked in the margins of the established knowledge production centers, with therefore little political and ideological support from the decision makers. The figure of Paul Otlet, an important cultural reference in *The Obscure Cities* and a strong believer in the peace-shaping properties of international bibliographical work,[1] is characteristic of this relative marginality, and the same can be said of the inventors of artificial universal languages or never-before-thought-of transport and communication systems. Others, however, did have a real although not always universally appreciated influence, such as (although already in a post–World War I context) Walter Rathenau (1867–1922), a Jewish statesman and social reformer who served as German foreign minister during the Weimar Republic and who was assassinated by right-wing terrorists. His ideas on the integration of state and economy are often seen as foreshadowing the idea of "total war," a vital continuation of the dreams of unification and globalization of all aspects of

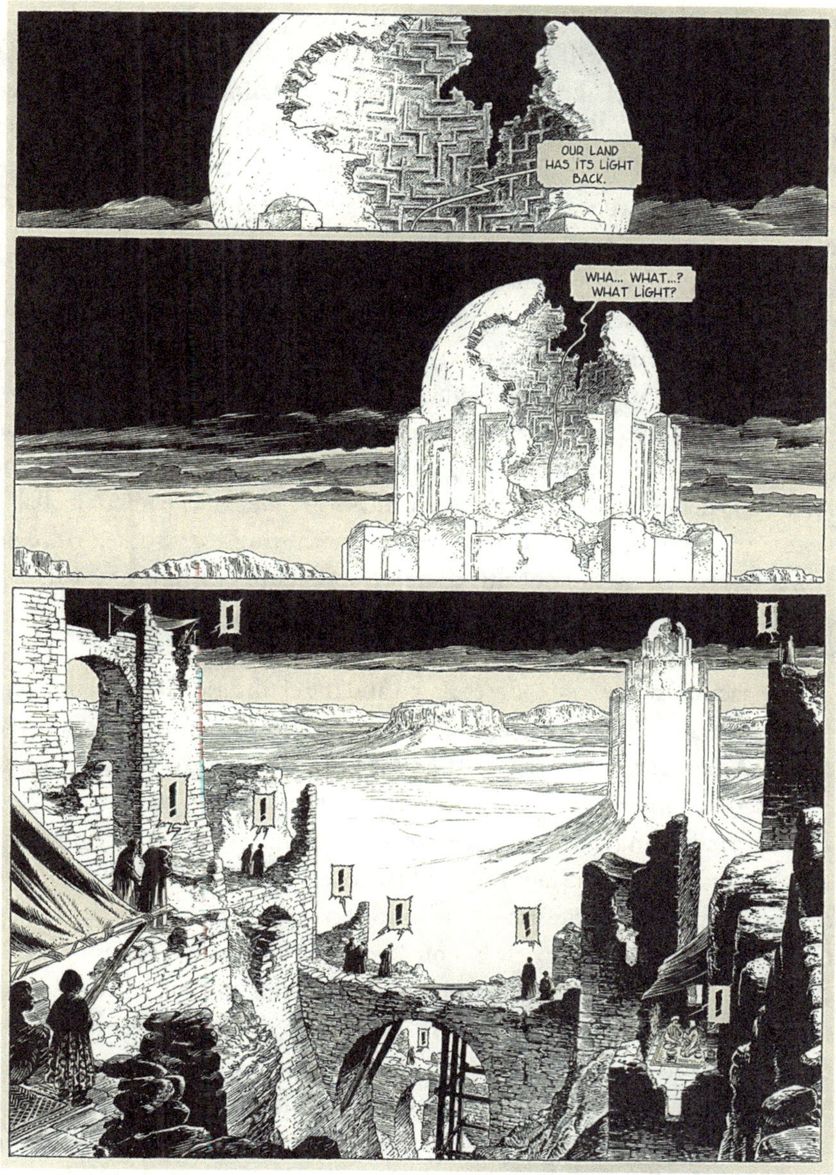

FIG. 7.2 The irruption of the East: *The Theory of the Grain of Sand*, page 106. Excerpt from *The Theory of the Grain of Sand*, François Schuiten and Benoît Peeters (© Casterman, with kind permission of the authors and Editions Casterman)

life. In *The Obscure Cities,* Walter Rathenau reappears as Mary von Rathen (see chapter 8), who will represent the humanist dimension of Rathenau's work and thinking that his assassination prevented him from fully realizing. As a matter of fact, all major characters of the series have much in common with the dream of unity and globalization that was at the heart of the historical stage of European civilization. Some of them tilt toward the more dictatorial sides of the big dreams of ordering, organizing, and rebuilding the world; others are clearly represented as stubborn yet innocent dreamers; still others, mainly those portrayed as artists, symbolize the dangerous and harmful effects of streamlining and (over)organization. Most of these figures are, however, not one-dimensional. Someone like Eugen Robick, one of the most important characters in the series, is at the same time the unconditional defender of rational city planning and a vulnerable character open to the secrets of the human heart. The very transformations of the uncontrollable system triggered by his calculations, a *cube* generating a networked *triangle,* symbolize the complexity of this character and more generally of the dream of a global order. This ambivalence is certainly an element that should not be forgotten when addressing a political reading of the series.

The pacified nature of Counter-Earth and the civilizational moment it represents can also be derived from a brief comparison to two other cultural creations that refer *grosso modo* to the same historical context: steampunk and Musil's *The Man without Qualities*. The former cannot take readers unaware. One of the leading authors of the steampunk movement, Bruce Sterling, clearly acknowledges the family resemblances between *The Obscure Cities* and this subgenre of the fantastic—"the art of Francois Schuiten, creator of *Les Cités Obscures* (together with Benoit Peeters), a fantastical series of books about an alternative reality, obsessively detailed and chronicled. The sort of thing that might be lumped in with Steampunk, although the emphasis is more on urbanism and technology" (Sterling 2008, n.p.).

The presence of the latter, a masterpiece of high modernist literature, instead may seem less self-evident, since Musil's novel is situated in a different time frame (it takes place in the Austro-Hungarian monarchy's last days, just before 1918) and in a very realist setting (Vienna). Yet there exist interesting structural correspondences between *The Man without Qualities* and *The Obscure Cities,* which single out Musil's work as a good comparison point. Musil's novel is also about world making, not in a material but in an ideological way. The preparations for a celebration in honor of seventy years of the Austrian emperor Franz Joseph's reign generate an endless number of ideas and discussions, all of them finally meaningless and abandoned, to

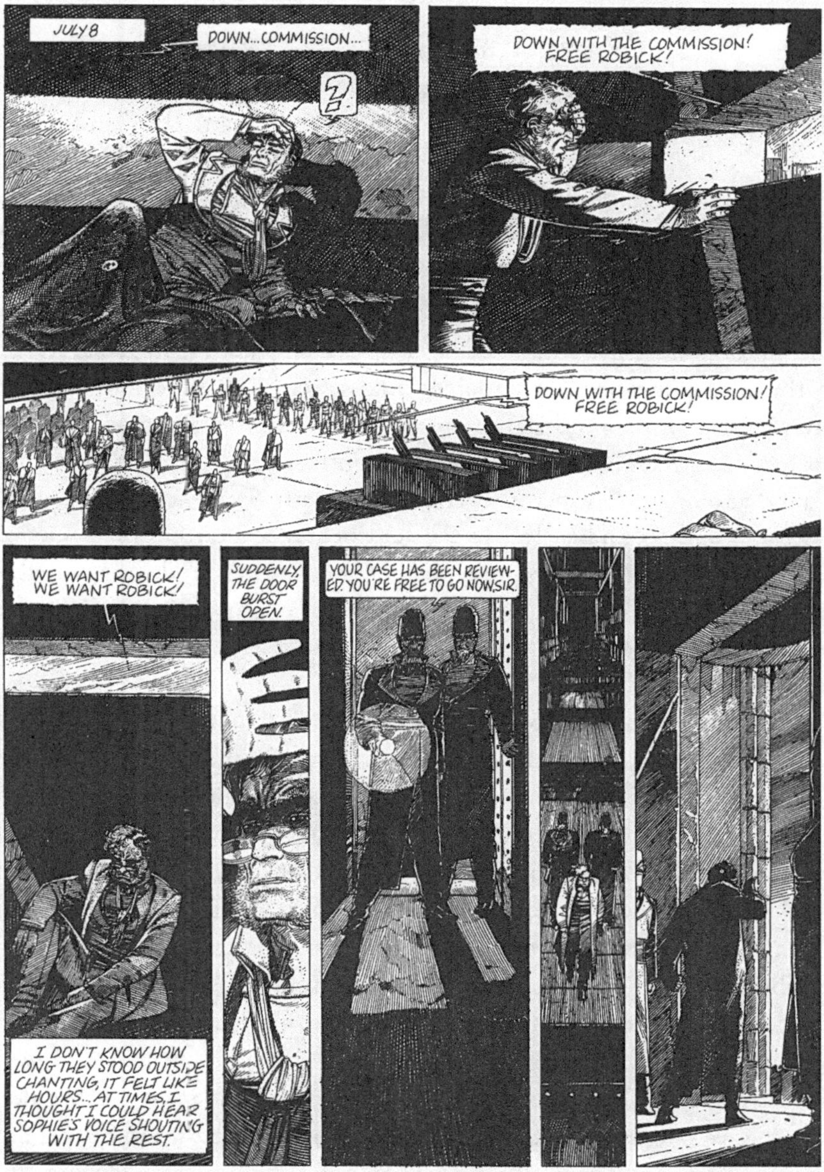

FIG. 7.3 Eugen Robick in jail, *Fever in Urbicand*, Integral Edition, vol. 1, p. 146. Excerpt from *Fever in Urbicand*, François Schuiten and Benoît Peeters (© Casterman, with kind permission of the authors and Editions Casterman)

"rebrand" the nation ("The Austrian Year 1918," "The World Year 1918," "The Austrian Peace Year 1918," or "The Austrian World Peace Year 1918") and to desperately find a way to give shape to an empire that is slowly dissolving in the air (and that the end of the First World War will radically dismantle). It is the accumulation of these ideas as invented possible worlds and the oscillation between fiction and reality that make Musil's novel a relevant counterpoint, together with some other elements that will be detailed below.

Originating in the 1960s but appearing as a real genre label only in the 1980s as a nod to the then very hot "cyberpunk," steampunk is an aesthetic and cultural movement that is a subgenre of science fiction. Its major feature is the incorporation of technology and aesthetic artifacts inspired by nineteenth-century industrial steam-powered machinery. Steampunk is often set in an alternative history of the nineteenth century's Victorian era, and from that point of view perfectly comparable with *The Obscure Cities*, whose historical background is close to the continental equivalent of late Victorianism. Steampunk is well represented in comics as well, as demonstrated by the successful series written by Alan Moore (the famous author of *Watchmen*) and illustrated by Kevin O'Neill, *The League of Extraordinary Gentlemen* (1999–; a movie adaptation was made in 2003).

In retrospect, for steampunk was not much debated in the early 1980s, the correspondences between steampunk and the work by Schuiten and Peeters are mainly the following: First, there is of course the central presence of technology: both worlds are full of inventors, tools, machines, corporations, sponsors, agencies, frauds, politicians, and the sometimes explosive cocktail of all these ingredients. Second, both steampunk and *The Obscure Cities* have a clear love of anachronisms and an equally blatant craving to make these anachronisms relevant for a contemporary reframing of stories, situations, and characters. Third, in either case one also finds a particular combination of fiction and nonfiction, a certain form of carefully documented and well-researched historical realism, and a return to the classic—that is, wildly imaginative—forms of science fiction, more turned also toward the conflict between science and utopia than toward Gernsback-inspired "amazing" and "astounding" space adventures, not to speak of today's cunning variations on space swashbuckling stories relying on CGI technology and other special effects. Fourth and finally, there is also the frequent reuse of traditional visual and narrative techniques based on nineteenth-century illustrations and adventure novels, which all serve as springboards to new forms of storytelling and world building. The time and space travel plots between Earth and Counter-Earth could figure without any problem in a modern steampunk novel or movie, while the influence of the historical Jules Verne illustrations is similarly visible in *The Obscure Cities*—or in other illustration art by Schuiten—as well as in steampunk movies and comics.

Yet in spite of sharing many of these and other characteristics, steampunk and *The Obscure Cities* also diverge on various points. *The Obscure Cities* is not only defined by a craving for technological and historical cohesion that is lacking in steampunk, but the latter is in general much more open to a direct political interpretation than the work by Schuiten and Peeters. "In general," obviously, given the fact that more than one album of *The Obscure Cities* has indeed a strong political subtext, if not text. *Brüsel* is the example that immediately springs to mind, but at least two other albums foreground the negative impact of medical disciplinarization: *The Leaning Girl* (see chapter 8) and *The Shadow of a Man*, which tackles similar issues of medical mismanagement and exclusion of nonmainstream bodies (in this case a man whose body turns transparent after an unsuccessful pharmacological treatment). And of course not all steampunk-inspired works promote a political reading. Nonetheless, the difference remains, and most readers would agree that in comparison with steampunk, *The Obscure Cities* series is less visibly politicized.

The second point of comparison may seem more surprising, in spite of the numerous German references, such as Blossfeldt's natural form aesthetics or Fritz Lang's expressionist cinema influences, but it will help to elucidate the specific take on politics as displayed in *The Obscure Cities*. In *The Man without Qualities* (published between 1930 and 1943), Robert Musil has written a ruthless satire of what he calls Cacania—the double hard "C" sound (read "caca," meaning "excrement") referring to the first letters of the German words "königlich" (royal) and "kaiserlich" (imperial)—which in fact refers to the Austro-Hungarian dual monarchy, the quintessence of old Europe before it would be swept away after World War I (Perloff 2016). Although the world caricatured by Musil is that of pre–World War I Europe and thus slightly posterior to the underlying civilizational model of steampunk as well as *The Obscure Cities*, the similarities with the world invented by Schuiten and Peeters are not difficult to pinpoint: the asphyxiating presence of bureaucracy; the general awareness of living in a machine age where calculations and mathematics appear to make sentimental and interior life almost meaningless; the burden of history and tradition; the impossibility for an individual not belonging to the ruling class to fully shape her or his own life, except in the margins of society; the discrimination against all those whose mind and body does not obey the general rules (in Musil: criminals, women, Jews, nonaristocrats; in *The Obscure Cities*: children, adolescents, loners, lovers); and the general sense of immobility and the end of history (a dangerous illusion in *The Man without Qualities*, a vastly political book; a kind of implicit background in *The Obscure Cities*, where it takes various forms, such as boredom or lack of historical consciousness). In comparison with steampunk, the differences between *The Obscure Cities* and *The Man without Qualities* are easier to describe. These differences are stylistic as well as narrative. Contrary to Musil, Schuiten and Peeters rely upon a more traditional form of storytelling (and drawing, if one might compare visual drawing style and verbal syntax), although it certainly makes sense to read *The Obscure Cities* as exhibiting some family resemblances with Musil's essay-novel. It is not a coincidence, for example, that some readers find the comics series somewhat cold and intellectual (Groensteen 1994), a reaction that can be explained by the tension between storytelling (the "novel" side) and world building (the "essay" side). But it is obvious that the difference between the two creations also concerns the political dimension, ubiquitous and biting in Musil, intermittent and less sarcastic in Schuiten and Peeters.

At the same time, however, *The Man without Qualities* offers the possibility to tackle in new ways one of the most salient features of Schuiten and Peeters's work. In chapter 4 of his novel, Musil develops the theory of the "sense of possibility":

> To pass freely through open doors, it is necessary to respect the fact that they have solid frames. This principle, by which the old professor had lived, is simply a requisite of the sense of reality. But if there is a sense of reality, and no one will doubt that it has its justifications for existing, then there must also be something we can call a sense of possibility. Whoever has it does not say, for instance: Here this or that has happened, will happen, must happen; but he invents: Here this or that might, could, or ought to happen. If he is told that something is the way it is, he will think: Well, it could probably just as well be otherwise. So the sense of possibility could be defined outright as the ability to conceive of everything there might be just as well, and to attach no more importance to what is than to what is not. The consequences of so creative a disposition can be remarkable, and may, regrettably, often make what people admire seem wrong, and what is taboo permissible, or, also, make both a matter of indifference. (Musil 1955, chap. 4)

Even if the way Musil uses this theory to substantiate his vision of modern man as a man without qualities and qualities as qualities without man is very unlike what one finds in *The Obscure Cities*, where the characters are generally not flat but round, the idea of a split between the real and the possible is definitely what drives the positive characters of the series. All of them are dreamers and builders, and although most of their plans are crushed by the ruling social order, paradoxically characterized by either blind innovation or complete immobility (in certain regards, the world of Counter-Earth is a frozen world), there is always the sense that another world is possible. The recurrent longing to get in touch with the invisible world behind the world as known is the best symbol of that "sense of possibility." The presence of something else or something more is not experienced in terms of outright discovery and exploration—the dream of a non-Counter-Earth is anything but a colonial dream in *The Obscure Cities*—but in terms of regeneration. Schuiten and Peeters's series may render an unmoving culture, with many parts such as its mythical Tower that are nothing else than archeological relics, but the encounter with other forms of life and worlds is a rejuvenating experience, a way of reanimating the past of a world that has come to a standstill.

From this perspective, one better understands the choice of a classic drawing style for *The Obscure Cities* and a type of storytelling that maintains many traditional elements, such as causality in plot structures, characterization and psychological motivation, and the attempt to invent a strange but attractive and reliable fictional universe. The objective of Schuiten and Peeters is less to showcase complete new forms of visual and narrative style than to demonstrate other ways of using existing material. In other words: the series is radically on the side of the "sense of possibility," not on that of the "sense of reality," and the best way to make this point is of course to take existing styles, themes, plots, and characters as the building blocks of a series that eventually produces something really different. In that sense, the social and political commitment of Schuiten and Peeters is undeniable throughout the whole series, even in works that do not emphasize social or political themes. Granted, city planning and building are frequently associated with the dehumanizing policy of dictatorial regimes, demonstrable in the multiple analogies between the city and art of Urbicand and the creations of Nazi German architect and city planner Albert Speer or architect and sculptor Arno Breker. And granted, the humans in such a world are sometimes nothing more than puppets on a string, deprived of any agency and defenseless victims of disciplinary higher forces, while gender, disability, and ethnicity are clearly markers that exclude rather than include (Hansen 2019). Except for the case of *Brüsel* or short stories such as "The Strange Case of Dr. Abraham" (see chapter 2), all works on the satire of urban nonplanning, or *The Shadow of a Man*, which it is not impossible to read as a transposition of Franz Kafka's biographical struggle with the injustices of the insurance services that employed him, the presence of these elements remains, after all, rather discreet.

There is, however, next to the relative absence of political themes at surface level and the generally pacified representation of Counter-Earth throughout the series, a third reason to be watchful when undertaking a political reading of *The Obscure Cities*. True, numerous passages from the series bring into play the tension between the crushing administrative powers and the helpless individual, the limited possibilities of resistance of people confronted with overwhelmingly disruptive phenomena (often identified as such—"phenomena"—the same way some people call "events" an ongoing war) or the endlessly continuing battle between the desire to live one's life and the functional logic of systems and fields. But in all these intrigues with their happy or unhappy denouements and painful or comic twists—for there is also a lot of humor and joy on Counter-Earth—the thematic dimension of the story can never be isolated from a reflection on the medium and the properties of its visual and verbal parameters. A narrative like *The Road to Armilia*, which could be framed in directly political terms as a variation on the emancipatory powers of fiction in a dehumanized and dehumanizing environment based on child labor and ecological disaster, is explicitly transposing a compositional technique by Raymond Roussel, the author of a constraint-based type of writing that he (partially) explains in his famous *How I Wrote Certain of My Books* (1935). The unfolding of the story obeys the figure paronomasia applied to a nursery rhyme, a typical example of Roussel's play with homophone doubles that both open and close a narrative (some of his texts are written by bridging the gap between an opening sentence that triggers the story and a near-identical sentence that brings the story to its end). We have already several times underlined the organic intertwining of a strong self-reflexivity of the series and a no-less-stronger sensibility to social issues. *Brüsel* may be a parable on greed, but it cannot be separated from the overall presence of the spreading network, as generated by the multiplication of geometrical forms in modern architecture, which in turn is a thematic translation of the work with straight lines and angles in comics layout. Logically, this kind of exchange also works the other way around, and the mechanism of the oblique line, which we will close-read in the next chapter, can also be read as symptom of a social and historical situation. In his groundbreaking rereading of the birth of comics, more precisely of its permanent rebirth in contact with other media (literature, photography, cinema) since the eighteenth century, Thierry Smolderen has suggested a political reading of the historical work by Rodolphe Töpffer, nowadays considered the founding father of the comics medium. For Smolderen, Töpffer, creator of Mr Pencil and other barely adapted Romantic dreamers, has introduced in comics a certain treatment of the arabesque that is not only a possible graphic equivalent of the typical narrative demarche of Laurence Sterne but also a strong critique of galloping rationalization:

> By creating a new hybridization of literature and drawing, Töpffer came closer to the romantic ideal of the arabesque than had any of his predecessors. *Festus* and *Cryptogame* [characters of Töpffer's comics] even returned to the graphic sources of the romantic concept by taking up the most important characteristic of the whimsical decorative frescoes in the ruins of Rome and Herculaneum. . . . As in these frescoes, the characters of *Festus* and *Cryptogame* float in a world where "the reality given to the impossible"[2] plays with the laws of nature in general, and those of gravity in particular. In Töpffer's albums, bodies often fly through the air; given the slightest pretext, they take flight, madly swirling at the speed of the wind. (Smolderen 2014, 49)

The close reading in the next chapter will put some meat on the bones of the political analysis of *The Obscure Cities*. To briefly conclude, it is possible to argue that in spite of the rather restrained presence of political issues at the thematic level, the series presents another take on social and political commitment that is both all-pervading and no less radical. For what does not remain discreet is the permanent awareness that it is possible to build a new world out of the old. The key political dimension of *The Obscure Cities* has to be situated at that level, which is not that of explicit themes but that of the implicit political reframing of visual forms and narrative structures.

8

Close-Reading *The Leaning Girl*

The sixth volume of the *Obscure Cities* series, *The Leaning Girl*, presents the traumatic youth of Mary von Rathen, daughter of the leader of the city-state of Mylos, the *Metropolis*-like industrial heart of Counter-Earth, before her inheriting the ruling powers of her father and her successful attempts to bring social reform to a city that one of the previous albums, *The Road to Armilia*, had presented as the epitome of ruthless and dehumanizing industrialization and mechanization. In *The Leaning Girl*, young Mary is a victim at age thirteen of a strange incident on a roller coaster that occurs after a weird and frightening eclipse. The accident leaves her literally inclined, and the rest of the story will show that she is attracted by another yet invisible planet, Earth. When leaving Counter-Earth with eccentric inventor-scientist Axel Wappendorf, a recurring character in the series, in search of that mysterious planet, she lands on an "unknown place" where she meets and falls in love with a lonely and misunderstood painter enigmatically escaped from planet Earth, Augustin Desombres, also a habitual character, well known to readers of *The Obscure Cities* as one of the chief "contacts" between Earth and Counter-Earth (his first appearance was in *Le Musée A. Desombres*).

At the heart of the story one finds the core element of the series' organization as well as of its narrative structure: on the one hand, a planet that is actually built by the mutual attraction as well as dissimulation of two

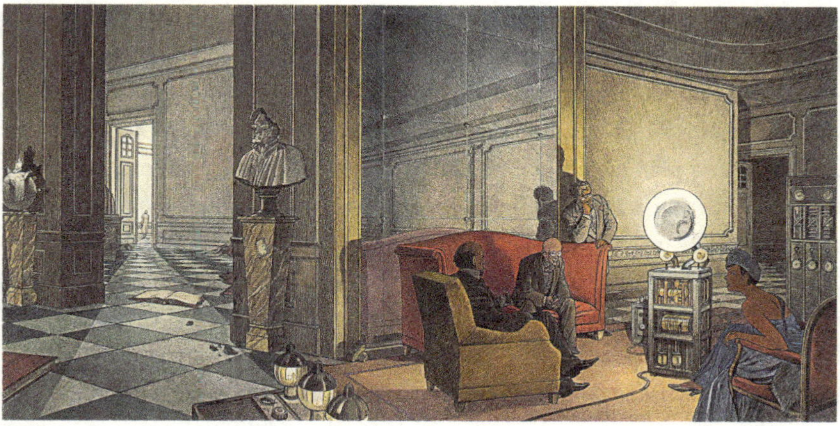

FIG. 8.1 Axel Wappendorf's first appearance (character sitting on the sofa and facing the reader), cover illustration of *Le Musée A. Desombres* (© François Schuiten)

planets, Earth and Counter-Earth; on the other hand, the possibility and eventually the actual realization of the crossing of their boundaries. In this volume the meeting occurs via the space travels of Mary and Augustin, whose encounter takes place in an unknown region, one imagines in between Earth and Counter-Earth or somewhere inside Earth. Besides, the album is extremely rich and dense as far as cross-referential and intertextual elements are concerned. The number of allusions to and borrowings from other volumes is incomparable, and the same goes for the references made to art history and literary history. *The Leaning Girl* is, however, not only a highly representative album in the series; it also contains a certain number of characteristics that give it a special position in *The Obscure Cities*. First of all, it is the only volume that features a woman as a main character. The book describes five years of her adolescence, before ending with a brief sequence on Mary as an adult, the new leader of Mylos. Compared to her, Augustin Desombres, although clearly not just a side figure, is certainly not the same type of protagonist. But *The Leaning Girl* is also a story where another key element of the series, namely, architecture, seems relatively absent—at least at first sight. Granted, the ontological crossing of spatial boundaries is strongly related with chronotopical elements, such as the isolated manor (Augustin Desombres is painting murals in a mansion lost in the middle of nowhere) and the empty wall hiding a great void (after her trauma Mary von Rathen becomes a runaway child and travels with a circus company in a world that is becoming in the end dramatically flat and two-dimensional, a world made of façades of buildings ready for their final demolition). Yet contrary to other volumes, architecture is less prominent here. In addition, *The Leaning Girl* is also the story where the contact between Earth and Counter-Earth is shown in a very direct and visual way. And last but not least: the book introduces a material dimension that had not yet been exploited in the series, namely, the combination of drawings and photographs, the former used to portray Counter-Earth, the latter to represent Earth, the blending of both media actually producing the fusion of both worlds.

If there are good reasons to choose *The Leaning Girl* for a close-reading chapter, the special position of the book does not impose a single or privileged reading perspective. The easiest choice would be of course to focus on the meeting of the two characters and their respective worlds, Counter-Earth and Earth, as performatively "induced" from the melding of two sign systems or media. As suggested in the analysis of the fantastic in chapter 5, the mix of drawing and photography is not what demonstrates or *illustrates* the crossing of the ontological gap between the two universes; it is instead what makes it possible and eventually *produces* it. However, this kind of reading would signify an analysis by leaps and bounds, which risks the possibility of missing the fine-grained structure and mechanisms of the comics language invented by Schuiten and Peeters. In order to do justice to these details, a funnel-shaped reading, starting from some general observations on time and space and progressively disclosing more minute operations at the level of the page, the panel, and eventually even the line, is more appropriate.

The chronotopical structure of *The Leaning Girl* is strongly put forward from the start of the book. Each chapter opens with a full-page image, which combines narrative and illustrative elements and contains, at the top of the page, a large caption specifying time and place. The captions, which are actually chapter titles, immediately establish the blending of time-travel and world-crossing, the movement back and forth between Earth and Counter-Earth, each of them with its own chronology and topology.[1]

A closer view of the structure of the intertwined geographies and calendars instantly shows the presence of a "third space," neither Earth nor Counter-Earth, which is also situated outside time. This new chronotope, labeled "unknown" but perhaps also utterly unknowable, connects as well as separates the two worlds of *The Obscure Cities*, displaying both the discordances and the similarities between them. Despite the clear symmetries of the two story lines and the two story worlds, the differences are even starker. On Counter-Earth, the main character, Mary von Rathen, travels from one place to another, and the story is a whirlpool of characters and events. On

Earth, the plot has only one character and is confined to one singular place, an isolated manor in a desert region of Central France where almost nothing happens. In addition, the comparison of the two series suggests a less immediately visible but far-reaching difference in the structure of time.

Two elements induce a simultaneity between the timing on Earth and the timing on Counter-Earth: first, the alternate montage of the two story lines and, second, the use of a comparable vocabulary as far as calendar time is concerned. The names of the months are the same on Earth and in Counter-Earth, and both worlds seem to measure hours, days, months, and years in comparable ways, even if their starting point is not the same, time on Counter-Earth starting to run "since the Tower," an intertextual wink to the Latin *ab urbe condita*, since the foundation of Rome. This suggested simultaneity is deceptive, however. Actually, time seems to go faster on Counter-Earth than on Earth, if one compares the first and last dates of the two story lines, except the coda on Green Lake: 2 September 747–24 January 751 (three years and more than four months) on Counter-Earth versus 28 October 1898–Spring 1900 (indications that are somewhat vaguer but can be read more or less as a year and a half). Various comments within the integral version of the series address the complex relationships between the two temporal and chronological systems of Earth and Counter-Earth.

The general tension between symmetry and dissymmetry of the two worlds also determines the two essential plot elements. First of all, Mary von Rathen's accident is provoked by a mysterious eclipse, a motif that defines the material contact, or should we say noncontact, between Earth and Counter-Earth in the series as a whole. In *The Leaning Girl*, an eclipse invokes a short-circuit in the roller coaster system on which Mary is taking a ride before being struck by a strange electric eruption. Second, the oblique or leaning position of Mary on Counter-Earth is explained in the album by the attraction of an invisible planet, Earth, and her recovery will only be possible thanks to the actual encounter, a loving one, with a denizen of Earth in an "unknown place." Third, a brief but important chapter added almost immediately after the publication of the first French version and now inserted in the integral French edition, just before the chapter telling of Mary's accident, shows Desombres covering his canvas with black paint, which gives him almost demiurgic powers, since the erasure of all figures in his painting on Earth seems to be at the origins of the eclipse on Counter-Earth.

The thickening plot elucidates, motivates, and eventually naturalizes the ontological gap between the two worlds, which meet through the encounter of two outcasts or freaks. Although this encounter seems impossible in realistic terms, the story tells not only how it happens, but how it is to a certain point inevitable, each of the two major characters, Mary von Rathen and Augustin Desombres, breaking down from their own world and thus bumping into each other in the same "outer space." The temporal indications at the head of the chapters accompany if not install a countdown mechanism that leads toward the both impossible and perfectly expected denouement.

But how does *The Leaning Girl* express the initial separation of its two worlds, and how does it visualize the third space that opens beyond their limits? At first glance, the difference between Earth and Counter-Earth manifests itself in terms of a difference in medium. The world of Counter-Earth is drawn, that of Earth is photographed (the third space is drawn as well, but in a different style, while after the return of Augustin Desombres to Earth, the hand with which he continues to paint is no longer photographed but drawn as a kind of living proof of his extraterrestrial adventure).

In the cosmology of *The Obscure Cities*, the choice of photography as an alternative medium makes perfect sense. Given the fact that the mutual invisibility of the worlds is framed in terms of "eclipse," the sudden outburst of "another" world within the "normal" world—read: the disruption of drawing by photography—highlights the "ecliptic" nature of this change, photography being a medium that is fundamentally based, at least in its traditional forms, on a kind of eclipse, or the sequential arrangement of light and dark, as materialized by the transition from opening to occluding via the camera's shutter. What this shutter is performing is exactly that: *an artificial yet highly productive eclipse*. And although black-and-white photography is not in itself a criterion that accentuates the mechanism of the eclipse, it nevertheless helps foreground the play with light and shadow that is equally at the heart of the photographic medium. In this regard it is important to observe that quite a few photographs in *The Leaning Girl* are striving for a certain balance between black and white that may refer to the principle of the negative-positive technique of classic photographic prints, which are "positive" versions of an underlying "negative" recording on a glass plate or a celluloid strip, for instance.[2] The negative-to-positive inversion can be seen as another form of eclipse, and this supplementary reference to an essential feature of the medium powerfully stresses the link between the key motive of the eclipse in *The Obscure Cities* and the role being played by photography in the visualization of this eclipse in a fictional world initially composed of drawings only. The chromatic balance of black-and-white zones and elements in the photographs of *The*

Leaning Girl strengthens the self-reflexive dimension of these pictures and, more generally, it increases the idea that the presence of photography in a comic can be interpreted, as already argued in the discussion on metalepsis in chapter 5, in relationship to a material subtext, in this case the mechanism of the eclipse.

The difference between comics drawings and photographic pictures may seem unbridgeable. On closer inspection, though, it proves quite thin, and this should not come as a surprise in a work that aims at crossing the boundaries between the two worlds that are visualized with the help of either of these media. As a matter of fact, drawings in *The Leaning Girl* are transformed into photographs, and vice versa.

Let us first analyze this mutual attraction and imitation for the medium of photography and see how the author of these pictures, Marie-Françoise Plissart,[3] succeeds in stylizing her views in such a way that they can almost be seen as drawn images. Two techniques are crucial in this regard, and each of them has logically as much to do with subject matter choices as with strictly photographic features, the latter ones being much more difficult to turn into drawing elements than the former.

First of all, Plissart focuses on objects that can be represented to look as if they were drawings made in the so-called Clear Line style, with strong contour lines, a spare use of shadow lines, and above all monochromatic color fields of neatly separated black, white and gray. The façade of Augustin Desombres's manor is a good example of this Clear Line photography, but so too are the clothes of the protagonist and the preference given to sharply delimited abstract figure versus background in patterns in endlessly repeated floor tiles and wall tiles. Second, Plissart's pictures increasingly zoom in on the paintings made by Augustin Desombres, which progressively become the painted doubles of the drawn props and settings of Counter-Earth in *The Leaning Girl*. In doing so, the album slowly immerses its photographic images of Earth into the drawn images of Counter-Earth. Most of these pictures have been retouched by Schuiten in order to stress the transition from photograph to drawing and vice versa. And it is of course anything but a detail that the photographic sequences tell the story of a painter, more precisely a painter incapable of actually representing the face of the young woman who occupies his dreams.

Similar observations can be made as far as the drawings are concerned. All of them seem made in order to evoke the medium of photography. The stark black-and-white contrasts as well as the frequent use of white contour lines on black surfaces are a direct reference to the language of photography, more precisely to the negative/positive type of photography as shown above. In addition, the systematic display of hatching lines and crosshatches is a direct intertextual hint at the fundamental stylistic property of the medium that was in charge of the reproduction in print before the commercial exploitation of the duotone technique in the 1880s, namely, *woodcut engravings* (see Sandweiss 2004 for a detailed analysis of the modifications from photography to drawn prints in the second half of the nineteenth century). Yet this period is exactly the one that is systematically evoked by *The Obscure Cities*, whose fictional universe is situated by most critics in the years prior to the great modernist turmoil of the early twentieth century. Finally, most readers will immediately be sensitive to the numerous allusions to, if not outright quotations of, photography in any volume of *The Obscure Cities*.[4] In *The Leaning Girl* there are, for instance, direct redrawings of famous pictures by Paul Strand, while one of the most important side figures of the book is Michel Ardan, an anagram of Nadar, pseudonym of Gaspard-Félix Tournachon, one of the founding fathers of French photography, but also, and of course not by chance, an outstanding draftsman and caricaturist. And we should not forget that the shift from illustration to photography was already at the heart of one of the first albums of the series, *L'Echo des cités*, which tells the story of a journal, *La Lumière* (Light), which was also the title of an authentic and historically very important French photo magazine (1851–1867).

The media analysis of drawing and photography in *The Leaning Girl* confirms the general principle of the induced or inferred fantastic as expounded on in chapter 5. I would like to add now a brief example of close reading of a singular page to show how these general devices are implemented at the micro level and how Schuiten and Peeters succeed in bringing together the two strands of medium-specificity and technical awareness while maintaining suspense, surprise, and storytelling. Just as their work on architecture establishes a permanent back-and-forth between a sharp reflection on style and composition in comics and a no less sharp commitment to social critique, the treatment of the leaning girl motif is the starting point of a multilayered thinking on both the production process of a comic and the salient theme, which clearly has to do with issues of gender and biopower.

Mary von Rathen's "illness" is a very complex phenomenon. It is certainly a symbol of puberty, and more generally of bodily change in a pivotal period in the life of a young woman, a crisis that can only be superseded by the free access to a new step in her development, in this case that of adult sexuality. The encounter between Mary von Rathen and Augustin Desombres is definitely a sexual one, and the healing dimension of sexual intercourse is clearly, although unobtrusively, shown in the album. At the same time, Mary's leaning position is also discarded as a simulation by her parents and the adult world of Mylos, the center of industry and power on Counter-Earth. Her physical singularity is negatively seen as a form of stubborn resistance to social streamlining, which Mary's parents will try to domesticate with the help of a variety of disciplinary systems: Mary is excluded from ordinary social life; she is more or less imprisoned in what looks like a private boarding school but what is in fact a youth detention center where she is bullied by her fellow students and terrorized by the staff; and she is forced to take part in all kinds of gymnastics that cruelly exhibit her body's singularities. Mary's liberation from these violent attempts to punish and discipline her body and behavior can only be obtained by her becoming a runaway and joining an ambulant freak show, where she is sheltered by an interspecies community of other not always self-chosen outcasts. But soon there is trouble in paradise, as represented by a greedy and exploitative manager whose dictatorial behavior forces Mary to be a fugitive once more. She finds a provisory home at Mount Michelson, where she is taken care of by Axel Wappendorf, the prototype of the absent-minded and somewhat lunatic scientist, before managing to perform a final breakout into the "third space" as a stowaway in the rocket Wappendorf has built to discover the invisible planet Earth. A die-hard believer in the existence of this planet, which, although completely invisible, explains certain strange phenomena on Counter-Earth, such as the leaning position of Mary, this unconventional inventor will play a crucial role in the healing of the freaky child and thus prepare her eventual access to the role of ruler of Mylos, many years (in Counter-Earth time) after her visit to the third space.

The following page (page 61) is set on Mount Michelson and stages a discussion between the bizarre inventor and Fritz, a scientist at the observatory supportive of Wappendorf's interplanetary travel project. It introduces the motif of the spaceship that will travel to the invisible planet, an irrational project according to Fritz, who cannot believe that the spaceship can ever return to Counter-Earth and who therefore wants to launch an unmanned flight, but a perfectly cogent project according to Wappendorf, who counts on the opportunities open to discovery on Earth to find a way to come back to his home base on Counter-Earth. In *The Leaning Girl*, this page is certainly not the most spectacular one. Neither is it the page that, although describing the ultimate preparation for the flight to Earth, describes the meeting of the two worlds, an event that at this point in the story still belongs to the sphere of wishful thinking and that only many pages later will spectacularly materialize. It is nevertheless a very interesting page, for it helps foreground the interweaving of a vital story element, namely, the clash between rationality and passion, control and risk taking, discipline and freedom, normalcy and unconventional behavior, on the one hand, and a set of formal devices that shape the story and thus show the importance of materiality and medium-specificity in the construction of the thematic layers of the narrative, on the other.

The general composition of the page is a mix of sequential arrangements, with three panels that I will call here panel A, panel B, and panel C, and translinear configuration. The three panels have to be read one after another, but it is clear from the very first glance that the page layout exceeds the principles of panel-to-panel transition and instead presents the three images as part of a larger structure, one that should be processed as a whole. The position of the captions, here on top of the first row (panels A and B) and at the bottom of the second row (panel C), "brackets" the whole page, whereas one can also easily recognize an underlying visual continuity in the management of lines and color zones, all elements that convert the string of three panels in one global image. The whole page thus appears as a network of overlapping and crisscrossing straight and curved lines, all tied together in more than one way. Here are some examples: the left stringer of the ladder in panel A is prolonged by the inner circle of the launch tower built at the observatory in panel C, while the inner circle of the same on the right side of panel C continues in the railing holding the ladder in panel B. But there are also many visual rhymes that are internal to each panel, such as, for instance, the symmetry between the curved lines inside the launch tower in panel B and Wappendorf's jacket. Their parallelism is underlined by a chromatic parameter, for the symmetrical elements of this panel are dark, and they are separated by a lighter zone where the nonsymmetrical elements are concentrated. Another example, in panel C, is given by the clouds that simultaneously veil and exhibit a section of the sky. The surface of these clouds rhymes with the black zones on the left and right sides of the image. As a matter of fact, this whole panel can be seen as a symbolic as well as a literal variation on the usual theme of the curtains of a stage that are opened one after the other to finally disclose what will be at the center of the play: the starry sky.

In addition, the central theme of page 61 powerfully hints at the idea of totality. Panel C is a clear reworking of the romantic cliché of the dreaming character lost in meditation in front of an almost infinite panorama, well known from the paintings by, for instance, Caspar David Friedrich. Here as well, the small characters are seen from the back and represented as sunk in

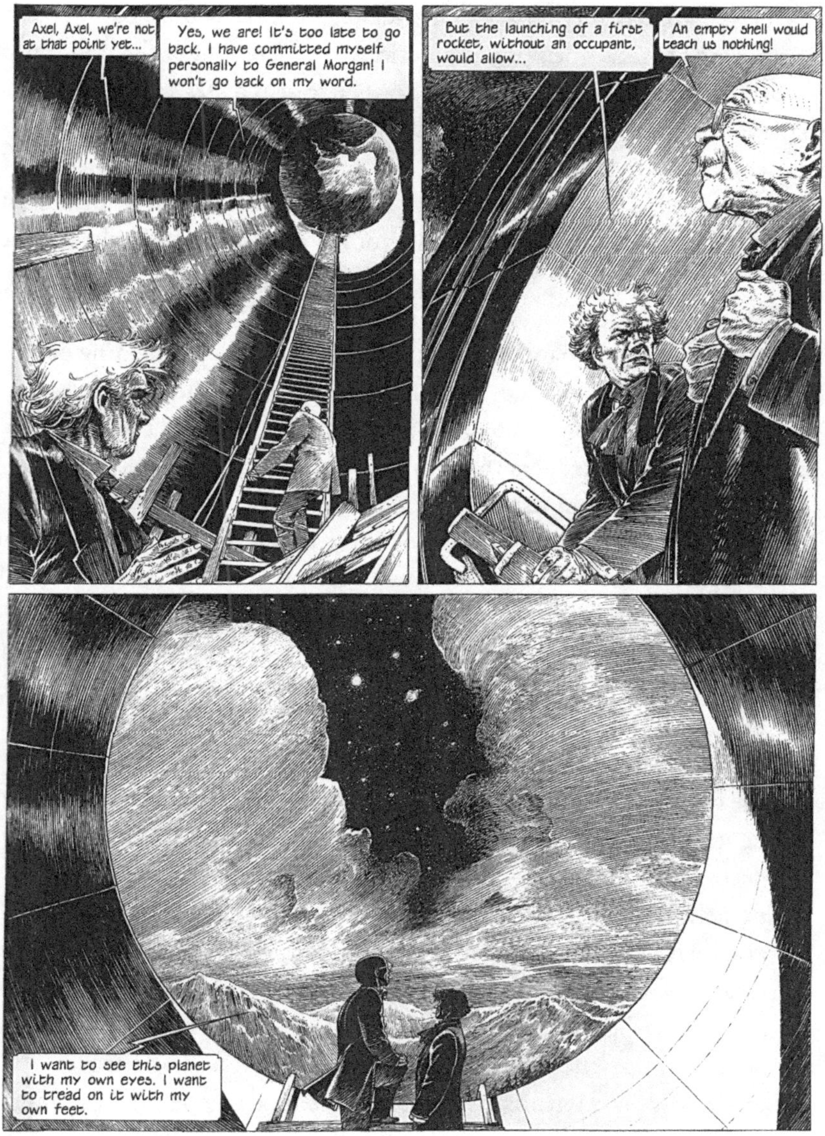

FIG. 8.2 *The Leaning Girl*, page 61. Excerpt from *The Leaning Girl*, François Schuiten and Benoît Peeters (© Casterman, with kind permission of the authors and Editions Casterman)

contemplation in front of a virtually infinite landscape: mountains, clouds, skies, stars, and so on. Panel C thus acts as a reminder that the page itself has to be watched as a kind of unity in diversity.

The result of this overall composition is a leveling of differences—anything but a detail in a creative enterprise that stages the crossing of boundaries between apparently incompatible universes. From that point of view, the intertwining of visual antinomies functions as a metaphor of the bridging of thematic differences. More precisely, it can be read as a user's manual to start exploring the meaning of formal mechanisms in the decoding of narrative and thematic layers.

On page 61 of *The Leaning Girl*, the range in nature of these formal differences is all-encompassing. They have, for instance, to do with the distinctions between

- big and small: in panel A the sky as seen through the opening of the launch tower is nothing more than a tiny circle, almost lost in a corner of the image; in panel C, the same sky occupies the center of the images and reduces the previously large characters to the minor role of small figurants;
- square and curved or circular lines: in addition to the analysis briefly sketched above, one easily sees how all panels multiply these kinds of forms and figures, first by dramatically increasing the number of drawn lines within each object or character, second by sticking to an etching-type style of drawing that underscores the dynamic presence of these countless curved and square lines;
- figurative and abstract: if one looks at the play of light and dark on the interior face of the launch tower in panel A, one cannot help but be struck by the multiple readings allowed by these apparently simple decorative elements: the concentric lines can be read as just that, namely, reflections of the moonlight inside the tower, but they can also be read as abstract motifs or, more symbolically, as the representations of a hidden star or planet whose form and vibrating light rays are "hidden" underneath the combined image of the tower's upper circle and the reflections on its interior (just as one can discover words inscribed within other words or sentences, one can hear and see emerge a radiant star within or under the literal representation of the tower); look also at Wappendorf's head in panel B: it directly mirrors—the same size and position—the opening of the launch tower in the panel, thus provoking a kind of overlap that is at the same time purely material and perfectly symbolic, for it shows what is on the inventor's mind. These kinds of readings foster of course the exchanges between abstract and figurative as well as literal and symbolic;

- black and white: these two colors are here used in such a way that the overall page composition offers a perfect balance of their respective chromatic tonalities; moreover, certain elements shift from black to white and from white to black (Wappendorf's jacket is white in panel A, black and white in panel B, white in panel C, for instance), and the systematic use of etching style techniques enables Schuiten to maintain or introduce multiple black lines on white surfaces and vice versa.

The sophisticated but perfectly readable exchanges between these antagonistic properties of the images prepare the fusion of Earth and Counter-Earth to come. At the same time, however, this fusion will remain temporary and incomplete. In that sense, the very persistence of the visual differences can be read as a forecast of the eventual limitations of this fusion. Small and big, straight and curved, figurative and abstract, black and white: all enter into a fruitful dialogue, but their merger is never complete; it does not engender a final and stable middle ground.

Other examples, more visible in other parts of the book, bring to the fore similar antagonisms: between left and right, far away and close, surface and depth, positive and negative, or inside and outside. In all these cases, the visual language of *The Obscure Cities* oscillates between difference and repetition, between the blurring of boundaries and the exacerbation of the difference between poles. Image-wise, such a mix can be summarized in two key structural figures: first, that of the oblique line, in between curved and straight lines, and essential to what happens to the main character of the narrative; second, that of the Möbius strip, the 3-D interpretation of obliqueness and the perfect illustration of what happens to the worlds of Earth and Counter-Earth, which ceaselessly touch each other without ever coinciding with their opposite invisible.

Let us, to end this close reading of page 61, have a look at the page that gives a rather synoptic view of the "third space" (page 131; see figure 8.3). This astonishing plate, the symbolic abstract of an impossible place, does not surprise careful readers of *The Leaning Girl*. One immediately recognizes the image of the cloudy sky that Fritz and Wappendorf contemplate from the inside of the launch tower on page 61. The sky has now morphed into a solid spectacle, which is also a variation on the fundamental tensions and characteristics as shown by the close reading: obliqueness is ubiquitous; the "third place" is structured like a universe where inside and outside

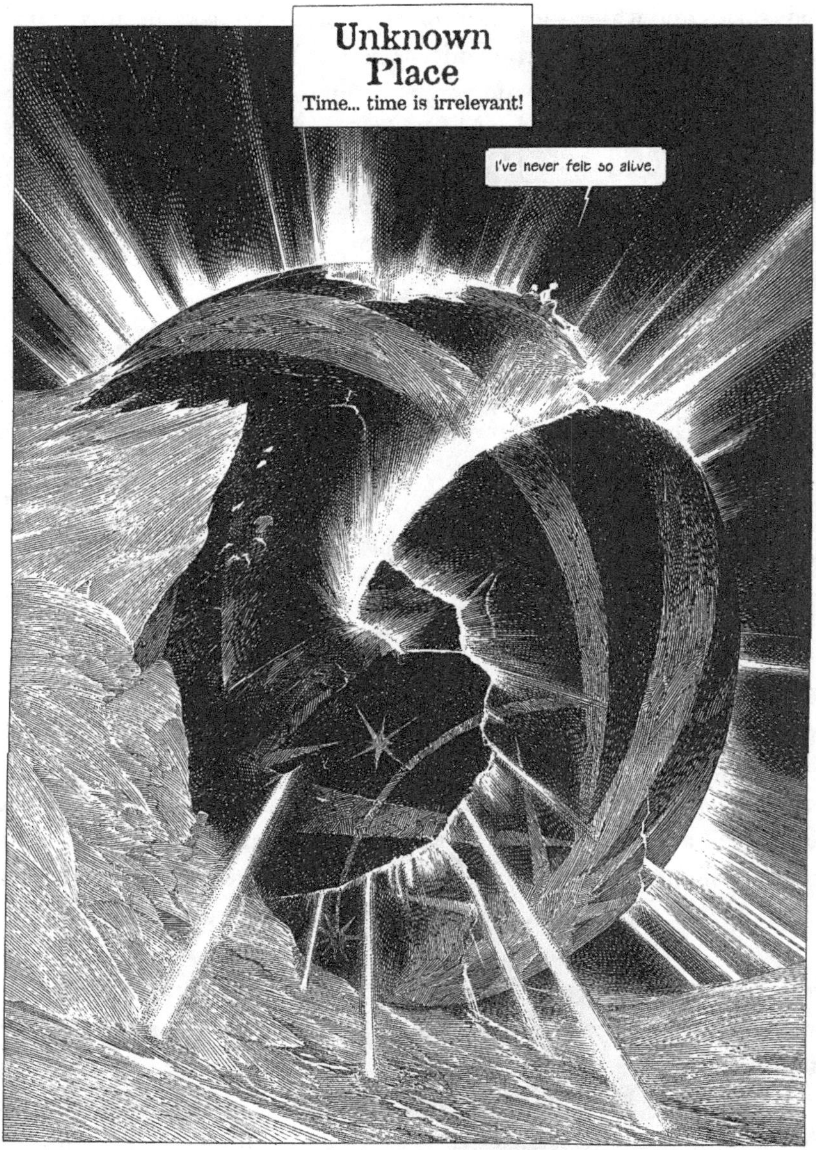

FIG. 8.3 *The Leaning Girl*, page 131. Excerpt from *The Leaning Girl*, François Schuiten and Benoît Peeters (© Casterman, with kind permission of the authors and Editions Casterman)

or inward and outward become as indistinguishable as the two sides of a Möbius strip. The impossible space of the encounter between Counter-Earth and Earth is also a world that is both immense and ridiculously small (the characters on top of the sphere are as big as human figures represented next to a building, to give an idea of the height and volume of the spaces they inhabit, in this case the space of a world that is no larger than a sizable building).

Page 131 is perhaps the ultimate image, not of *The Obscure Cities* as a fictional and imaginary universe, but of the series as a book, something we can hold in our hands but that at the same time fully dominates us; something that keeps us in the palm of its hand, in a permanent oscillation which is the gift and the power of all great works, which always master us when we think that we master them most.

9

A Conversation with Benoît Peeters

The first album of *The Obscure Cities* was published in 1983, but things must have started well before, no? For instance, your friendship and collaboration with François Schuiten?

Definitely. As you know, I was born in Paris in 1956, but in 1958 my parents moved to Brussels for my father's work, at the moment of the Brussels World Fair and the early years of the European Union. I was enrolled at the European School, where I had launched a small school magazine, which I wrote and edited all on my own. My parents were so dismayed at the time and energy it took me to make that journal that they decided to send me to another, Belgian Catholic school, which they hoped would put me back on the right track again. It is there, in the symbolic year 1968, that I met François Schuiten. We immediately became friends, in spite of or thanks to our differences. François, who was the son of an important architect and painter, was incredibly gifted at drawing and painting. For his age, his technical skills were amazing. Thanks to his family background he already had a solid knowledge of art history and visual culture, both classic and modern. Very soon we started making plans together, and the first one that materialized was a . . . school magazine, which we wrote and illustrated together. These years were not only formative to our collaboration, which from the very beginning ignored the strict division of labor, for we worked together on the texts as well as on the images, but also of my interest in painting and art history. Under the guidance of François's father, who liked to take us to museums and galleries, I even took Sunday classes and seriously tried to start painting, unfortunately without great success. François and I were the only pupils, and he was much ahead of me, but this experience has been vital for me and my love of the image. At age sixteen, I went back to Paris with my parents and I lost sight of François, but when for sentimental reasons I returned to Brussels in 1978, still a student (I then studied with Roland Barthes, who was supervising my thesis on Hergé) but already a published author (a first novel, *Omnibus*, had appeared with the famous Minuit publishing company in 1976), our friendship and collaboration rapidly resumed—and all that continues until today. I am now living in Paris once again, but the frequency and intensity of our collaboration are still the same.

When you came back to Brussels, in 1978, François had already started making comics, I believe.

Yes. After high school he had taken the first specialized BA-MA program in comics that existed in Belgium, in the St-Luc art school, and perhaps in the whole world, and as a student he was already publishing in the trendsetting *Métal Hurlant* magazine, founded and coedited by Moebius. Although I had a pretty good knowledge of classic comics, François introduced me to this line of work, more specifically to Moebius. Nineteen seventy-eight was also the first year of *(À Suivre)*, the legendary monthly that completely renewed graphic narrative in Europe, and the editors, who had been invited as experts on the exam panel of the art school, had in turn invited him to participate from #3 on. Very soon François and I were making projects for a collaborative work, which from the very start we saw as a typical *(À Suivre)* narrative, that is, an author comic to be serialized chapter by chapter (the notion of "chapter" was then very new), no longer in black and white, as in the first issues of the journal, but in color. And our project, which eventually became *Samaris*, was rapidly accepted, after we had shown the editors some ten more-or-less finished pages. The actual serialization started in 1982, and the book came out one year later. It had an excellent critical reception and has been translated very rapidly in *Heavy Metal*.

How did the collaboration actually go, and was it already the way you collaborated later on in the series and in other projects?

We frequently met, mainly in his studio, and we spent a lot of time discussing not only the general idea of what we wanted to do, but also the visual

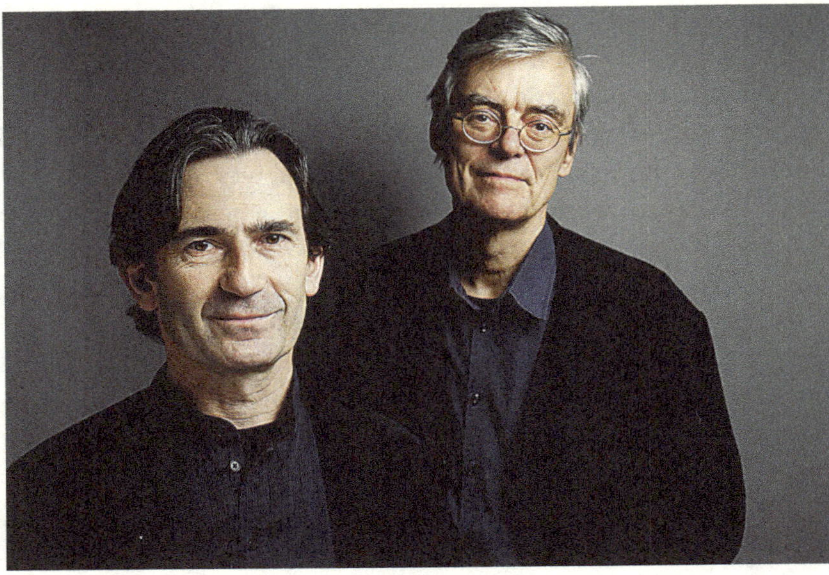

FIG. 9.1 Schuiten and Peeters, photograph by Isabelle Franciosa (© Isabelle Franciosa)

design of both story world and page layout. We did everything together, permanently merging and rethinking the visual aspects of the comic as well as its story line. We put my first narrative ideas and François's first visual sketches together, and then we made not one but various storyboards. We really invented everything together and worked step by step, never knowing exactly in advance how the story would end. This way of working was compatible with the serialization policy of the magazine and suited very well François's slow way of working. François has always been doing everything himself, from the initial research (his documentation is impressive and has always been a great source of inspiration) and first sketches till the "post-pencil" steps that are the inking, the lettering, and the coloring, always in a very artisanal way, everything by himself, with no help of any assistant at all. Yet this open way of proceeding is also key to the way we have been elaborating the fictional world of *The Obscure Cities*. First, we only had a very open idea of the universe we were inventing, and even in later phases of the series it has been essential for us that this story world was not determined or circumscribed by a "bible." Just as we have never worked with already-finished or cast-in-stone scenarios, we wanted a world that remained open to changes and even more a world that would never be complete or homogeneous. And this has been our way of working even today.

I think it is important to remind readers that both of you, who may be the perfect example of fruitful collaboration, are also developing a lot of personal, often also collaborative, projects—in your case for instance the photo novels co-written and realized with Marie-Françoise Plissart, who by the way is also involved in several parts of the *Obscure Cities* work.
Sure. Even if my collaboration with François started from the simple fact that we were also friends, this friendship has been strengthened by our collaborative work. But it is not possible to collaborate if those working together feel as if they were prevented from giving the best of themselves, as happens in collaborations where one partner feels exploited or misrepresented by the final result. A good collaboration does not put between brackets the specific input of each partner. Instead I like to consider it as the intersection between what each of them is doing, sometimes outside of their specific collaboration. François is a great visual artist, who has always had many other projects (posters, silk prints, scenography productions). As far as I am concerned, I have been publishing essays and biographies all my life. But our talents have met in *The Obscure Cities*, which has given us the opportunity to realize something we would never have done just on our own. In addition, one should not forget that our respective expertise is really very different: François's visual culture and drawing competences are breathtaking, while I have a strong literary but also philosophical background (my academic training was philosophical, more than literary).

***The Obscure Cities* is an open world, not just as fiction, but also as an editorial project. It is a kind of rhizome that seems to exceed any attempt to totally embrace it. At the same time, there is now, at least in French, a so-called integral version in four volumes. Was it your and François's idea to bring the series to a close, or does this complete version do something else?**
No, it was not our idea at all. After the success of some of our books in Japan, a local young publisher came up with the idea to offer the material that existed on the Japanese market in a handy and accessible "complete works" format. She did a tryout with a first volume, which sold very well and obtained the Grand Prize Manga (awarded for the very first time to non-Japanese authors) and allowed her to publish the four-volume edition she had in mind. The object was so visually appealing that many French fans and readers of the series also wanted to buy the books, even if they had not the slightest knowledge of Japanese. The Japanese example encouraged us to emulate the initiative in French, which we also saw as an opportunity to publish our work in a

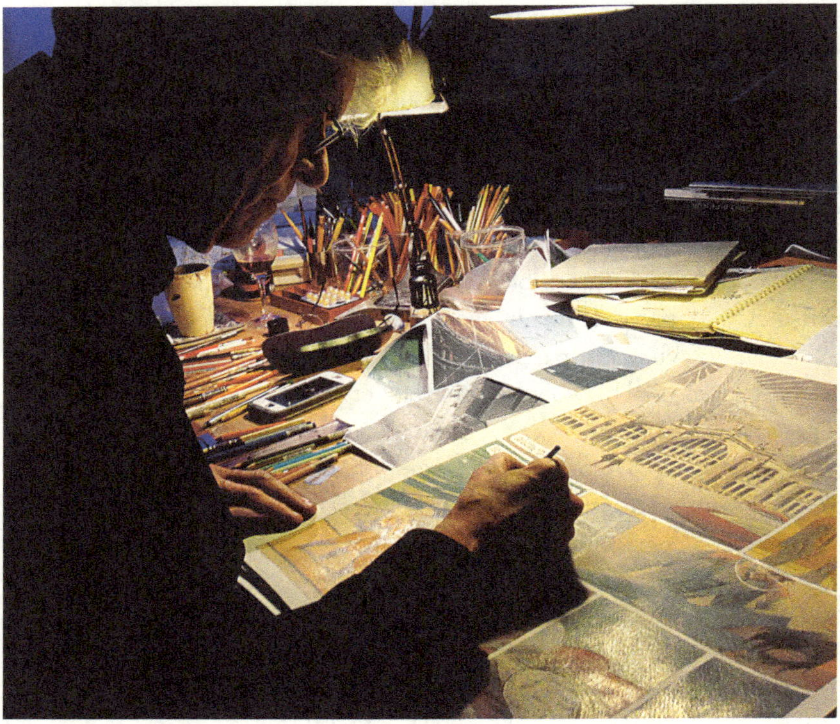

FIG. 9.2 François Schuiten at work, photograph by Benoît Peeters (© Benoît Peeters)

way that had not been possible, technically speaking, at the moment of the books' first publications. Since François had conserved his initial artwork, we could make new and much better scans, just as we could work with the most up-to-date color print technology and choose the best possible paper quality, etc. And I must confess we are both very happy with the result.

I certainly agree, but at the same time, this complete version is much more than a technical achievement. It is also a way of continuing the permanent transformation of the *Obscure Cities* world. How do you see the major differences between previous editions?
First of all, there is indeed that perhaps strange effect of unification. Strange, because one of the salient features of the series had always been—and to a certain extent continues to be—the great heterogeneity of its materials, whose format and nature have always been changing. You may compare it with the formal and other metamorphoses of Chris Ware's *Acme Novelty Library* in its first years. François and I have tried to expand as much as possible the limits of diversification of what it was possible to do without leaving the world

of trade publishing, and we have been very lucky that our publisher, Casterman, has always supported us in this regard. But now in the complete version, the opposite phenomenon seems to happen: there is a single format for all works; the books also include works that had never been published as autonomous book projects or that only existed as special editions or collector['s] items and that are now juxtaposed with traditional albums, and in addition there is also that overarching structure, more or less based on the "city guide" structure that had been the model of a previous side project of the series. But all this is only one side of the story. For on the one hand, we did not include all available material, much of which is not print-related. On the other hand, we also poked fun with the false dream of totalization, for instance by introducing some jokes in the list of characters at the end of the last volume.

The continuing presence of the previous versions, which are planned to remain in print, and the ceaseless expanding of side projects support of course the essential openness of the series. However, the biggest change in the complete version seems to be that of the "framing" of the fictional world, no?
Yes, in the complete version, we really put a strong emphasis on making the *Obscure Cities* world as relatable as possible. We do not present the various works as fictions, but as stories taking place in a world that we want to make as consistent and trustworthy as possible, even if we know—and we hope our readers know as well—that the series is a work of fiction. But much more than in the individual publications, we play with the willing suspension of disbelief of the audience.

An important dimension of this fictional world is the Altaplana website, which currently entails more than 3,000 pages, and which can be seen as part of the *Obscure Cities* world.
Yes and no. Altaplana.be ["be" for Belgium], which is a site that we authorize and support, is not an example of fan fiction, even if it is completely managed by committed readers. The ambition of Altaplana is to offer all available information on the *Obscure Cities* world and to present it in a way that makes it as easily consultable as possible, which is by definition very different from the way readers of the books experience it. In the latter case, information may be scarce and partial and not always easy to summarize and structure. However, Altaplana is not a site that publishes creative expansions or continuations—which does not mean that it is not creative itself. As a matter

of fact, Altaplana is an encyclopedic project that has progressively replaced our own, first attempts to bring *The Obscure Cities* to the Internet. In the late nineties, François and I had created a site, Urbicande, which aimed at providing the reader with a digital equivalent of the *Obscure Cities* experience; that is, the experience of entering an unknown world where the idea of permanent discovery and labyrinthine surprise was more important than that of traveling through an already-charted territory. One of the specific features of the site was for instance that each new visit was necessarily different from the previous ones, an experience some readers found not only bewildering but almost incomprehensible. They actually thought it was a bug.

The way you describe it is very appealing. Why does Urbicande no longer exist?

The management of the site proved technically difficult, very expensive, and extremely time-consuming, and we soon realized that our priorities lay elsewhere, but some traces of it remain on Altaplana.[1] Nevertheless, François and I share a deep interest in the way readers interact with our work. We see this interaction as a kind of gift, the most stunning example being of course that of Mary von Rathen, one of the characters of our work who started a real correspondence with us, while keeping her own identity a complete secret through to today. A startling story, but one that reveals a perfect understanding of our play with fiction and reality in the series. For the same reason, we were very happy to welcome and encourage the initiative by a great Dutch fan, Eilko Bronsema, to develop the Altaplana site, which we closely follow but without having it under our control.

Strangely enough, the world of *The Obscure Cities* has not yet been exploited in many different formats. Has this to do with the fact that this world is already touching upon so many different formats and media and that, by including for itself so many other influences and inspirations, it becomes a paradoxically self-supporting unity?

As the example of Altaplana and the permanent dialogue with our readers demonstrate, we do not consider ourselves the absolute owners of the world we created. After all, the complete version, which has brought various key changes in our work, was not our idea but the expansion of the idea of our Japanese editor, Misato Sawada! And we are certainly open to expansions and continuations by others. It is possible that there will be no other albums, at least not at the core of the series, for there will always be new side projects, and given the specific nature of *The Obscure Cities*, which is totally dependent on the collaboration between François and me, it seems implausible that there will ever be a reboot. Moreover, François's style and technique, so meticulous and time-consuming, do not really fit today's ways of making comics and graphic novels, where authors are not always given the time that is necessary to enact this kind of detailed, technically difficult, and time-consuming drawings. Nevertheless, outside the world of comics, many things are of course possible, and we are certainly open to proposals. The *Obscure Cities* world is not a finished world; there is room for new explorations in other formats. The Mary von Rathen adventure is a real-life example of it, and it is clear that the visual design of our series is having an impact on scenographers, for example, but it is true that there has never been for instance a blockbuster adaptation.

This lack has always surprised me. It should be attractive to film such a fabulous world, no? And aren't the stories the kinds naturally appealing to a very large audience?

I think that there are two main reasons for that, one that is very easy to understand, and one that as far as I know has never really been addressed. Let me explain. One of the reasons that *The Obscure Cities* does not have multiple adaptations is, next to the difficulty of appropriating the complexities of François's style, the fact that our fictional world is already absorbing and reworking so many elements borrowed from so many other media and contexts. Our work is a patchwork of countless influences and sources of inspiration. So that's one reason. But the other element is I think more important, namely, the absence of evil, I mean absolute evil, and it is intriguing to notice that it remains hardly debated. Obviously, in *The Obscure Cities* there are bad characters, and even good characters do not always behave well, but the dark dimension of their acts is never crucial to the story, and there is always some humor in the way they are presented. In addition, there is in the whole series not the slightest presence of real or absolute evil, in the metaphysical or religious sense of the word. In *The Obscure Cities*, bad characters are never totally bad; they are rather characters with some negative aspects. What is totally missing is a Manicheist world vision. In *The Obscure Cities*, one does not find what authors such as Shakespeare or Dostoyevsky or, in a different field of cultural production, characters like the Joker, so powerfully embody—and which all great actors, and I am thinking here of Orson Welles for instance, adore to personify—namely, the destructive power of evil as an independent and uncontrollable force. This is a limitation of my and François's imaginary. I simply do not have that Manicheist worldview, and I do not believe in absolute evil as such, in spite of the many terrible things that have always happened throughout history and which are such an exceptional driving force in most popular fictions, certainly in the United States.

Coming back to the unifying moment in the complete edition and more precisely to the fact that the older versions of the series continue to be available—and for those who do not read French or Japanese, these are still the only ones—what do you think of the wishes of some artists to revise their previous work, and in certain cases even try to give full priority to the updated version?

It is true that the complete edition brings this issue to the fore, certainly given the fact that *The Obscure Cities* has always been thought of, by us as well as by our readers, as what Umberto Eco calls an "open work"; that is, a work that changes with each new experience of it. By offering a complete version, however incomplete it remains in many regards, we seem to have introduced a kind of closure, not only by suggesting that it will be difficult from now on to add new albums to the series, but also by reframing the existing works in a new and unified way. One is certainly entitled to ask whether artists actually have the right to do so and, if they do, whether the new perspective they impose upon the already existing material is by definition better or more valuable than the previous one. We know for instance that in the last years of his life, Degas tried to overpaint works already sold to private collectors, who were afraid of letting him enter their houses. We also know, to take an example from the culture of comics, that Hergé strongly preferred the redrawn and colorized versions of his first black-and-white albums, an opinion that has only much later proved open to debate. It is a very complex issue, where the ideas of the makers and those of the audience may diverge. Nevertheless, even the complete edition of *The Obscure Cities* is a work that can be seen as radically open. François and I certainly do not claim to be in total control of the world we built or explored, as shown for instance by the fact that readers frequently confront us with interpretations and discoveries we had either totally forgotten or even never dreamt of. Needless to say of course that we feel very proud when readers draw our attention to hidden meanings, references, allusions, metaphors, etc., that they clearly derive from our work but that we had never made explicit or even been aware of ourselves.

As you already hinted at before, the success of a collaboration also depends on the possibility of each partner in exploring his own talents and desires. How would you analyze that special relationship between the

collaborative work with François and your other work, be it individual or equally collaborative but with other artists?

At first sight, one may think that the success of *The Obscure Cities* has prevented me from having a career as a novelist. Before launching the collaboration with François, I had already published two short novels. Yet I never experienced the decision to focus on something else than the novel as a loss—and definitely not as a failure. There are many reasons why I did not choose to follow that path: writing a novel is a lonely job, over which I preferred various forms of collaboration; it is also a risky business, financially speaking, and since I had to earn a living, it was safer to work in the comics industries than to spend two years on a novel that may not sell at all; next, there is also the fact that I feel personally more attracted to the writing of other genres, mainly essays and biographies, than to the writing of a novel; and finally, I am probably one of those who no longer believes that the novel is the central literary and cultural form of our times (today, it is probably the television series). Yet this negative way of thinking is somewhat deceptive: I may not consider the novel the dominant genre, but I adore narratives, and I could perfectly fulfill my wish to tell stories by collaborating with François on *The Obscure Cities* and with others on other types of stories.

However, *The Obscure Cities* seems to have been crucial in the realization of another dimension of your literary and philosophical formation. You are not only the key biographer of, for instance, Jacques Derrida, but the intellectual environment of your formative years, which the French call "*la modernité*" and the Americans quite deceptively the "French Theory," is ubiquitous in the series. How would you describe that influence, and can you give some examples of it?

You are right, and this is certainly a good example of the way our collaborative work has given me the opportunity to develop my own interests. I think that the most important influence of my intellectual training and interests concerns the global structure of *The Obscure Cities*, which presents a world that fundamentally resists unity, uniformity, cohesion—and all attempts to systematize this world can only lay bare its fundamental "difference." From that point of view, the notion of rhizome as coined by Deleuze and Guattari, who use it among other things to challenge the unitary and monolithic structure of the tree, has been highly influential, just as their insistence on the inevitable presence of holes and lacks in any living structure. In a similar vein, there is certainly also a direct influence of Lacan's thinking on visual and conceptual paradoxes in his later seminars—which as a student I passionately followed, like many young people of that period. Lacan's work on the Borromean knots and more generally on structures that both contain themselves and are contained by one of their components is something that has inspired the way in which we built the *Obscure Cities* world. Deleuze and Guattari, Lacan, but also Douglas R. Hofstadter's *Gödel, Escher, Bach*, a book that analyzes similar spatiotemporal paradoxes, Robbe-Grillet, on whom I have written extensively, and Freud's notion of the uncanny are permanently on my mind when working on the form and structure of our fictional world. The refusal of unity, the intertwining of order and disorder and, more specifically, of conflicting orders such as the vegetal and the mineral or the living and the nonliving, are undoubtedly linked with my fascination with that kind of modernity. When Jacques Derrida had accepted to analyze another collaborative project, the photo novel *Right of Inspection* I made with photographer Marie-Françoise Plissart, I had offered him *Fever in Urbicand*, whose theme he considered close to his own take on deconstruction. So, yes, *The Obscure Cities* may have turned me away from my first steps as a novelist, but they certainly allowed me to appropriate in new and personal ways many other aspects of my literary mind.

Not only the general structure but the whole world of *The Obscure Cities* seems full of scholars and scientists, and some of them do seem to illustrate quite well the tension between order and disorder, logic and madness, difference and repetition (to quote the title of a famous book by Deleuze).

Sure, and I would like to stress that these scientists are never presented as mad or evil scientists and that the tone of the series is never parodic or aggressive in this regard. What all these characters have in common is the confrontation with a world they do not fully understand and their desire to make rational meaning out of it. To a certain extent, they are not so different from the experience of our fictional world itself: we invite readers to willingly suspend their disbelief and try to organize the partially uncharted, definitely labyrinthine, and frequently self-contradictory universe they are entering, yet always with humor.

Although deeply rooted in nineteenth-century European culture, *The Obscure Cities* has succeeded in becoming a globally appreciated series. How do you explain that success, and how do you analyze its reception in different cultures?

The success in non-European countries has come quite rapidly recently. Certainly in Asia, with many translations in Japanese, Chinese, and Korean, *The*

Obscure Cities has seduced wide audiences from different backgrounds and generations. For us, this success first came as a mystery. To Asian readers, references to futurist and Nazi architecture (*Fever in Urbicand*), the disintegration of former Yugoslavia (*The Invisible Frontier*), or cultural icons such as Peter Brueghel, Orson Welles, or Napoleon (*The Tower*) will probably be lost. In a country like China, contrary to Japan or Korea, comics culture is also something rather new, so even the visual and narrative comics languages our series is hinting at will certainly go unnoticed. Nevertheless, the public's reactions have always been very enthusiastic. Today, I am tempted to believe that what attracts readers from other cultural settings and other reading habits is fundamentally the power of certain metaphors, such as exemplarily the figure of the leaning girl, to create both a strong visual image and a touching psychological character, which seems to appeal to very different audiences. We tried to achieve something similar with the transparent body in *The Shadow of a Man*, but for reasons that I would be incapable of explaining, this metaphor has not had the same impact on the readers' imagination.

The Obscure Cities have never indulged in becoming pure fantasy or pure science fiction. Do you think that is part of their force as well?
It is certainly part of the DNA of the series. *The Obscure Cities* does not present a world in which anything becomes possible or thinkable, as may be the case in science fiction, or where the notion of reality is more or less discarded, like in fantasy. With our series, we wanted to respect a more challenging problem and create a world as well as a number of situations and characters that, although totally fictional, remain nevertheless plausible. We want our readers not only to relate to the *Obscure Cities* universe, but also to at least accept the hypothesis that such a world might really exist. As a matter of fact, such a play with the unreal is probably part of the comics medium in general, which does not address reality the same way it happens in cinema or literature. In comics, the limits of what looks real or unreal are easier to stretch.

Is this also what makes _The Obscure Cities_ a series that we associate more with classic comics and not with the more recent phenomenon of the graphic novel? The series is not an example of mainstream comics, far from that, but its essential praise of fiction and imagination also makes it very different from the autobiographical or semiautobiographical stance of most graphic novels.
Yes, I can agree with that, although it is dangerous to address the history of comics in these overwhelmingly generalizing terms, as if there was nothing

left of the energetic and joyful sense of storytelling in older comics in today's graphic novel and as if the more self-reflective dimension of the latter were absent in the former. I would like to formulate it in a more cautious way and underline the fact that the *Obscure Cities* novels are above all works of imagination, a work that aims at offering a complex and challenging world which does not pretend to look for safe and simple answers, but also a work that is not afraid of humor and emotions.

(Brussels, 3 January 2019)

10

Birth of an Album

The Theory of the Grain of Sand

BENOÎT PEETERS

TRANSLATED BY JAN BAETENS

Preparatory Notes

Some of our books are born from a single idea that organizes the whole story. *Fever in Urbicand*, *The Tower*, and even *The Leaning Girl* belong to this type of work. Other albums, like *Brüsel*, evolve more freely, as if the story had to discover its own direction en route, when we had already started telling it. *The Theory of the Grain of Sand* is an example of this second category. There was, at first, the desire to make an album in black and white wherein fantastical phenomena would play a major role. Then there was, one summer, a horizontal sketchbook in which François Schuiten made a large number of sketches, freely inventing situations he found attractive.

This "holiday sketchbook" contained several ideas I liked very much: the man in levitation, the invasion of the sand, the pile of stones. . . . Others did not have the same appeal to me; nevertheless some of them could be used in the script as examples of wrong tracks. The way the story was progressively being shaped was thus triggered by the fantastic situations sketched by François. What I did was, among other things, to articulate these various ideas by making this as credible as possible. I tried, for instance, to make the reader accept that it was "normal," if not "logical," that a character could fly away and fly over the city. I also wanted to come back to the city of Brüsel, many years after the album that we had devoted to it, and do something new with the character of Mary von Rathen, the "Leaning Girl." I was also tempted by a more "choral" composition than in our previous albums and to follow simultaneously various groups of characters. These were the elements that helped elaborate the story.

In order to draw the protagonists, François wanted to find his ideas in the people we know and frequently meet. He wanted to find his inspiration in their faces and gestures, while also looking at their life as well as their way of being. In certain cases, he even asked some of them to pose, like the draftsman Alain Goffin (for Maurice), Eric de Kuyper (for Constant), or the politician Cécile Jodogne (for Elsa), since he wanted to avoid repeating what he had already done before. In a similar vein, one of the recurrent settings of *The Theory of the Grain of Sand*—one might even say one of its principal characters—is the Autrique House, built in Brussels by the great architect Victor Horta in 1893. During several years, we have been deeply involved in the protection, the restoration, and also the scenographic organization of this art nouveau building. This place, which is now open to the public, plays a key role in the story. It is both part of the fantastical dimension of the story world and faithfully represented in its tiniest details. It is thanks to these somewhat blurry and very fragile elements, as well as to the permanent shifts between them, that François and I have been able to produce here what is so crucial for us: the uncanny.

The Theory of the Grain of Sand

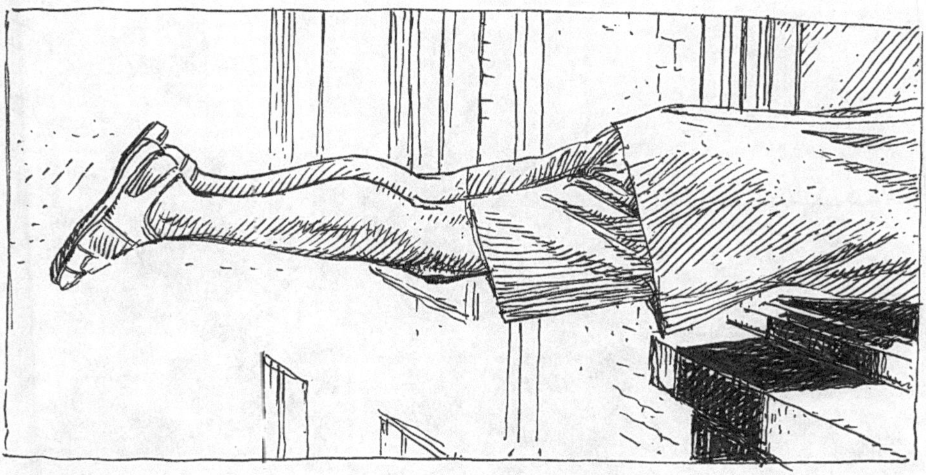

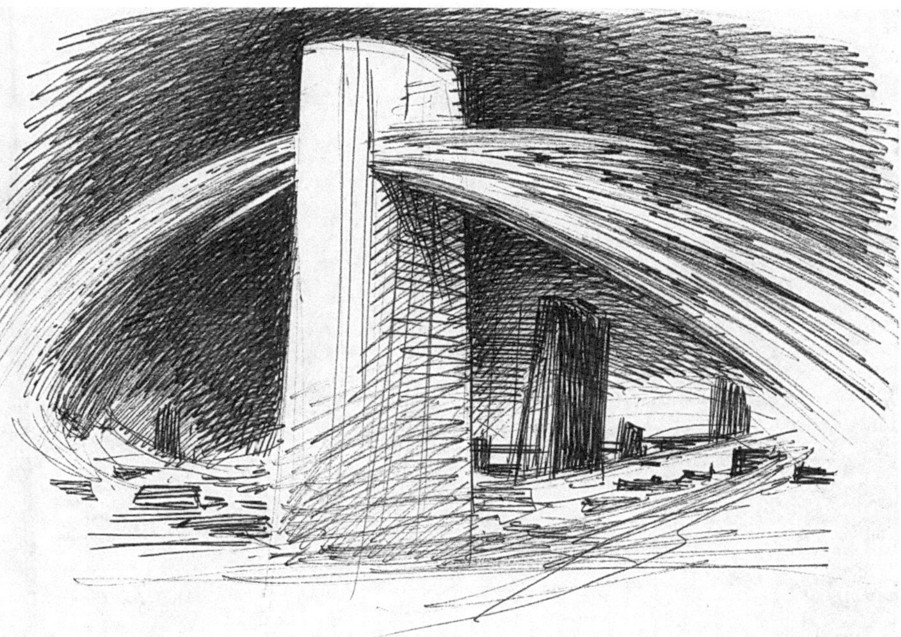

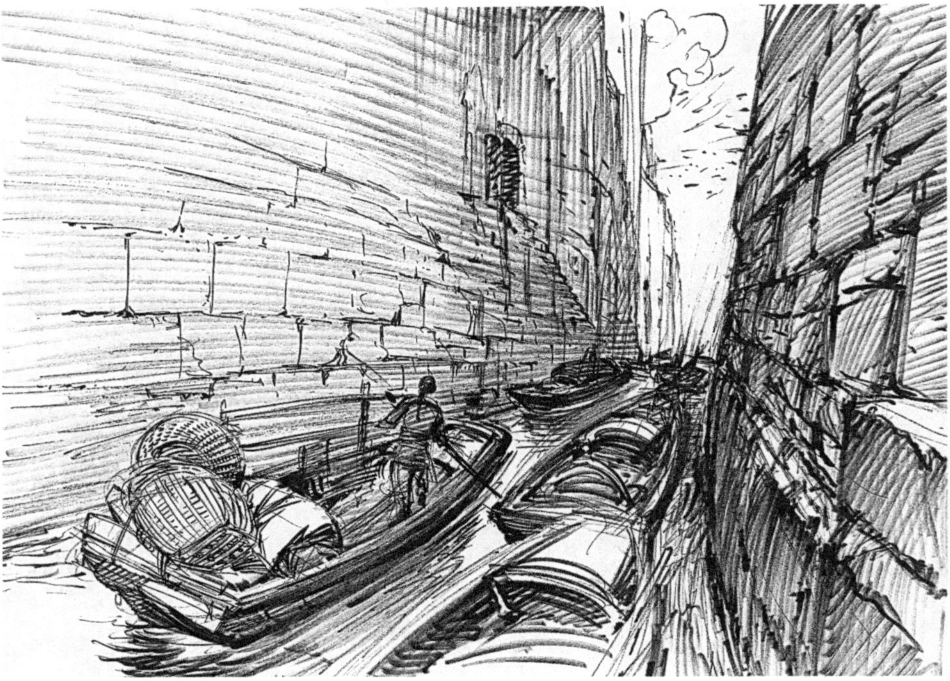

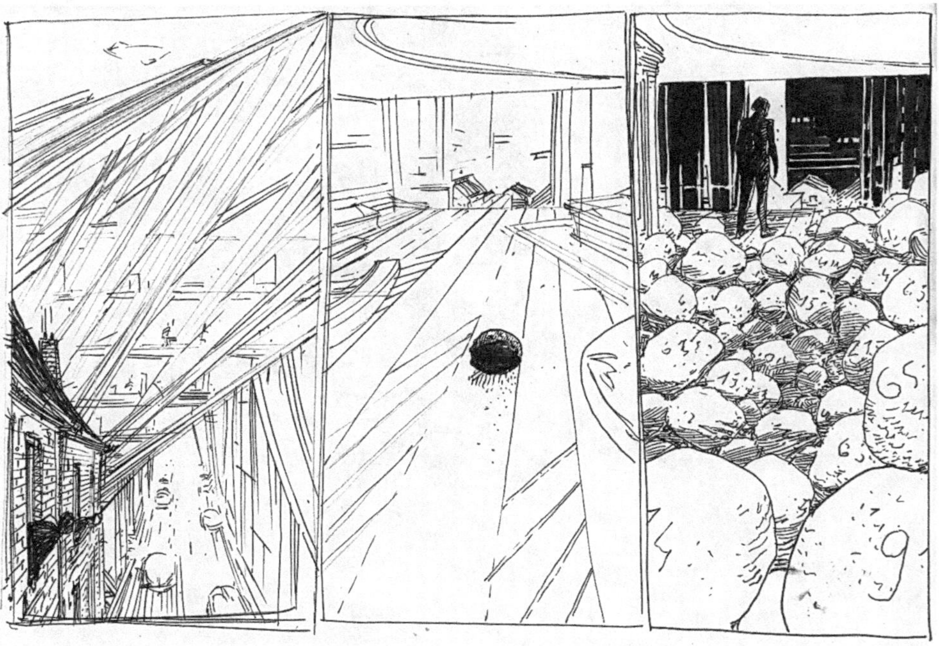

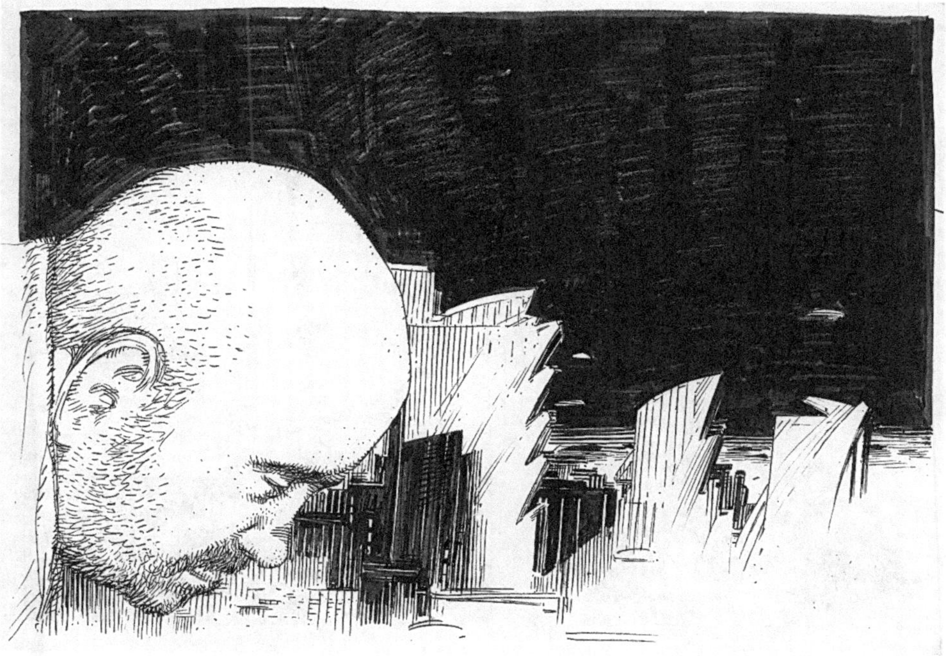

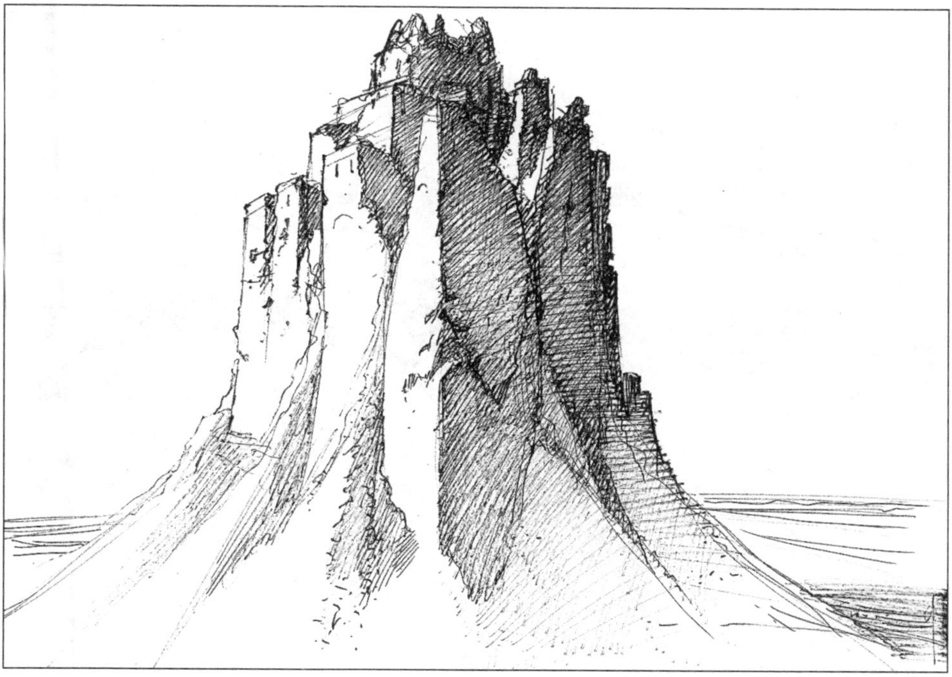

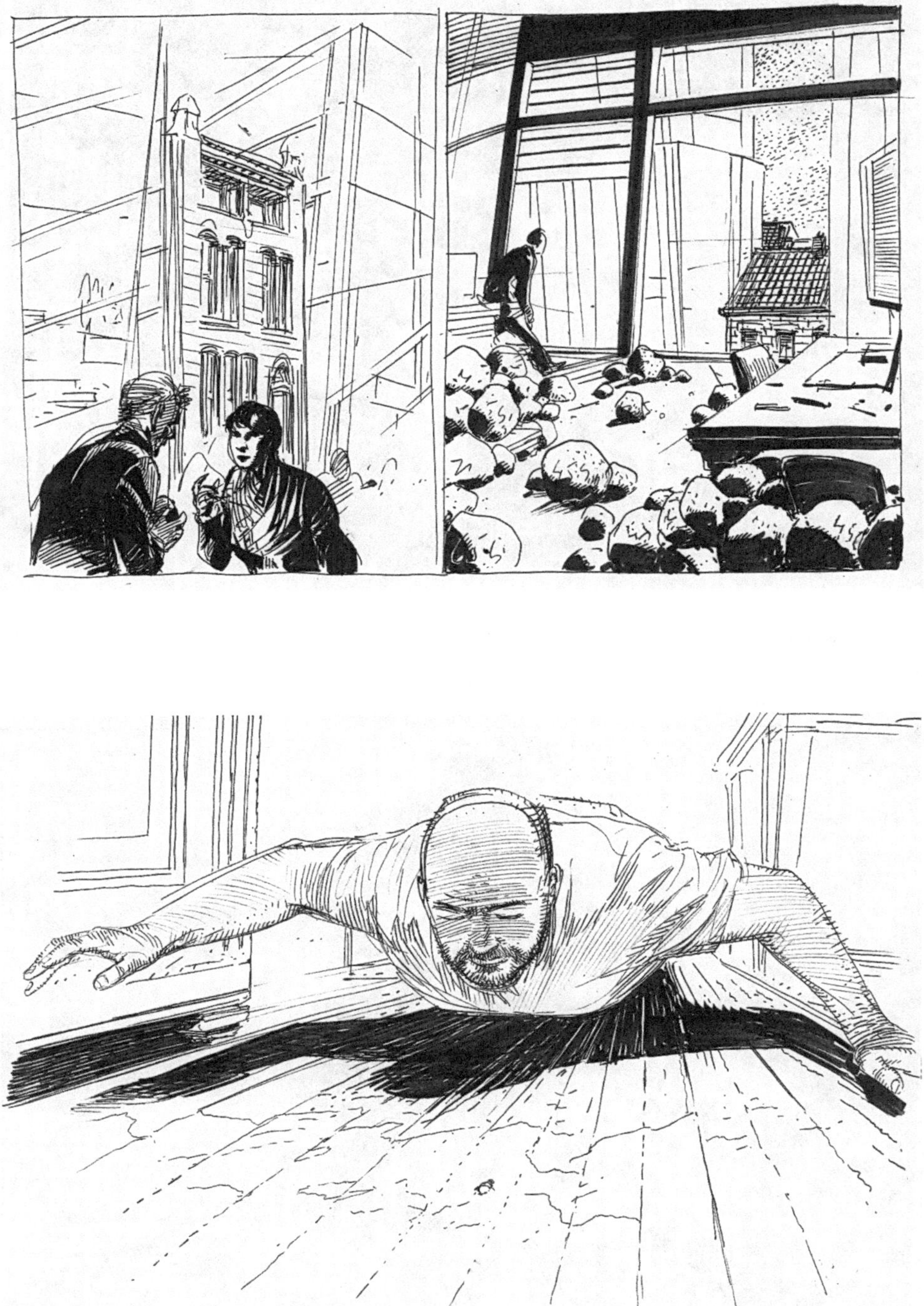

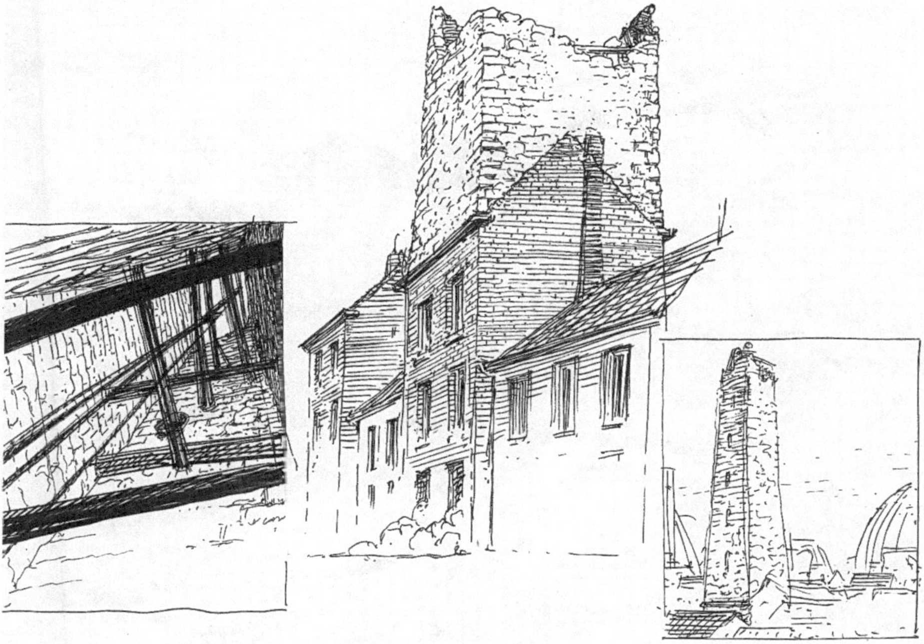

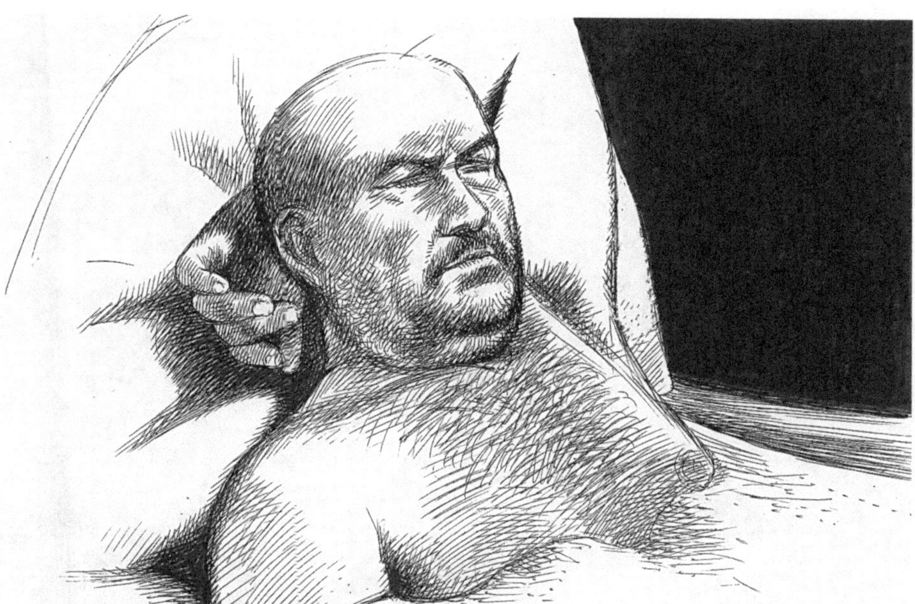

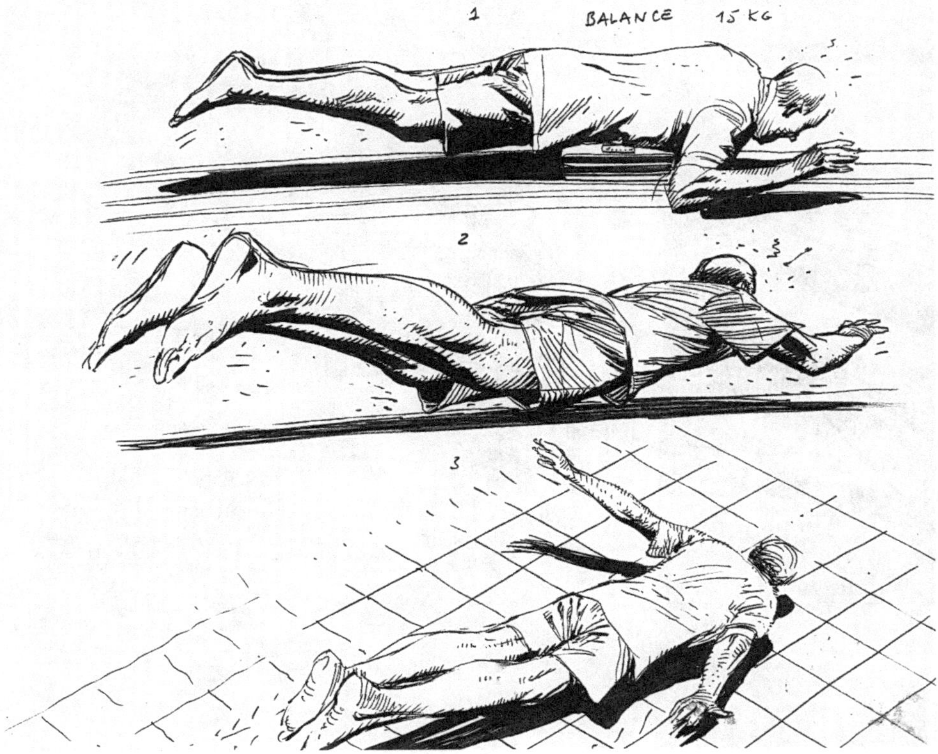
1
BALANCE 15 KG
2
3

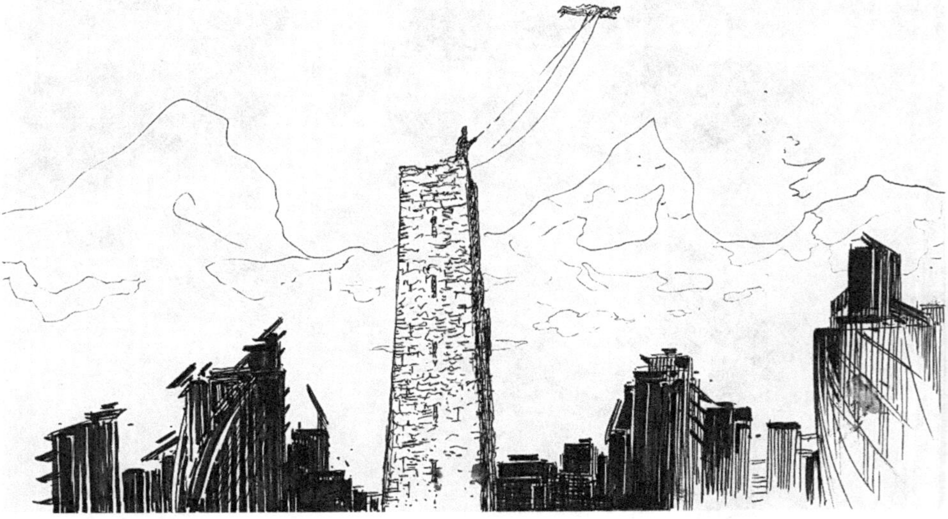

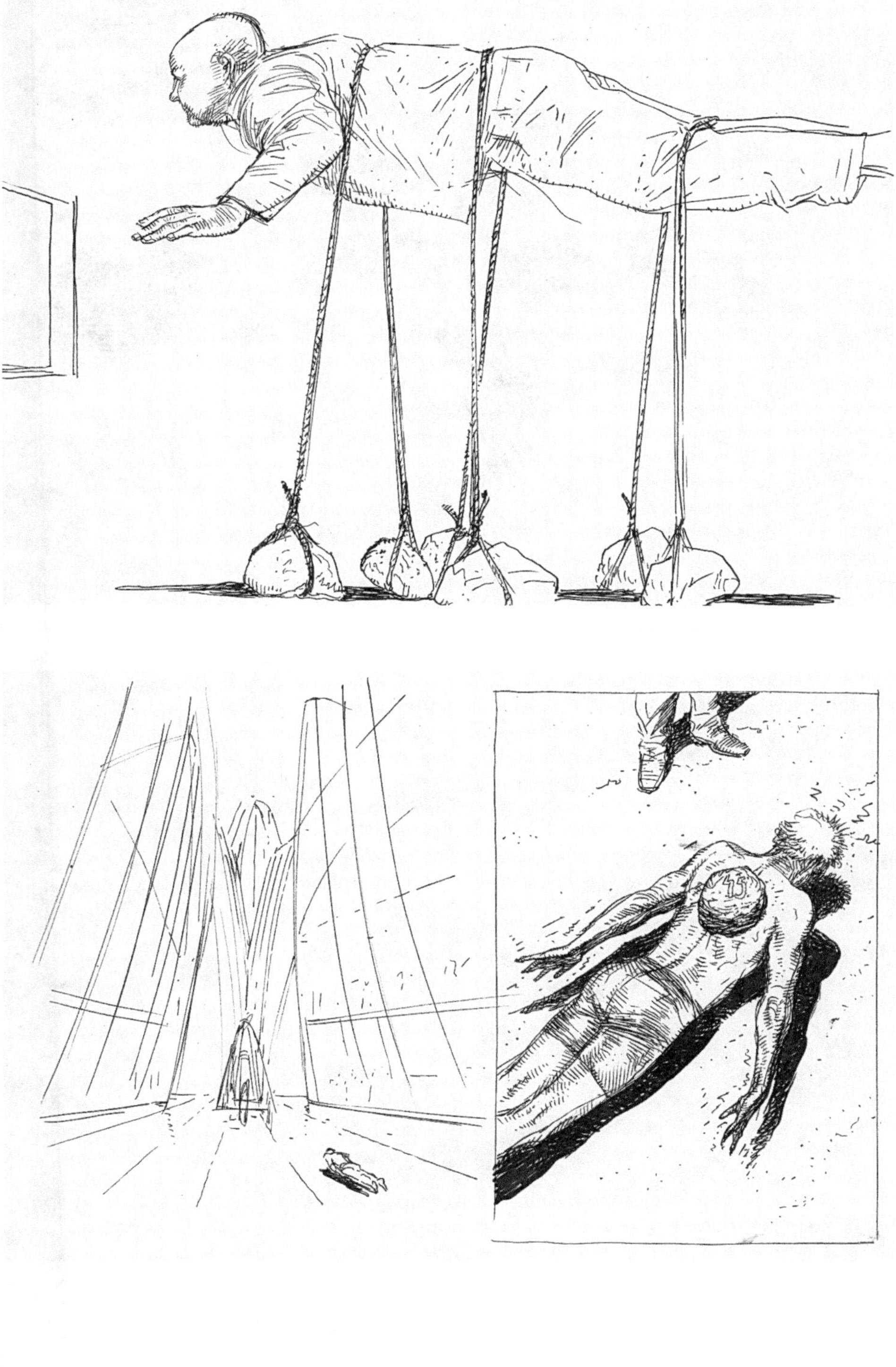

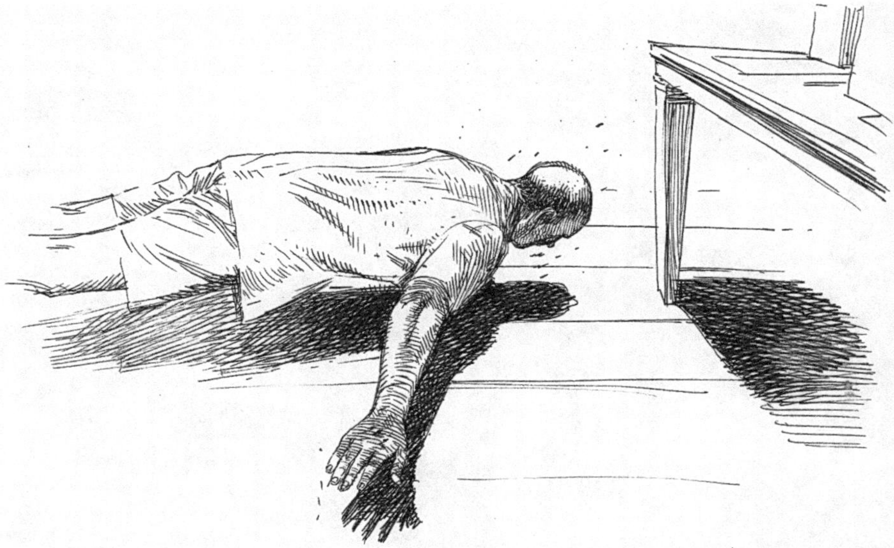

Page 24

IMAGE 1
24 juillet
11 H 50
Il y a maintenant 30 ou 40 pierres de même taille dans l'appartement de Constant. Il a commencé à vider certaines étagères de leurs livres, pour y placer les pierres et, juste en dessous, une étiquette indiquant les circonstances de leur découverte. Une pierre dans les mains, Constant prend un peu de recul pour regarder son travail.
Constant : **Ah, ça prend tournure ! Reste à voir ce que je vais faire de tous ces livres…**

IMAGE 2
15 H 33
4 ou 5 enfants (dont les deux déjà vus) font un concours de château de sable.
La fille : **Dommage qu'on n'ait pas de coquillages…**
Un garçon (tout occupé à son château) : **Tu vas voir celui-là, ce sera le plus beau !**

IMAGE 3
17 H 05
Elsa dans le jardin fleuri. La façade arrière de la maison derrière elle. La bonne apporte un plateau avec le thé.
Léonie : **Voilà le thé, Madame… Quel beau temps, n'est-ce pas ?**
Elsa : **Oui, Léonie, j'ai l'impression que ce sont les premiers vrais beaux jours.**

IMAGE 4
20 h 45
Maurice dans la cuisine du restaurant, tout guilleret. Il s'apprête à prendre deux assiettes.
Maurice : **Laissez, je vais les apporter moi-même !**
La serveuse : **Vous avez l'air en pleine forme, Patron.**
Maurice : **Je me sens des ailes ce soir…**

Page 56

IMAGE 1

Plan large. Mary, l'échevin Sleeckx et son jeune adjoint arrivent devant la maison de Constant. Les pierres continuent à s'accumuler.

L'adjoint : **Quelle quantité incroyable ! Et tout cela viendrait d'un seul appartement ?**

IMAGE 2

Mary, de trois-quarts dos, s'adresse aux deux officiels.

Mary : **C'est ce que je me suis évertuée à expliquer au Divisionnaire. Sans grand succès, je dois le reconnaître...**

IMAGE 3

Constant se dirige vers eux. Il a enfilé une veste par-dessus son pyjama, mais ne semble pas se rendre compte de son allure insolite.

Constant : **Bonjour, Mary ! Bonjour, monsieur l'échevin ! Je suis très heureux de vous voir.**

IMAGE 4

Plan plus serré sur l'échevin et son adjoint.

L'échevin : **Ah, monsieur Abeels ! Alors, que se passe-t-il ? Racontez-nous ça...**

IMAGE 5

Plan serré sur Constant. Mme Josette arrive, à l'arrière-plan.

Constant : **Eh bien, comme vous le constatez, le rythme d'apparition des pierres s'est accéléré de manière dramatique. Je n'ai même plus le temps de faire des relevés...**

IMAGE 6

Plan plus large sur le groupe. Mme Josette les a rejoints.

Mme Josette : **Mon plancher s'est écroulé ! Un trou grand comme ça... Je croyais que c'était la guerre.**

Constant : **Si on ne se dépêche pas de nous aider, c'est tout l'immeuble qui va s'effondrer.**

IMAGE 7

L'échevin serre la main de Mme Josette, avec l'air préoccupé d'un vieux professionnel de la politique.

L'échevin : **Ne vous en faites pas, madame, la situation est sous contrôle...**

L'adjoint : **Nous allons envoyer des camions, tout ça va être évacué très vite.**

IMAGE 8

Le petit groupe d'officiels est impatient de se remettre en route.

Mme Josette : **Et pour mon plafond, qu'est-ce que... ?**

L'adjoint : **Il faut prendre contact avec votre assurance, madame.**

La Théorie du grain de sable

Résumé de la deuxième partie

1. Petit matin. Elsa descend, très fatiguée, peut-être encore en peignoir. (Ou alors, on commence par suggérer sa mauvaise nuit, les bruits qu'elle entend sans pouvoir les situer, etc.)

Quand Elsa descend, Léonie, déjà au travail, ramasse des verres sales, vide des cendriers, etc., comme au lendemain d'une grande réception. Elle est à bout de nerfs.

Léonie : J'en peux plus, moi, Madame... Tous ces verres sales, ces cendriers ! Qu'est-ce qui se passe ici ? Avant, vous ne faisiez pas des fêtes comme ça !

- Mais je vous assure, Léonie, je n'ai pas organisé la moindre fête.

- Allons, allons ! Et tout ce bruit en pleine nuit, la voisine m'en a parlé...

- Ecoutez... je...

- Vous n'êtes plus la même, Madame. Toujours fatiguée, toujours énervée... Du temps de vos parents, des choses comme ça ne seraient jamais arrivées.

- Je dois le reconnaître, il se passe des choses un peu bizarres... Je suis un peu dépassée...

- Je le vois bien, moi, ce qu'il y a... Allez vous regarder dans la glace ! Avec vos poches sous les yeux, vous faites peine à voir ! N'essayez pas de me faire croire que vous passez vos nuits à dormir !

- Ça suffit, Léonie.

- Parfaitement, Madame, ça suffit... Je n'ai pas été engagée pour m'occuper d'une salle des fêtes. Je vous rends mon tablier...

- Mais... ce n'est pas possible... je...

Léonie joint le geste à la parole et commence à défaire son tablier.

- Oh que si, Madame, c'est parfaitement possible. Je ne resterai pas une heure de plus... Une si jolie maison, si c'est pas malheureux.

2. Même jour, un peu plus tard. Le Divisionnaire revient trouver Mary, à son hôtel. Il lui parle de cas absurdes, qui n'ont rien à voir. Il a apporté une série de documents : « J'ai sorti de nouveaux dossiers qui devraient vous intéresser. »

Storyboard

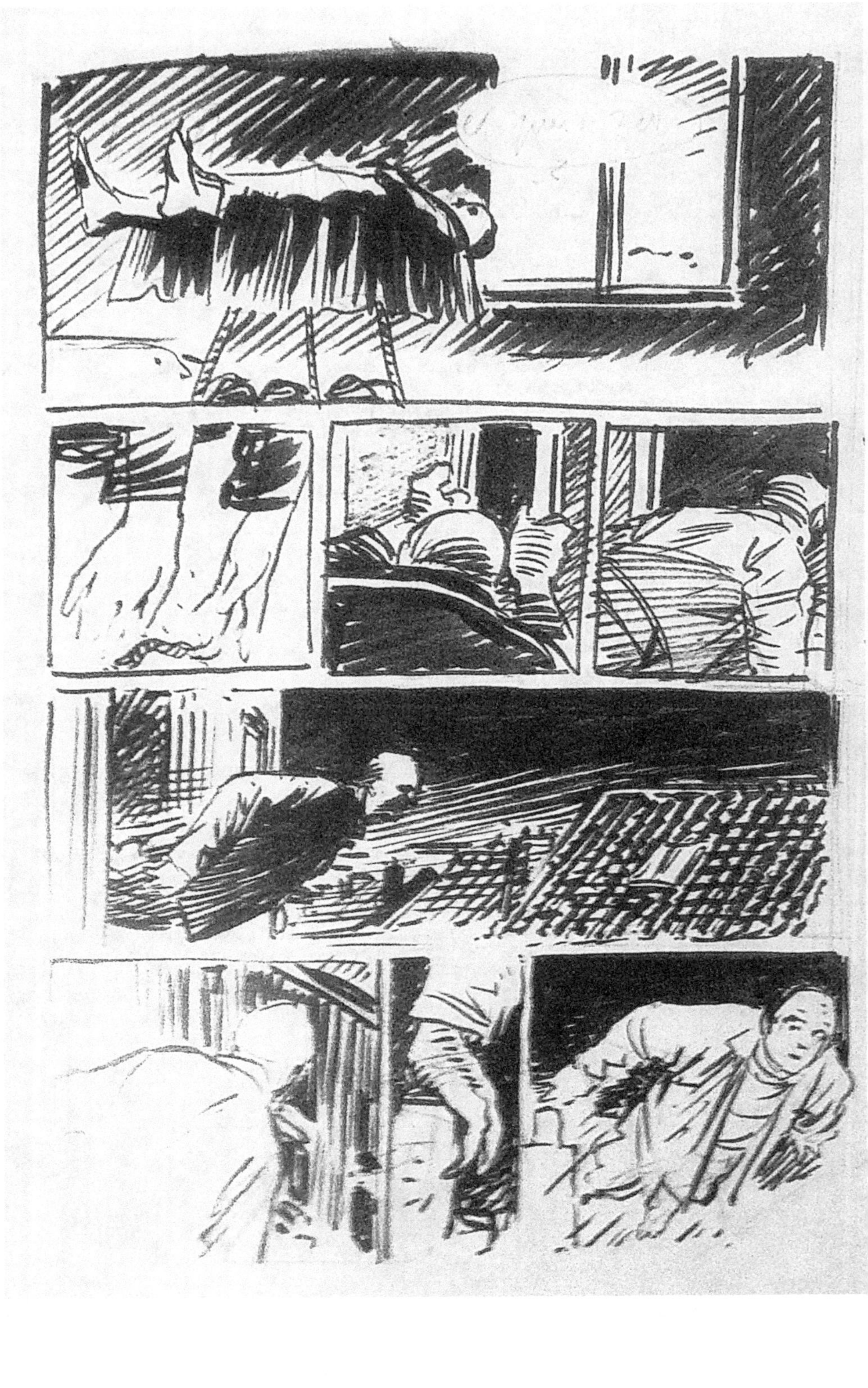

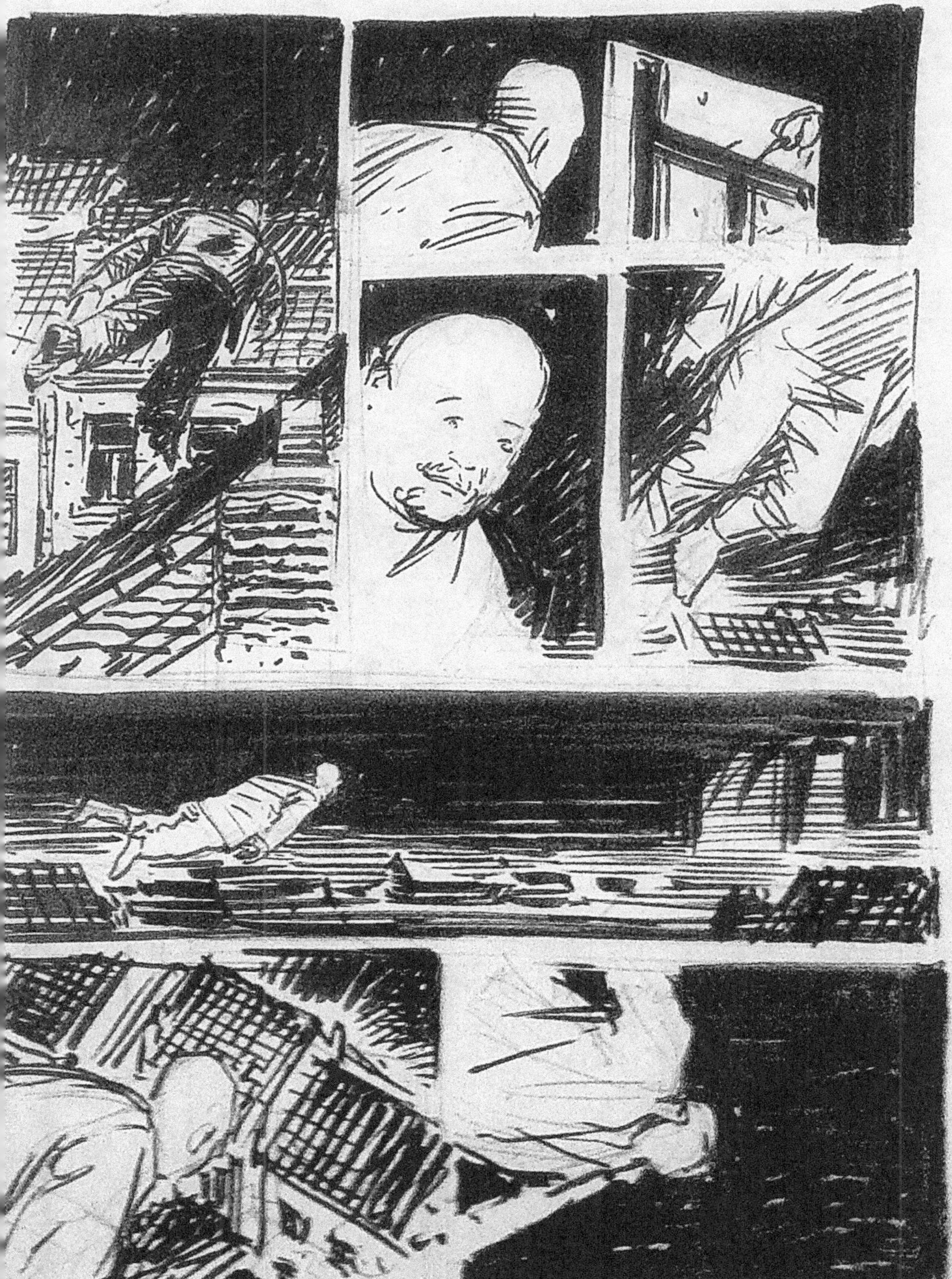

Cover Ideas and Sketches

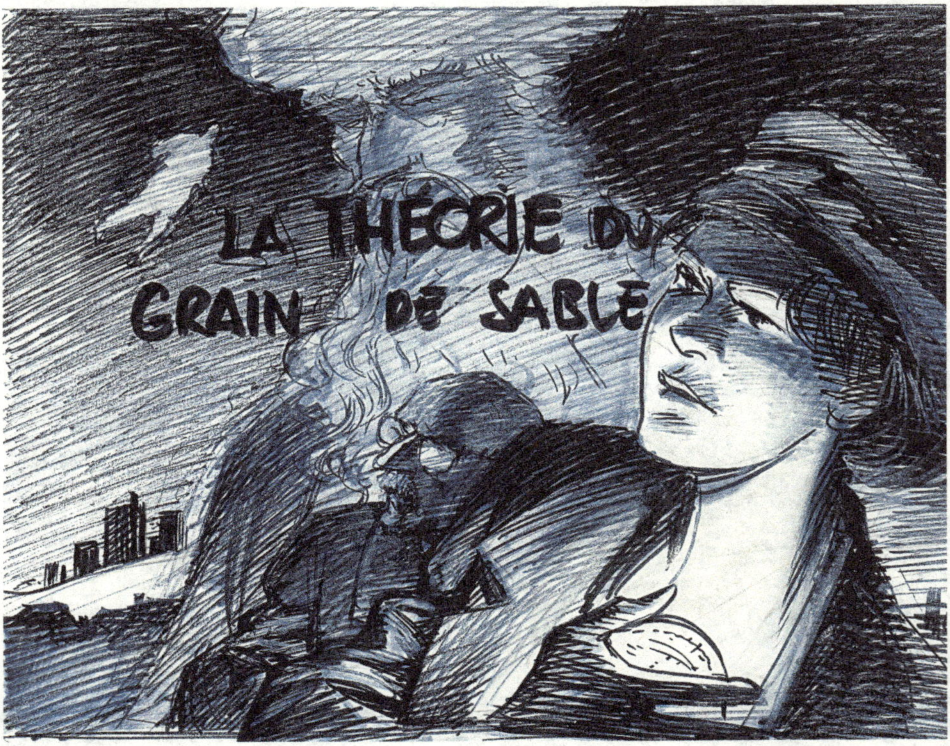

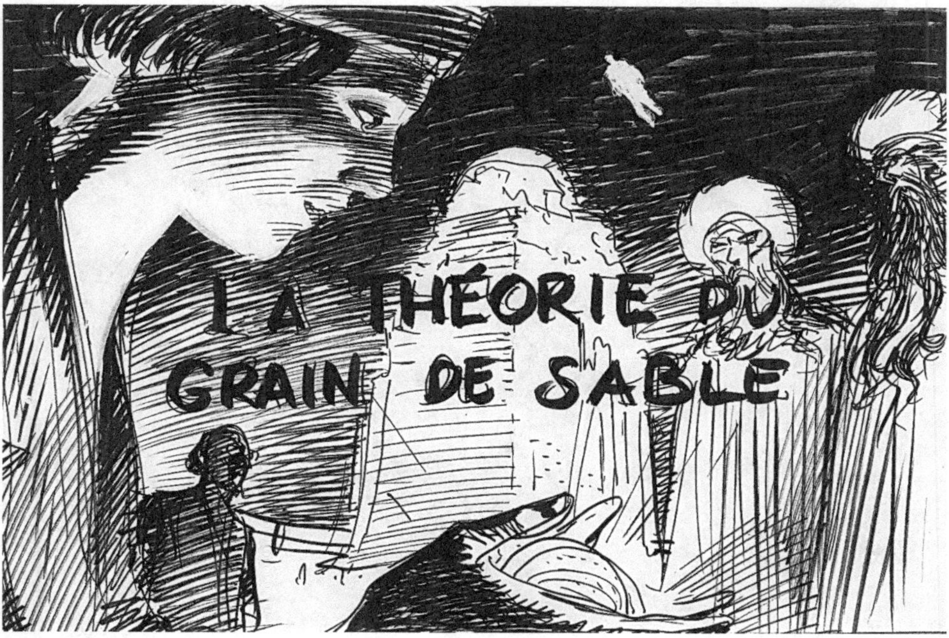
LA THÉORIE DU
GRAIN DE SABLE

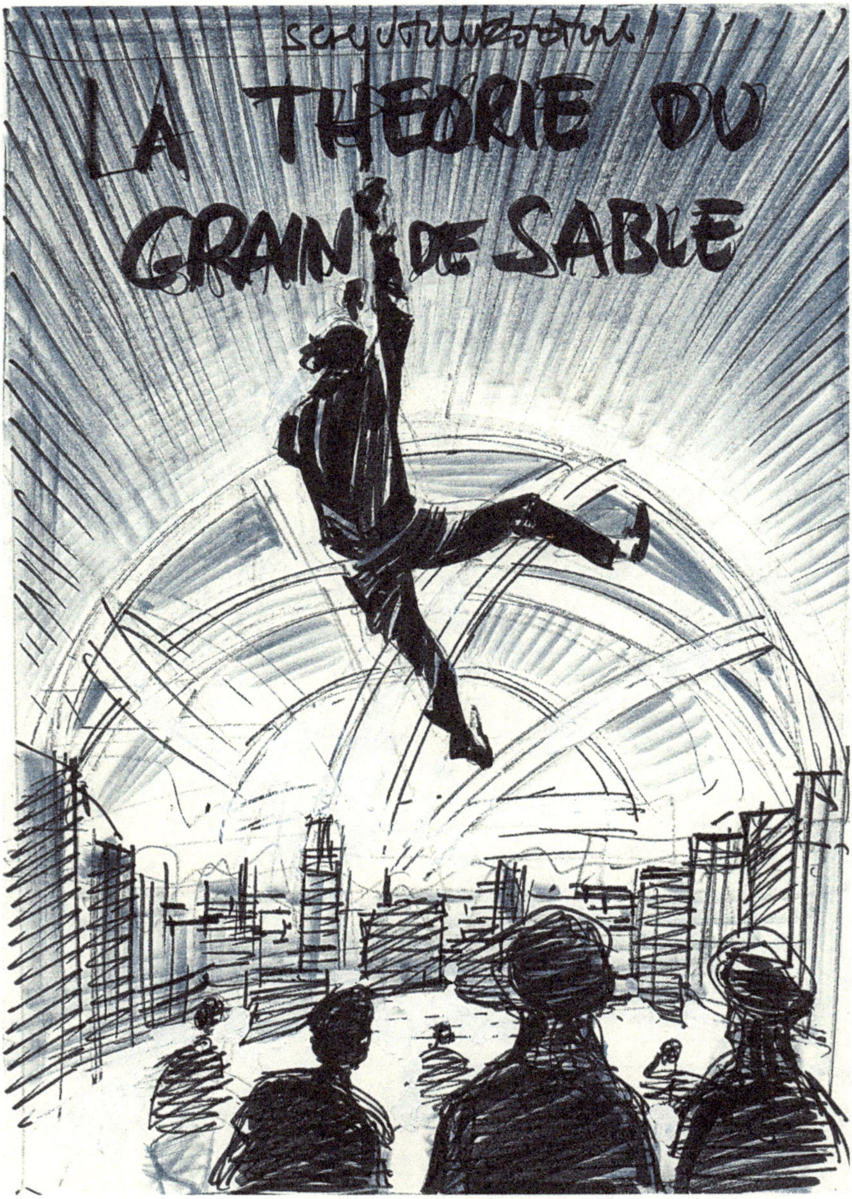
LA THEORIE DU
GRAIN DE SABLE

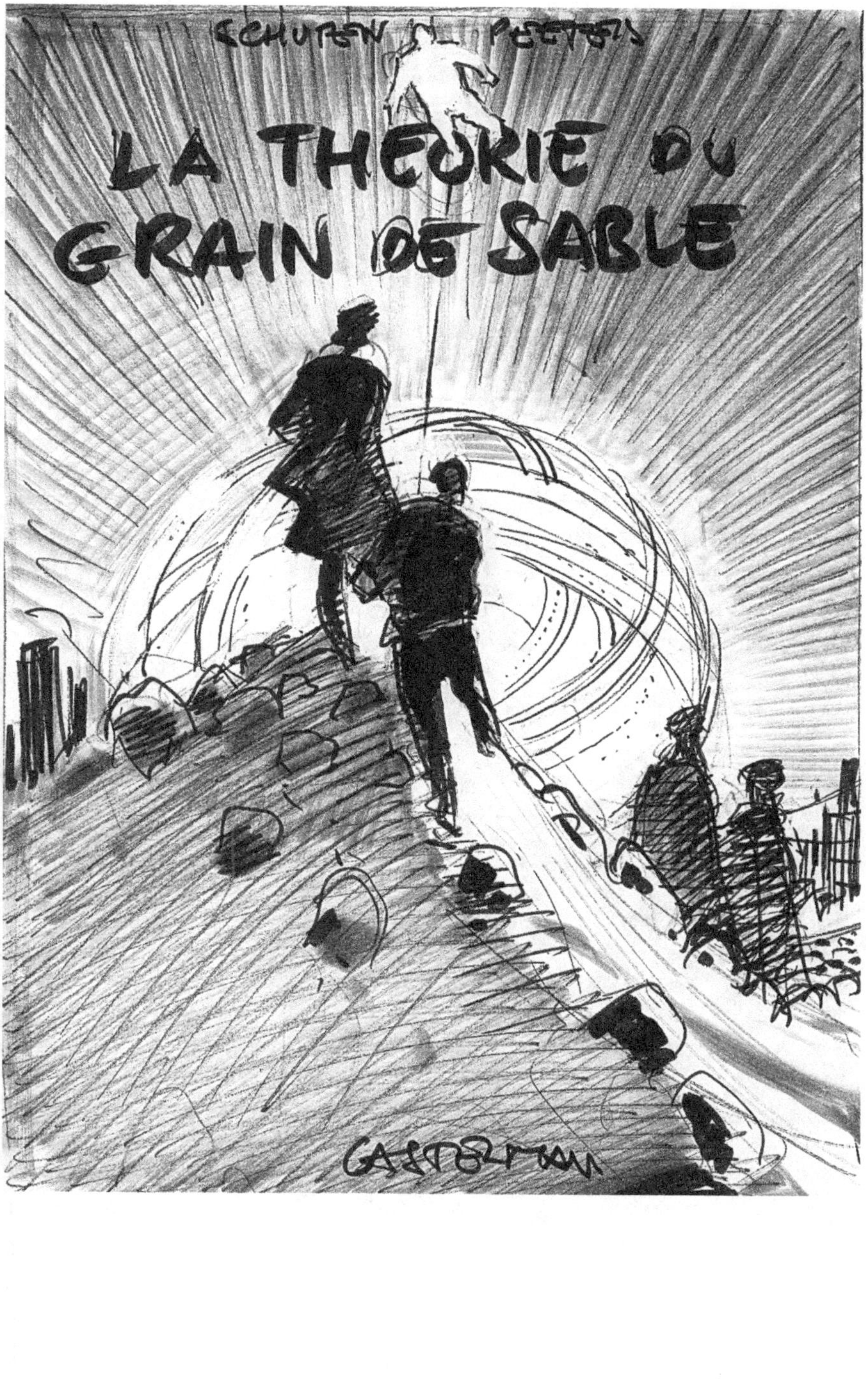
SCHUITEN PEETERS
LA THEORIE DU GRAIN DE SABLE
CASTERMAN

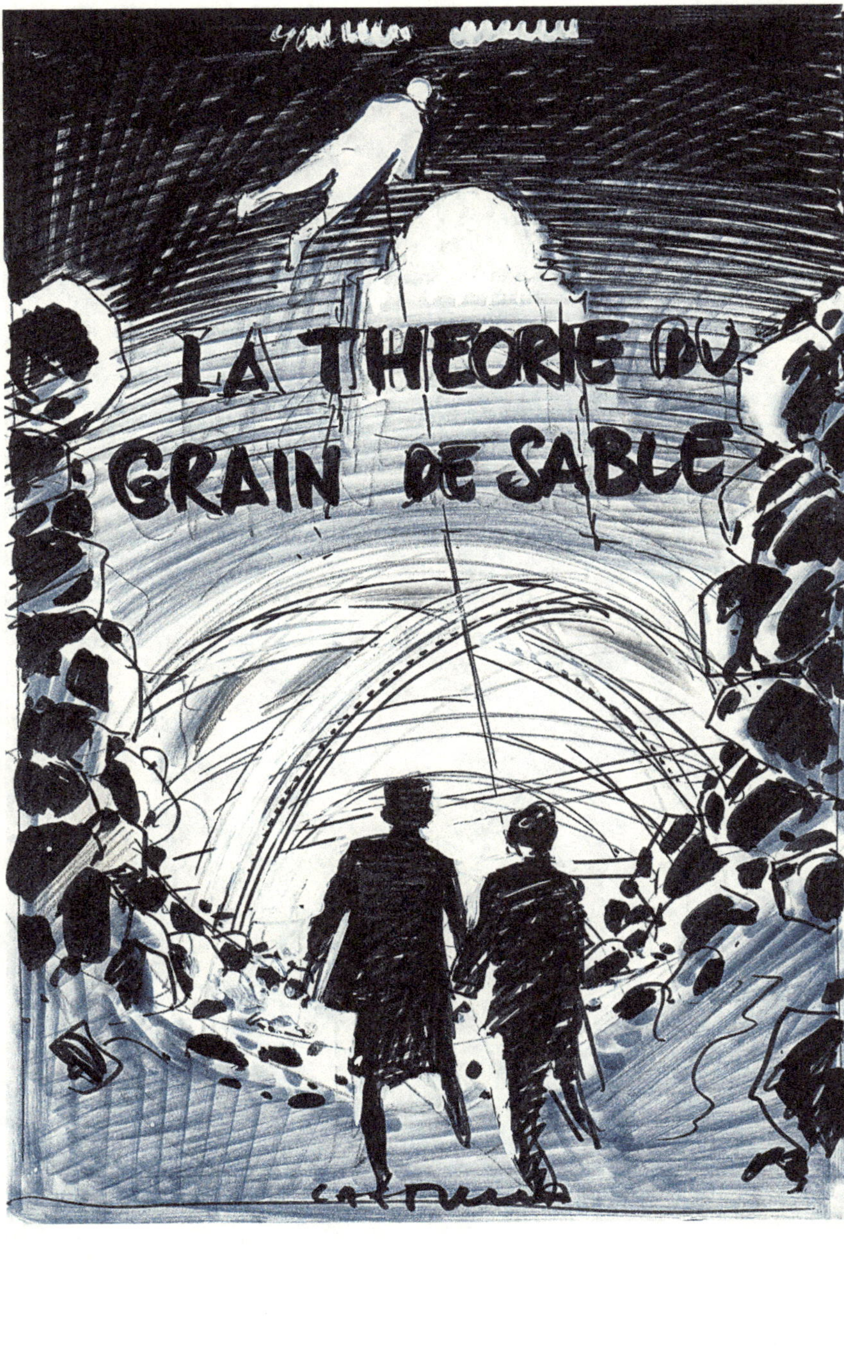
LA THEORIE DU
GRAIN DE SABLE

Acknowledgments

My most sincere thanks to the many people and friends who have made this book possible: Frederick Aldama, who encouraged me to initiate its writing; Benoît Peeters, who followed its various steps and kindly accepted to engage in the conversation in the last chapter of this book; Harry Thorrington, who was my first proofreader; Philippe Marion and Raphaël Baroni, whose work on comics and narrative has been helpful throughout the whole work; François Schuiten, who generously allowed me to reproduce his artwork; Marie-Françoise Plissart, Vladimir Peeters, and Isabelle Franciosa for the generous sharing of their photographs; Steve Smith, who kindly granted the permission to reuse the U.S. material of *The Obscure Cities*; the Editions Casterman for their kind authorization to reuse French material; the reviewers and staff of Rutgers University Press; and in general all those who continue to make the comics scholars world such an open and warm community.

Notes

Chapter 1. A New Series, a New Type of Author

1 The first American publisher of the series had chosen this title. The new publisher, IDW, has rapidly managed to impose the correct translation. Chapter 5 of this book gives an in-depth discussion of the specific meaning of the "fantastic" in the *Obscure Cities* context.

2 https://www.altaplana.be/en/start. For a complete overview of the series components, see the references at the end of this book. *The Obscure Cities* currently comprises ten albums, six spin-offs, a number of short stories, and a wide range of differently published or realized works. All print-related materials are gathered in four "integral" volumes, published in French between 2017 and 2019. As will become clear over the course of this book, the fact that no new albums have been announced does not mean at all that the *Obscure Cities* project is therefore closed. In the United States, *The Obscure Cities* has been translated in two waves, with two publishers having started to translate the series, but never in a systematic or complete way (one can only hope that the translations currently issued by IDW will soon put all the albums at the public's disposal). This situation strangely differs from that of all other parts of the world, since the series is available in all major European and other languages (including Russian, Chinese, Japanese, and Korean).

3 However, one should be aware that in the European context this distinction does not automatically overlap with that which exists between low art and high art or popular culture and elite culture.

4 https://www.altaplana.be/en/dictionary/chronicles#integrals.

5 Typical examples would be *L'Echo des savanes*, created in 1972 by authors such as feminist Claire Brétecher, who had started in *Pilote* but were deeply disappointed by the timid political line of the magazine, or *Métal Hurlant*, founded in 1975, which even tried for some time to produce an American translation, *Heavy Metal* (see Labarre 2017 on the multiple metamorphoses of this magazine).

6 "A security element operating to the flank of a moving or stationary force to protect it from enemy ground observation, direct fire, and surprise attack" (*Department of Defense Dictionary of Military and Associated Terms*, 2005). See Lacroix 2013 for an application of this concept to literary history.
7 Since 2012, Casterman has been part of the French Gallimard group.
8 His books *Hergé: Son of Tintin* (2011) and *Derrida* (2012b), both translated into English, are reference works.
9 His critical writings on the language of comics have rapidly become trendsetting in the emerging field of comics studies; see Peeters 2003 [1991] and 2015 [1984].
10 In 2015 he was appointed as the UK's first-ever comics professor at the University of Lancaster.
11 http://www.trainworld.be/en.

Chapter 2. A World of Its Own

1 This point of view, that of the actual witness and no longer that of the author of a work of fiction, prevails in the Integral Edition. It clearly tends toward strengthening the blurring of boundaries between fact and fiction in the series.
2 In one of his letters to his fiancée, Freud wrote in 1885: "Brussels was beautiful, a huge city, splendid buildings, the street inscriptions French and Flemish . . . I came to a steep hill, where a building stood, of a mass development and column splendor, . . . I really thought it was the royal palace. . . . It was the Palace of Justice." See https://www.theviennapsychoanalyst.at/index.php?wbkat=1850.
3 Later that year the same show was also presented in Paris.
4 The French title is a clear allusion to the famous installment novel by Eugène Sue, *Les Mystères de Paris* (1842–1843), the first great novel of the socially committed "mystery city" genre, which would grow to exert great influence on authors such as Charles Dickens. At the same time, the title of the short story refers as much to Poe's "The Facts in the Case of Mr. Valdemar" as to Stevenson's *The Strange Case of Dr Jekyll and Mr Hyde*. Mystery and case genres, so to speak, are the perfect backdrop for a series that establishes a dialogue between fiction and documentary.
5 For this scene, Schuiten has redrawn the painting *A Clinical Lesson at the Salpêtrière* (1887) by Pierre Aristide André Brouillet.

Chapter 3. More Than a Possible World

1 For a more detailed presentation of the notion of "transmedia storytelling," see chapter 6.
2 For the time being, Peeters and Schuiten's story world has not been commercialized as a real "franchise"; see the interview with Benoît Peeters in chapter 9 of this book.
3 Which, by the way, has its own calendar and its own time line, more similar to that of the Roman *ab urbe condita*, "since the foundation of the city," than to other ways of structuring eras.
4 Readers of Jules Verne will equally recognize this character, who appears in various of his novels.
5 See the discussion thread on "Fauxtations" at https://fauxtations.wordpress.com/2015/01/04/augustine-the-world-is-a-book/.

Chapter 4. Between Chapter and Series

1 Storyteller and not just scriptwriter, since the auteur aesthetics of serious comics tended to defend the model of the "complete author," that is, the artist in charge of both the drawings and the scriptwriting and thus in total control of the work (Baetens and Frey 2014, 134–143 and passim).

2 In the 1984 edition, two pages were added, three were modified, and the authors briefly introduce the character of Eugen Robick, the protagonist of the second album, which was then being serialized.

Chapter 6. In and Out the Medium

1 As a matter of fact, a team comprising Schuiten, Peeters, and two architects participated in the contest for the renovation of the museum. Their project eventually ranked second and was the starting point for the complete makeover of the Arts et Métiers subway station in Paris.

2 The author of this book gratefully acknowledges the exceptional generosity of the authors in this regard.

3 The complete files of the "Mary affair" can be consulted at the Altaplana website under the title "Mystery of Mary": https://www.altaplana.be/en/dossiers/mystery-of-mary?s%5B%5D=correspondances.

4 His major theoretical work, *Le Livre sur le livre: Traité de documentation*, was reissued in 2015, with a preface by Benoît Peeters and a cover illustration by François Schuiten.

5 Readers of Borges may recall that Otlet is hinted at in his famous essay "The Analytical Language of John Wilkins," where after some ironic comments on the best ways of "dividing" knowledge, he continues as follows: "The Bibliographic Institute of Brussels exerts chaos too: it has divided the universe into 1000 subdivisions, from which number 262 is the pope; number 282, the Roman Catholic Church; 263, the Day of the Lord; 268, Sunday schools; 298, Mormonism; and number 294, Brahmanism, Buddhism, Shintoism and Taoism. It doesn't reject heterogenic subdivisions as, for example, 179: Cruelty towards animals. Animal protection. Duality and suicide seen through moral values. Various vices and disadvantages. Advantages and various qualities." See Jorge Luis Borges, *Other Inquisitions, 1937–1952*, trans. Ruth L. C. Simms (Austin: University of Texas Press, 1993).

Chapter 7. Doing Politics in Comics

1 A conviction he shared with one of his initial sponsors, the Belgian socialist politician Henri La Fontaine, Nobel Peace Prize winner in 1913. After World War I, these kinds of "universalizing" dreams came under great pressure, as can be seen from the fiasco of the League of Nations (1919–1946).

2 A quotation from Töpffer's essay "Notice sur l'histoire de Monsieur Jabot" (1833).

Chapter 8. Close-Reading *The Leaning Girl*

1 For a comparison of the correspondences between time on Earth and time on Counter-Earth in *The Leaning Girl*, see the section "Timelines" in the Altaplana

page on the album: https://www.altaplana.be/en/albums/leaning-girl?s%5B%5D=leaning&s%5B%5D=girl.

2 The Belgian semiotician Henri Van Lier has argued that it is possible to reread the history of photography by establishing a systematic although not mechanical relationship between changes in style and subject matter, on the one hand, and technological changes, on the other. As far as the negative-positive technique is concerned, his main examples are given by the work of Hill and Adamson (Van Lier 2004, 17).

3 Plissart is a leading photographer in the field of narrative photography and the photo novel and was in charge of the photographic elements of *The Leaning Girl* and other accompanying material of *The Obscure Cities*. Her own work includes a landmark photonovel published with a long commentary by Jacques Derrida: *Droit de regards* (1985; English translation with Monticelli in 1998: *Rights of Inspection*).

4 For practical reasons I will not expand here on the particularly dense network of visual intertextualities in *The Leaning Girl*. In *The Obscure Cities* series, this album is probably the one that reworks and appropriates more than the others our cultural visual memory. The starting element of the plot is borrowed from *The Shooting Star*, the tenth volume of *The Adventures of Tintin* (1942), also haunted by the near-collision of two planets (Earth and a gigantic meteor); the traveling life of Mary von Rathen as circus attraction is largely indebted to Tod Browning's *Freaks* (1932), but also to literary sources such as novels by Dickens and Hector Malot's 1878 *Nobody's Boy*, a classic of French youth literature. Moreover, as in many other volumes, a number of panels are inspired by various illustrated Jules Verne editions (for an overview, see http://jv.gilead.org.il/rpaul/). Verne himself makes an appearance in the book, bluntly declaring that he has borrowed the inspiration for his *Extraordinary Voyages* from . . . *The Obscure Cities*!

Chapter 9. A Conversation with Benoît Peeters

1 https://www.altaplana.be/en/dossiers/urbicande.be/start.

References

Primary Sources

The Obscure Cities (Paris: Casterman)

ALBUMS

Les Murailles de Samaris, 1983 ("Samaris," IDW, 2017; first edition: "The Great Walls of Samaris," Nantier Beall Minoustchine, 1987)
La Fièvre d'Urbicande, 1985 ("Fever in Urbicand," Nantier Beall Minoustchine, 1992)
La Tour, 1987 ("The Tower," Nantier Beall Minoustchine, 1993)
La Route d'Armilia, 1988
Brüsel, 1992 ("Brüsel," Nantier Beall Minoustchine, 2003)
L'Enfant penchée, 1996 ("The Leaning Girl," IDW, 2017)
L'Ombre d'un homme, 1999 ("The Shadow of a Man," IDW, 2020)
Souvenirs de l'Eternel Présent, 1999
La Frontière invisible, two volumes, 2002 and 2004 ("The Invisible Frontier 1/2") (Nantier Beall Minoustchine, 2002 and 2004)
La Théorie du grain de sable, two volumes, 2007 and 2008 ("The Theory of the Grain of Sand," IDW, 2016)

SPIN-OFFS

L'Archiviste, 1987 (album, illustrated fictional essay)
Le Musée A. Desombres, 1990 (multimedia show: book, CD, radio drama)
L'Echo des cités, 1993 (album, illustrated fictional essay)
Mary La Penchée, 1995 (youth literature album)
Le Guide des cités, 1996 (album, illustrated fictional essay)
L'Affaire Desombres, 1999 (album with DVD)

SHORT STORIES AND OTHER PRODUCTION

See Altaplana website: https://www.altaplana.be/en/start.

INTEGRALS: FOUR INTEGRAL ALBUMS RELEASED BETWEEN 2017 AND 2019
Les Cités obscures 1, 2017
Les Cités obscures 2, 2018
Les Cités obscures 3, 2018
Les Cités obscures 4, 2019

Secondary Sources

Adorno, T. W., and Max Horkheimer. 2002 [1947]. *Dialectic of Enlightenment*. Translated by Edmund Jephcott. Stanford: Stanford University Press.

Alber, Jan. 2013. "Unnatural Narrative." In *The Living Handbook of Narratology*. http://www.lhn.uni-hamburg.de/article/unnatural-narrative (accessed 10 December 2018).

Allen, Rob, and Thijs van den Berg, eds. 2014. *Serialization and Popular Culture*. New York: Routledge.

Altaplana (official website of *The Obscure Cities*). https://www.altaplana.be/en/start.

Altman, Rick. 1999. *Film/Genre*. London: BFI.

Andrews, Chris. 2019. "Paranoid Interpretation and Formal Encoding." *Poetics Today* 30(4): 669–692.

Baetens, Jan. 2018. "Adaptation: A Writerly Strategy?" In *Comics and Adaptation*, edited by Benoît Mitaine, David Roche, and Isabelle Schmitt-Pitiot. Jackson: University Press of Mississippi, 31–46.

Baetens, Jan, and Hugo Frey. 2014. *The Graphic Novel: An Introduction*. New York: Cambridge University Press.

———. 2018. "Continued Comics: The New 'Blake and Mortimer' as an Example of Continuation in European Series." In *The Edinburgh Companion to Contemporary Narrative Theories*, edited by Zara Dinnen and Robyn Warhol. Edinburg: Edinburgh University Press.

Bakhtin, M. M. 1981. *The Dialogic Imagination: Four Essays*. Translated by Caryl Emerson and Michael Holquist. Austin: University of Texas Press.

Baroni, Raphaël. 2011a. "Généricité ou stéréotypie?" *Cahiers de Narratologie* 17. http://narratologie.revues.org/1090 (accessed 1 October 2018).

———. 2011b. "Le Récit dans l'image: Séquence, intrigue et configuration." *Image & Narrative* 21(1). http://www.imageandnarrative.be/index.php/imagenarrative/article/view/136.

Baroni, Raphaël, and Françoise Revaz, eds. 2015. *Narrative Sequence in Contemporary Narratology*. Columbus: Ohio State University Press.

Barthes, Roland. 1974 [1970]. *S/Z: An Essay*. Translated by Richard Miller. New York: Farrar, Straus and Giroux.

Baudry, Julien. 2018. *Cases-Pixels: Une histoire de la BD numérique en France*. Tours: Presses Universitaires François-Rabelais.

Beaty, Bart. 2012. *Comics versus Art*. Toronto: Toronto University Press.

Belting, Hans. 2014. *An Anthropology of Images*. Princeton, NJ: Princeton University Press.

Chollet, Laurent. 2000. *L'Insurrection situationniste*. Paris: Dagorno.

Crucifix, Benoît, and Bjorn-Olav Dozo. 2018. "E-Graphic Novels." In *The Cambridge History of the Graphic Novel*, edited by Jan Baetens, Hugo Frey, and Stephen E. Tabachnick. New York: Cambridge University Press, 574–590.

De Kosnik, Abigail. 2016. *Rogue Archives: Digital Cultural Memory and Media Fandom*. Cambridge, MA: MIT Press.

Denson, Shane. 2014. "The Logic of the Line Segment: Continuity and Discontinuity in Serial-Queen Melodrama." In *Serialization and Popular Culture*, edited by Rob Allen and Thijs van den Berg. New York: Routledge, 65–79.

Duplan, Olivier. 2018. "Les Cités obscures, c'est un puzzle, mais un puzzle infini." *Le Temps*, 14 December 2018. https://www.letemps.ch/culture/cites-obscures-cest-un-puzzle-un-puzzle-infini (accessed 16 November 2019).

Dürrenmatt, Jacques. 1998 [1976]. *The History of Sexuality*. Vol. 1, *The Will to Knowledge*. Translated by Robert Herley. London: Penguin.

———. 2013. *Bande dessinée et littérature*. Paris: Garnier.

Foucault, Michel. 1995 [1975]. *Discipline and Punish: The Birth of the Prison*. Translated by Alan Sheridan. New York: Vintage Books.

Frey, Hugo, and Jan Baetens. 2019. "Comics Culture and Roy Lichtenstein Revisited: Analysing a Forgotten 'Feedback Loop.'" *Art History* 42(1): 126–153.

Garcia, Tristan. 2013. "Que sont les Cités obscures?" http://www.la-galerie.ch/wp-content/uploads/2013/05/Que-sont-les-Cites-obscures-©Tristan-Garcia.pdf (accessed 1 December 2018).

Gardner, Jared. 2012. *Projections: Comics and the History of Twenty-First-Century Storytelling*. Stanford: Stanford University Press.

Genette, Gérard. 1983 [1972]. *Narrative Discourse: An Essay in Method*. Translated by Jane E. Lewin. Ithaca, NY: Cornell University Press.

GREBD (Groupe de Recherches sur la Bande dessinée, Université de Lausanne). 2013. "La BD avant l'album." Exhibition catalogue. https://wp.unil.ch/grebd/evenements/expositions-du-grebd/ (accessed 8 December 2018).

Groensteen, Thierry. 1993. *Direct Color*. Thurn: Kunst der Comics.

———. 1994. "La Légende des Cités." *Le Neuvième Art*, n.p. http://neuviemeart.citebd.org/spip.php?article802 (accessed 5 December 2018).

———. 2013 [2011]. *Comics and Narration*. Translated by Ann Miller. Jackson: University Press of Mississippi.

Hall, Stuart. 1993 [1973]. "Encoding. Decoding." In *The Cultural Studies Reader*, edited by Simon During. London: Routledge, 507–517.

Hansen, Lene. 2019. "Gender, Agency and the Politics of Subjectivity in *La Frontière invisible*." In *Rethinking Silence, Voice and Agency in Contested Gender Terrains*, edited by Jane L. Parpart and Swati Parashar. London: Routledge, 27–49.

Hergenrader, Trent. 2018. *Collaborative Worldbuilding for Writers and Gamers*. London: Bloomsbury.

Hesmondhalgh, David. 2012. *The Cultural Industries*. 3rd ed. New York: Sage.

Jenkins, Henry. 2007. "Transmedia Storytelling 2007." http://henryjenkins.org/blog/2007/03/transmedia_storytelling_101.html (accessed 1 October 2018).

Kelleter, Frank. 2017a. "Five Ways of Looking at Popular Seriality." In *Media of Serial Narrative*, edited by Frank Kelleter. Columbus: Ohio State University Press, 7–34.

———, ed. 2017b. *Media of Serial Narrative*. Columbus: Ohio State University Press.

Krajewski, Markus. 2014. *World Projects: Global Information before World War I*. Minneapolis: University of Minnesota Press.

Kunzle, David. 1973. *The Early Comic Strip: Narrative Strips and Picture Stories in the European Broadsheet from c. 1450 to 1825*. Berkeley: University of California Press.

Labarre, Nicolas. 2017. *Heavy Metal, l'autre Métal Hurlant*. Bordeaux: Presses Universitaires de Bordeaux.

Labio, Catherine. 2015. "The Architecture of Comics." *Critical Inquiry* 41(2): 312–343.

Lacroix, Michel. 2013. "Le Pas de côté de la flanc-garde: *La Nouvelle Revue française*." *L'Esprit créateur* 52(3): 9–25.

Lecigne, Bruno. 1983. *Les Héritiers d'Hergé*. Brussels: Magic Strip.

Leroy, Fabrice. 2018. "European Literary and Genre Fiction: The *(À Suivre)* Magazine and the 'Adventure' and 'Science Fiction' Traditions (Pratt, Tardi, Moebius)." In *The Cambridge History of the Graphic Novel*, edited by Jan Baetens, Hugo Frey, and Stephen M. Tabachnick. New York: Cambridge University Press, 251–268.

Letourneux, Matthieu. 2017. *Fictions à la chaîne: Littératures sérielles et culture médiatique*. Paris: Seuil.

Levie, Françoise. 2006. *L'Homme qui voulait classer le monde: Paul Otlet et le Mundaneum*. Brussels: Les Impressions Nouvelles.

MAM—Musée des Arts et Métiers, Paris. 2018. Visitor Information. https://www.arts-et-metiers.net/musee/visitor-information (accessed 1 December 2018).

Manovich, Lev. 2001. *The Language of New Media*. Cambridge, MA: MIT Press.

Marion, Philippe. 2009. *Schuiten filiation*. Ixelles: Versant Sud.

Mathews, Harry, and Alastair Brotchie. 2005. *Oulipo Compendium*. Los Angeles: Make Now Press; London: Atlas Press.

McCloud, Scott. 2000. *Reinventing Comics*. New York: Paradox Press.

Menu, Jean-Christophe. 2011. *La Bande dessinée et son double*. Paris: L'Association.

Michallat, Wendy. 2018. *French Cartoon Art in the 1960s and 1970s*. Leuven: Leuven University Press.

Motte, Warren F. 1986. *Oulipo: A Primer of Potential Literature*. Lincoln: University of Nebraska Press.

Musil, Robert. 1955 [1930]. *The Man without Qualities*. Vol. 1, *A Sort of Introduction, and The Like of It Now Happens (I)*. Translated by Eithne Wilkins and Ernst Kaiser. London: Secker and Warburg.

Pedri, Nancy, ed. 2018. "Mixing Visual Media in Comics." Special issue, *ImageTexT* 9(2). http://imagetext.english.ufl.edu/imagetext/archives/v9_2/ (accessed 30 July 2019).

Peeters, Benoît. 1985. "Échafaudages." *Cahiers Georges Perec* 1: 178–191.

———. 2001a [1976]. *Omnibus*. Paris: Les Impressions Nouvelles.

———. 2001b. *Robbe-Grillet: Entretiens avec Benoît Peeters*. Paris: Les Impressions Nouvelles. DVD.

———. 2003 [1991]. *Lire la bande dessinée*. Paris: Flammarion.

———. 2007 [1983]. "Four Conceptions of the Page." Translated by Jesse Cohn. *ImageText* 3(3). http://www.english.ufl.edu/imagetext/archives/v3_3/peeters/ (accessed 10 October 2018).

———. 2008. *Écrire l'image, un itinéraire*. Brussels: Les Impressions Nouvelles.

———. 2011 [2002]. *Hergé, Son of Tintin*. Translated by Tina A. Kover. Baltimore: Johns Hopkins University Press.

———. 2012a [1980]. *La Bibliothèque de Villers, suivi de Tombeau d'Agatha Christie*. Brussels: Espace Nord.

———. 2012b [2010]. *Derrida: A Biography*. Translated by Andrew Brown. London: Polity Press.

———. 2015 [1984]. *Lire Tintin: Les Bijoux ravis*. Paris: Les Impressions Nouvelles.

———. 2018. "Obscurs Chapitres." *Cahiers de Narratologie* 34. https://journals.openedition.org/narratologie/8632 (accessed 29 December 2018).

Peeters, Benoît, and François Schuiten. 2018. *Revoir Paris*. Paris: Casterman.

Peeters, Benoît, François Schuiten, and Marie-Françoise Plissart. 2004. *La Maison Autrique: Métamorphoses d'une maison art nouveau*. Brussels: Les Impressions Nouvelles.
Perloff, Marjorie. 2016. *Edge of Irony: Modernism in the Shadow of the Habsburg Empire*. Chicago: University of Chicago Press.
Ricardou, Jean. 1975. *Le Nouveau Roman*. Paris: Seuil.
Robbe-Grillet, Alain. 1992 [1963]. *For a New Novel*. Translated by Richard Howard. Evanston, IL: Northwestern University Press.
Roeder, Katherine. 2014. *Wide Awake in Slumberland: Fantasy, Mass Culture, and Modernism in the Art of Winsor McCay*. Jackson: University Press of Mississippi.
Roussel, Raymond. 2005 [1935]. *How I Wrote Certain of My Books*. Translated by Trevor Winkfield. Cambridge, MA: Exact Change.
Ryan, Marie-Laure. 2013. "Possible Worlds." In *The Living Handbook of Narratology*. https://www.lhn.uni-hamburg.de/node/54.html (accessed 30 July 2019).
Samson, Jacques, and Benoît Peeters. 2010. *Chris Ware: La Bande dessinée réinventée*. Paris: Les Impressions Nouvelles.
Sandweiss, Martha A. 2004. *Print the Legend: Photography and the American West*. New Haven, CT: Yale University Press.
Schuiten, François, and Benoît Peeters. 1997. *L'Aventure des images*. Paris: Autrement.
———. 2019. *Mondes Im-Parfaits*. Brussels: Les Impressions Nouvelles; Yverdon: La Maison d'ailleurs.
Smolderen, Thierry. 2014 [2009]. *The Origins of Comics: From William Hogarth to Winsor McCay*. Translated by Bart Beaty and Nick Nguyen. Jackson: University Press of Mississippi.
Sollers, Philippe. 1990 [1983]. *Women*. Translated by Barbara Bray. New York: Columbia University Press.
Sterling, Bruce. 2008. "The Obscure Cities." Wired. https://www.wired.com/2008/09/the-obscure-cit/ (accessed 30 July 2019).
Todorov, Tzvetan. 1973 [1970]. *The Fantastic: A Structural Approach to a Literary Genre*. Translated by Richard Howard. Cleveland: Case Western Reserve University Press.
van der Hoorn, Mélanie. 2012. *Bricks and Balloons: Architecture in Comic-Strip Form*. Rotterdam: NIA.
Van Lier, Henri. 2004 [1992]. *Histoire photographique de la photographie*. Brussels: Les Impressions Nouvelles.

Index

Italicized page numbers indicate illustrations.

About the Author

JAN BAETENS is a professor of cultural studies at the University of Leuven. His recent books on comics and visual studies are *The Cambridge History of the Graphic Novel*, coedited with Hugo Frey and Stephen E. Tabachnick; *Novelization: From Film to Novel*; and *The Graphic Novel*, coauthored with Hugo Frey.